LABOR AND EMPLO.

RELATIONS ASSOCIATION SERIES

Human Rights

*in Labor and Employment Relations:
International and Domestic Perspectives*

EDITED BY

James A. Gross and Lance Compa

First Edition

ISBN 978-0-913447-98-7

Price: $24.95

LABOR AND EMPLOYMENT RELATIONS ASSOCIATION SERIES
Proceedings of the Annual Meeting (published electronically beginning in 2009)
Annual Research Volume
LERA 2006 Membership Directory (published every four years)
LERA Newsletter (published quarterly)
Perspectives on Work (published twice a year in June and December)

Information regarding membership, subscriptions, meetings, publications, and general affairs of the LERA can be found at the Association website at www.lera.illinois.edu. Members can make changes to their member records, including contact information, affiliations and preferences, by accessing the online directory at the website or by contacting the LERA national office.

Cover photo: Children making firecrackers. Sivakasi, Tamil Nadu, India. Photographer: D.Brown. ©ILO

LABOR AND EMPLOYMENT RELATIONS ASSOCIATION
University of Illinois at Urbana-Champaign
School of Labor and Employment Relations
121 Labor and Industrial Relations Building
504 East Armory Ave.
Champaign, IL 61820
Telephone: 217/333-0072   Fax: 217/265-5130
Internet: www.lera.illinois.edu   E-mail: leraoffice@illinois.edu

CONTENTS

CHAPTER 1

Introduction

JAMES A. GROSS
LANCE COMPA
Cornell University

This volume is intended to collect the best current scholarship in the new and growing field of labor rights and human rights. We hope it will serve as a resource for researchers and practitioners as well as for teachers and students in university-level labor and human rights courses.

The animating idea for the volume is the proposition that workers' rights are human rights. But we recognize that this must be more than a slogan. Promoting labor rights as human rights requires drawing on theoretical work in labor studies and in human rights scholarship and developing closely reasoned arguments based on what is happening in the real world. Citing labor clauses in the Universal Declaration of Human Rights is one thing; relating them to the real world where workers seek to exercise their rights is something else. The contributors to this volume provide a firm theoretical foundation grounded in the reality of labor activism and advocacy in a market-driven global economy.

Separate Tracks

For most of the half-century after the Second World War, labor rights and labor standards were strictly a matter of national law and practice. Small groups of specialists in each country knew of the International Labour Organization and the dozens of "conventions" adopted since the ILO's founding in 1919. ILO conventions are meant to fashion common international labor standards around the world. ILO norms are nonbinding unless and until they are ratified and incorporated into national law, but they set out a marker of international consensus on workers' rights. In many countries, however—and especially in the United States—ILO standards traditionally have had little weight or relevance.

In similar fashion, labor advocates have rarely, if ever, looked to international human rights norms in their promotion of workers' rights. The "international bill of rights," consisting of the Universal Declaration of Human Rights (UDHR), the International Covenant on Civil and

Political Rights (ICCPR), and the International Covenant on Economic, Social and Cultural Rights (ICESCR), contains many labor-related clauses. They cover freedom of association, organizing, and bargaining; prohibitions on forced labor and child labor; nondiscrimination and health and safety in the workplace; decent wages and benefits; and other labor subjects. But trade unionists and their allies did not make the connection between international labor standards and their struggles in national settings. Human rights were disconnected from labor concerns and labor discourse.

During this same period, from the end of World War II to the 1990s, the human rights community hardly ever took workers' rights into its field of vision and activism. Human rights activists focused—with good reason—on outrages like genocide, torture, arbitrary arrest and imprisonment, and death squad killings, often perpetrated by U.S.-supported military dictatorships. Human rights supporters saw labor rights and labor standards lying more in the economic arena, not that of human rights. The long list of labor-related clauses in basic human rights instruments just did not translate into action by human rights promoters.

Two Paths Converge

In the 1990s the separate paths of labor rights and human rights advocacy began to converge. Each group came to see that its traditional boundaries were too narrow in a new context of political, social, and economic upheaval captured by the term "globalization." Trade unions looking to national labor law systems for organizing and bargaining gains found themselves undercut by a race-to-the-bottom global economy. Human rights advocates saw that their traditional agenda did not adequately address the consequences of economic globalization and the suffering it unleashed on victims of the "destruction" side of capitalism's creative destruction. Of course, globalization had winners as it rolled on, but millions of "losers" faced human rights abuses: child workers, trafficked workers, discriminated-against workers, workers forced into labor at the point of a gun, workers fired, jailed, and killed for trying to form unions, and many more.

One sign of a new connection between labor rights and human rights appeared with the introduction of labor clauses in trade agreements like the North American Free Trade Agreement (NAFTA) labor side accord and other U.S. pacts with trading partners. Although lacking strong enforcement mechanisms, these clauses and their reliance on ILO and international human rights standards created opportunities for labor and human rights advocates to work together filing complaints and backing them up with new forms of cross-border solidarity.

In one notable case filed under NAFTA's labor agreement in 1997, Human Rights Watch and allied labor and women's rights groups in Mexico challenged the widespread practice of pregnancy testing by U.S.-based multinational firms in the *maquiladora* region along the U.S.–Mexico border. Nothing in the NAFTA agreement empowered its trinational commission to order and enforce a halt to the practice, but a verdict in the court of public opinion, generated by the complaint and the joint advocacy campaign by American and Mexican labor–NGO alliances, put a stop to the practice in many of the factories supplying U.S. companies.

Another signal of a labor–human rights convergence came with other initiatives by Human Rights Watch (HRW). Beginning in 2000, HRW produced book-length reports on violations of workers' rights in the United States as well as in other countries. The U.S. reports covered household domestic workers, child labor in agriculture, meatpacking industry abuses, Walmart's interference with workers' freedom of association, and workers victimized across the country in many industries when they tried to exercise organizing and bargaining rights. Abroad, HRW labor rights reports addressed child labor in Ecuador, women workers in Guatemala, freedom of association in El Salvador, forced labor in Burma, migrant construction workers in the Middle East, migrant domestic workers in Indonesia and Malaysia, and more.

Other human rights groups have similarly taken up labor's cause. Amnesty International USA created a business and human rights division with extensive focus on workers' rights. Its parent organization, London-based Amnesty International, created a workers' rights program and engaged an experienced British trade unionist to direct it. Oxfam International broadened its development agenda to include labor rights and standards, and its Oxfam America group created a workers' rights program to take up these causes inside the United States. In 2003, Oxfam launched a "national workers' rights campaign" on conditions in the U.S. agricultural sector. In 2004, the group published a major report titled *Like Machines in the Fields: Workers Without Rights in American Agriculture* (Oxfam America 2004).

Labor's Turn to Human Rights

On the labor side, the AFL-CIO has launched a broad-based "Voice@Work" project designed to help U.S. workers regain the basic human right to form unions to improve their lives. Voice@Work stresses international human rights in workers' organizing campaigns around the country. In 2005, for example, the labor federation held more than 100 demonstrations in cities throughout the United States and enlisted signatures from 11 Nobel Peace Prize winners, including the Dalai Lama, Lech Walesa, Jimmy Carter, and Archbishop Desmond Tutu, supporting workers' human rights in full-page advertisements in national newspapers.

In 2004, trade unions and allied labor support groups created a new nongovernmental organization (NGO) called American Rights at Work (ARAW). ARAW launched an ambitious program to make human rights the centerpiece of a new civil society movement for U.S. workers' organizing and bargaining rights. ARAW's 20-member board of directors includes prominent civil rights leaders, former elected officials, environmentalists, religious leaders, business leaders, writers, scholars, an actor, and one labor leader (AFL-CIO president John Sweeney). The convergence of these movements is aptly illustrated in the figure of the group's international advisor, Mary Robinson, who is the former United Nations High Commissioner for Human Rights.

Many organizations are also turning to international human rights arguments in defense of immigrant workers in the United States. For example, the National Employment Law Project (NELP) includes an immigrant worker project under its rubric "workers' rights are human rights—advancing the human rights of immigrant workers in the United States." NELP has been a leader in filing complaints to the Inter-American Commission and Inter-American Court of Human Rights on rights violations among immigrant workers in the United States.

Working with Mexican colleagues, NELP sought an Inter-American Court Advisory Opinion on U.S. treatment of immigrant workers. The petition was prompted by the Supreme Court's 2002 *Hoffman Plastic* decision stripping undocumented workers illegally fired for union organizing from access to back-pay remedies (*Hoffman* 2002). The Inter-American Court issued the opinion that undocumented workers are entitled to the same labor rights, including wages owed, protection from discrimination, protection for health and safety on the job, and back pay, as are citizens and those working lawfully in a country.

Reaching out to the religious community, Interfaith Worker Justice (IWJ) is a national coalition of leaders of all faiths supporting workers' rights under religious principles. IWJ places divinity students, rabbinical students, seminarians, novices, and others studying for careers in religious service in union-organizing internships. Through a national network of local religious coalitions, IWJ also sponsors projects for immigrant workers, poultry workers, home-care workers, and other low-wage employees. IWJ gives special help when religious-based employers, such as hospitals and schools, violate workers' organizing and bargaining rights.

A new student movement that began against sweatshops in overseas factories has adopted a human rights and labor rights approach to problems of workers in their own campuses and communities, often citing human rights as a central theme. Students at many universities held rallies, hunger strikes, and occupations of administration offices to support union organizing and "living wage" and other campaigns among blue-collar workers, clerical and technical employees, and other sectors of the university workforce.

These initiatives suggest that the human rights and labor communities no longer run on separate tracks. They have joined in a common mission with enhanced traction to advance workers' rights.

Using International Mechanisms

The U.S. labor movement's new interest in international human rights law is reflected in its increasing use of ILO complaints and international human rights mechanisms. In 2002, the AFL-CIO filed a complaint with the ILO Committee on Freedom of Association (CFA) challenging the Supreme Court's *Hoffman Plastic* decision. In *Hoffman*, the Supreme Court had held, in a 5–4 decision, that an undocumented worker, because of his immigration status, was not entitled to back pay for lost wages after he was illegally fired for union organizing. The five-justice majority said that enforcing immigration law takes precedence over enforcing labor law.

The union federations' ILO complaint argued that eliminating the back-pay remedy for undocumented workers annuls protection of workers' right to organize, contrary to the requirement in Convention 87 to provide adequate protection against acts of anti-union discrimination.

The AFL-CIO's complaint was successful: in November 2003, the CFA announced that the *Hoffman* doctrine violates international legal obligations to protect workers' organizing rights. The committee concluded that remedial measures left to the National Labor Relations Board (NLRB) in cases of illegal dismissals of undocumented workers are inadequate to ensure effective protection against acts of anti-union discrimination. The CFA recommended congressional action to bring U.S. law into conformity with freedom of association principles, with the aim of ensuring effective protection for all workers against acts of anti-union discrimination in the wake of the *Hoffman* decision.

Supervisory Exclusion

In October 2006, the AFL-CIO filed another CFA complaint, this time against the NLRB's decision in the so-called Oakwood Trilogy (*Croft Metal, Inc.* 2006; *Golden Crest Healthcare Center* 2006; *Oakwood*

Healthcare, Inc. 2006). In *Oakwood,* the NLRB announced an expanded interpretation of the definition of "supervisor" under the National Labor Relations Act. Under the new ruling, employers can classify as "supervisors" employees with incidental oversight over co-workers even when such oversight is far short of genuine managerial or supervisory authority.

In its complaint to the ILO, the AFL-CIO relied on the ILO conventions, arguing that the NLRB's decision contravened No. 87's affirmation that "workers and employers, without distinction whatsoever, shall have the right to establish and . . . to join organizations of their own choosing without previous authorization." The AFL-CIO further argued that the NLRB's Oakwood Trilogy strips employees in the new "supervisor" status of protection of collective bargaining rights in violation of Convention No. 98.

In its March 2008 decision, the CFA found that the criteria for supervisory status laid out in the Oakwood Trilogy give rise to an overly wide definition of supervisory staff that would go beyond freedom of association principles, and it urged the U.S. government to take all necessary steps to ensure that exclusions are limited to workers genuinely representing the interests of employers.

TSA Airport Screeners

In November 2006, the CFA issued a decision in a complaint filed by the AFL-CIO and the American Federation of Government Employees (AFGE) against the Bush administration's denial of collective bargaining rights to Transportation Security Administration (TSA) airport screeners (International Labour Organization 2006). The administration argued that events of September 11, 2001, and concomitant security concerns made it necessary to strip TSA employees of trade union rights accorded to other federal employees.

Again, the CFA found the United States failing to meet freedom of association standards. The CFA said that persons who are clearly not making national policy that may affect security, but only exercising specific tasks within clearly defined parameters, should be able to exercise organizing and bargaining rights.

North Carolina Public Employees

In 2006, the United Electrical, Radio and Machine Workers of America (UE) filed a complaint with the CFA. The complaint charged that North Carolina's ban on public worker bargaining, and the failure of the United States to take steps to protect workers' bargaining rights, violated ILO's principles that "all workers, without distinction should enjoy organizing and bargaining rights, and that only public employees who are high-level policymakers, not rank-and-file workers, should be excluded from the right to bargain."

In April 2007, the CFA ruled in the union's favor and urged the U.S. government to promote the establishment of a collective bargaining framework in the public sector in North Carolina to bring the state legislation into conformity with the freedom of association principles (International Labour Organization 2007).

Employers Engaging the Human Rights Argument

The employer community recognizes the force (and, for some, the menace) of the labor rights as human rights argument. The National Right-to-Work Committee (NRTWC) sees the potential for ILO rulings to advance U.S. labor's cause: in February 2008, the NRTWC issued a briefing paper titled *Organized Labor's International Law Project? Transforming Workplace Rights into Human Rights* (Muggeridge 2008). The paper noted that trade union advocates have effectively argued that labor rights ought to be considered not as mere elements of economic policy, but as international human rights proclaimed and monitored by international bodies. It went on to warn that domestic courts may allow themselves to be influenced by the rulings of international tribunals and concluded that the United States should consider withdrawing from ILO membership because of the unions' use of ILO complaints.

In March 2009, the U.S. Chamber of Commerce and the U.S. Council for International Business issued public statements that Congress should reject the proposed Employee Free Choice Act because it violates ILO Conventions 87 and 98. This signaled a reversal of their long-standing position that these ILO standards do not apply to the United States and that the United States cannot ratify them.

Some Critical Voices

We are mindful of the fact that some analysts sympathetic to workers and trade unions have expressed skepticism about promoting labor rights as human rights as a strategy for advancing labor's cause. Some suggest that a focus on "rights" plays into the hands of anti-labor forces who assert, for example, the right to refrain from union membership, or the right to secret ballot elections, or employers' right to manage the business. Instead of arguing that labor rights are human rights, these friendly critics call for a focus on labor solidarity and industrial democracy.

These are healthy cautions from serious, committed scholars and defenders of trade unions and workers' rights. They contribute to a needed debate about the role and effectiveness of human rights activism and human rights arguments in support of workers' rights. But they do not convince the editors of this volume that a human rights argument should be jettisoned. The fact that anti-labor forces appropriate "rights talk" does not mean we should leave the field. This is contested terrain, and we should not yield it to anti-labor forces. We should not have to choose between human rights and solidarity as the touchstone of effective advocacy on behalf of workers. We can call for both, insisting that they go hand in hand.

Workers are empowered in campaigns when they are themselves convinced—and are convincing the public—that they are vindicating their fundamental human rights, not just seeking a wage increase or more job benefits. The larger society is more responsive to the notion of trade union organizing as an exercise of human rights rather than economic strength. The human rights argument pries open more space for workers' organizing and bargaining by framing them as a human rights mission, not just as a test of economic power between institutional adversaries.

The fact that international human rights arguments strain for a place in American political discourse is not a reason to shy away from their use. It's a reason to bring human rights into the discourse to connect with a natural sense of "rights" that all people have. In this spirit, we conceived and bring to press this volume.

The authors of the essays here constitute a diverse and accomplished group of human rights activists, practitioners, and scholars, all of whom have published extensively. James Gross sets the tone for the volume by emphasizing that the growing movement for promoting and protecting human rights at workplaces here and around the world posits a new set of values and approaches that challenge every orthodoxy in the employment relations field, every practice and rule rooted in that orthodoxy, and even the underlying premises and intellectual foundations of contemporary labor and employment systems. More specifically, his chapter discusses how the human rights movement challenges and is challenged by traditional conceptions of the sources of worker and employer rights, the philosophy and practice of the unregulated market, the long-standing opposition to the idea of economic rights, the wide-ranging consequences of cultural and moral relativism, and doctrines of national sovereignty—and even the still dominant industrial pluralism theory attributed to "Wisconsin School" pioneer John R. Commons. Finally, Gross describes the gap between U.S. labor laws and international human rights law and standards and explores the implications of these human rights challenges for labor and employment research.

Jeff Hilgert challenges industrial relations and labor economics to articulate a framework of workers' health and safety as a human rights concern. His chapter aims to establish a new foundation for industrial relations scholarship and to build a human rights foundation for labor policy. He uses workers' health and safety to illustrate the contrasts between institutional labor economics and human rights and shows that the human rights worldview offers a fundamentally different perspective than institutional economics particularly in regard to policy evaluation, the role of government and the analysis of government policy, and understanding human rights in a social context. Hilgert concludes that the human rights worldview poses a more significant challenge to the orthodoxy of neoclassical economics than does any other market-based economic philosophy, including the institutional labor economics school. He also finds that the history of how institutional economics has viewed worker health and safety disqualifies institutional labor economists from claiming the banner of universal human rights advocacy. That fact further illustrates, according to Hilgert, the need for a distinct human rights analysis in industrial relations scholarship that, in his words, would catch up with the reality of the suffering of many millions of workers.

Burns Weston sees child labor as not only a human rights problem but as a human rights problem that is multidisciplinary, multifaceted, and multisectoral. His chapter is premised on five interrelated propositions: that child labor is exploitive, hazardous, or otherwise contrary to children's best interest and constitutes a "blight on human civility"; that child labor begs to be abolished; that child labor manifests itself in complex ways demanding multidimensional approaches to its eradication; that no form or level of social organization can claim "business as usual"; and that change requires an ongoing commitment to the application of human rights law and policy, which includes the right of children to influence their own lives. Consequently, Weston advocates a rights-based approach that responds to skeptics' arguments, contests the claimed absence of a theory of human rights, and sets forth a nuts-and-bolts strategy that includes legal and "extra-legal" means to abolish child labor. Weston contends that "reorienting one's worldview," while essential, is not sufficient to bring about broad-based change without the practical measures he proposes.

Tonia Novitz addresses workers' freedom of association, particularly the conflict between collective action and individual choice. She focuses on two issues: whether the freedom of association encompasses not only the positive entitlement to associate with others but also the negative entitlement to refuse to do so and whether freedom of association extends beyond the ability of an individual to form and join an organization without state interference to the ability to have an organization engage in collective action with state support and protection. Novitz discusses these issues in the context of international law (including U.N. covenants, ILO conventions, and the decisions of the ILO's Committee on Freedom of Association) and the legal systems of Canada, the United Kingdom, and the United States. She finds that the laws of those countries do not comply wholly with ILO standards and that in the U.S. and Canada, this noncompliance has prevented ratification of key instruments relative to the freedom of association. Her essay has important implications for determining the most effective ways to gain protection for participation by workers' organizations in collective bargaining.

Rebecca Smith's chapter emphasizes the urgent and compelling need to protect the rights of migrant workers and forced laborers, so many of whom are the victims of wage exploitation, discrimination, and retaliation. She points out that models exist—in treaties, in judicial decisions, in the approaches of some governments, and in migrant communities themselves—that policy makers in the U.S. and around the world could find useful in dealing with these human rights violations. Smith describes a protection scheme that would redress the imbalance between migrant workers (documented and undocumented) and nationals of a country, including labor rights differences, and recommends aggressive measures to identify and protect victims of trafficking. Her conclusions are based on a thorough analysis of the decisions of the Inter-American Court of Human Rights, the ILO Committee on Freedom of Association, the European Court of Human Rights, and various national courts.

Edward Potter and Marika McCauley Sine reject the traditional business view that upholding internationally recognized human rights based on documents and treaties is not part of business activity. They maintain that business cannot thrive adhering to that position in a global economy. According to Potter and McCauley Sine, business cannot ignore its unique role concerning human rights despite the fact that primary accountability remains with government to protect its citizens and to enforce the law. The authors provide a historical perspective on the evolution of how human rights began to find its way into business through self-regulation in the form of codes of conduct that reflect ILO standards. Despite this progress, the authors lament, there is no clear path or pragmatic set of standards articulating the human rights obligations of employers. They also note that human rights topics are still absent from most boardrooms.

Although most discussions of employment discrimination law and policy treat the issue as one of civil rights or work law, Maria Ontiveros takes a different approach, using a human rights perspective to assess the strengths and weaknesses of discrimination law and policy. Her chapter begins with the reasons why employment discrimination is correctly understood as a violation of human rights and then discusses the ILO's principles regarding employment discrimination and its implementation of those principles. Ontiveros also discusses specific topics, namely, racial discrimination and affirmative action; discrimination based on sex, gender, and sexuality; religious discrimination; and discrimination based on national origin, citizenship, and migrant status. Her chapter concludes with a comparative and critical evaluation of U.S. employment discrimination law under human rights principles. Using human rights as the standard of judgment, Ontiveros finds that U.S. law "falls short of providing full protection of the human rights of American workers."

Susanne Bruyère and Barbara Murray explain the transition in focus when considering workers with disabilities from impairment and rehabilitation to the long-overlooked rights of those workers to participate at the workplace and in the world economy. It is a shift from a predominantly medical or welfare approach to a social rights–based model of disability. They emphasize that although the rights of workers with disabilities were ignored even in the International Bill of Rights (the Universal Declaration of Human Rights, the International Covenant on Civil and Political Rights, and the International Covenant on Economic, Social and Cultural Rights), change has come with the adoption of the U.N. Convention on the Rights of Persons with Disabilities (CRPD). In light of this recent human rights development, the authors review and discuss the status of disability laws in the U.S. and the European Union. They underscore the need for change in overarching philosophy to understand that employment is a key aspect of disability rights policy and empowerment. In addition to a discussion of specific changes that need to be made, the authors provide a valuable discussion of the implications of their work for labor and employment relations professionals and for further research.

References

Croft Metal, Inc., 348 NLRB No. 38 (2006).
Golden Crest Healthcare Center, 348 NLRB No. 39 (2006).
Hoffman Plastic Compounds, Inc. v. *National Labor Relations Board*, 535 U.S. 137 (2002).
International Labour Organization. 2006. Committee on Freedom of Association Case No. 2292, Report No. 343. Complaint against the United States.
International Labour Organization. 2007. Committee on Freedom of Association Case No. 2460, Report No. 344. Complaint against the United States.
Muggeridge, Matthew C. 2008. "Organized Labor's International Law Project? Transforming Workplace Rights into Human Rights." *Engage*, Vol. 9, no. 1 (February), pp. 98–108.
Oakwood Healthcare, Inc., 348 NLRB No. 37 (2006).
Oxfam America. 2004. *Like Machines in the Fields: Workers Without Rights in American Agriculture.* March.

CHAPTER 2

Takin' It to the Man: Human Rights at the American Workplace

JAMES A. GROSS
Cornell University

A New Perspective

Until recently, the international human rights movement and organizations, human rights scholars, and even labor organizations and advocates have given little attention to workers' rights as human rights. As I have written elsewhere:

> Historically human rights organizations have concentrated on the most egregious kinds of human rights abuses such as torture, death squads, and detention without trial. This lack of attention has contributed to workers being seen as expendable in worldwide economic development and their needs and concerns not being represented at conferences on the world economy dominated by bankers, finance ministers, and multinational corporations. As one United Nations document put it, "Despite the rhetoric, violations of civil and political rights continue to be treated as though they were far more serious, and more patently intolerable, than massive and direct denials of economic, social, and cultural rights" (Gross 2003:3).

This is particularly true in the United States, where labor and employment law practitioners and jurists rarely even refer to human rights instruments and standards, let alone utilize them. Those instruments and standards exist on nearly all aspects of work, including nondiscrimination; freedom of association; collective bargaining; safety and health; wages, hours, and working conditions; migrant labor; forced labor; child labor; employment security; social security; and training and technical assistance.

The current growing concern for the promotion and protection of human rights in labor and employment systems in the United States and around the world promises a new vision, exciting in its potential for

challenging not only every orthodoxy in the labor–employment relations field and every practice and rule rooted in that orthodoxy but
even the underlying premises and intellectual foundations of contemporary systems. This does not mean that the traditional concerns of
labor–employment systems would become unimportant, but that those
concerns—collective bargaining, conflict resolution, personnel policies, labor market institutions and their operation, and government
regulation—would be redefined by reconsidering those old labor problems from a new human rights perspective.

That new perspective, moreover, would constitute a standard of
judgment and a set of values different from and, in many crucial ways,
contrary to the commonly accepted standards and values that give dominance to efficiency, competitiveness, profitability, stability, economic
development, management rights, property rights, and cost–benefit
analysis. Conformity to the human rights standard would require fundamental changes in labor employment systems far different than the
changes proposed and anticipated on the basis of long-dominant standards and values (Kochan 1998).

Subjecting every rule and premise to a human rights test will also
demonstrate, more clearly than before, the central roles and influence of
values and moral choices and conceptions of rights and justice in the
determination of the worth of human life, workers' rights to participate in
the decisions that affect their lives at the workplaces and beyond, the
sources of worker and employer rights, and the basis for distributing workplace benefits and burdens. These are deliberate and conscious choices by
legislators, government agencies, judges, labor arbitrators, negotiators of
collective bargaining contracts, human resources departments, employers
(unionized or not), and other decision makers in these labor–employment
systems—they are not choices dictated by some unalterable economic
laws. Labor–employment systems are not deterministic.

The Universal Declaration of Human Rights

The Universal Declaration of Human Rights, or UDHR (Universal
Declaration of Human Rights 1948), although not a binding treaty,
has been the foundation of much of the post–World War II codification of human rights in covenants, conventions, protocols, and
regional treaties. The UDHR is considered the "moral anchor" of the
worldwide human rights movement and currently "there is not a single nation, culture, or people that is not in one way or another
enmeshed in human rights regimes" (Morsink 1999:x). The language
of the declaration was intended to proclaim, not merely to recommend or suggest.

The UDHR was the first statement of moral values issued by an assembly of the human community. The authors of the declaration considered themselves to be representatives of all humankind more than representatives of the 56 member nations of the United Nations (UN) in 1948. The changes in the tentative titles of the document from the "United Nations Declaration of Human Rights" to the "International Declaration of Human Rights" to the "Universal Declaration of Human Rights" reflect the international shift of attention away from states and their delegations to all men, women, and children in all walks of life in every culture around the world. In the document's operative paragraph, for example, the U.N. General Assembly proclaimed that the UDHR

[a]s a common standard of achievement for all peoples and all nations, to the end that every individual and every organ of society, keeping this Declaration constantly in mind, shall strive by teaching and education to promote respect for these rights and freedoms and by progressive measures, national and international, to secure their universal and effective recognition and observance, both among the peoples of the Member States themselves and among the peoples of territories under their jurisdiction (Morsink 1999:330).

There had been enormous pressure on the delegates to the founding conference of the United Nations in 1945 to include an international bill of rights in the UN Charter. Under the authority of the General Assembly, the Economic and Social Council established a Commission on Human Rights and directed the commission to write an international bill of rights. Two years later, the Third General Assembly adopted the UDHR. In that entire period, through proposals, revisions, debates, deletions, additions, and votes, the drafters never attempted to agree to a formal definition of what a human right is.

There was philosophical consensus, however, that human rights are inherent in people. The UDHR states in its preamble that "recognition of the inherent dignity and of the equal and inalienable rights of all members of the human family is the foundation of freedom, justice and peace in the world." It asserts in Article 1 that "all human beings are *born* free and equal in dignity and rights" (emphasis added). Human rights are literally the rights one has simply because one is a human being. The drafters of the UDHR intended to assert moral rights of the highest order that all human beings had and were entitled to enjoy without permission or assent and that were beyond the power of any person, group, government or otherwise to grant or deny (Donnelly 1996). This concept poses a direct challenge to existing institutions, practices, and values generally and to labor–employment systems, in particular—as will be discussed.

Economic Rights

Although the UDHR offers no specific definition of the individual and collective rights of human beings, it posits a set of values, a new ethic of human rights, in sharp contradiction to the values that powerfully influence the United States' labor–employment system. The UDHR sought to transform the moral awareness of all peoples by positing the dignity and worth of all persons and their inherent and inalienable entitlement not only to civil and political rights (Articles 1–21) but also to economic and social rights (Articles 22–28). At its core, the UDHR rejects the purest expression of evil in the modern world: "the ability to erase the humanity of other beings and to turn them into usable and dispensable things" (Delbanco 1995:192).

At one point in Arthur Miller's play *Death of a Salesman*, Willie Loman, the salesman about to be fired after 34 years with the firm, cries out, partly in anger and partly in desperation, "You can't eat the orange and throw the peel away—a man is not a piece of fruit" (Miller 1976:82). Loman had no claims against his employer based on legal rights, or contractual rights, or court precedent, or constitutional rights. He asserted a moral right, however, based on the value of human life. He claimed it was unjust for others to be indifferent to his suffering and to treat him as if he were expendable and counted for nothing unless he had something to sell. But the dominant free market value scheme considers workers to be commodities to be priced in the market no differently than any resource for production.

Classical economics' basic assumption defines human behavior as rational only when a person acts to maximize his or her own satisfaction. Each human being is an amoral, hedonistic, pleasure-maximizing acquisitive animal—or, as preferred by the philosophy of economics, "homo economicus." The each-versus-all individualism that drives the free market approach to life induces people to be preoccupied with their own private self-interests. This one-for-one-and-none-for-all value scheme is articulated by novelist Ayn Rand in *The Fountainhead*, a hymn to individualism, in which her heroes struggle against any restraint on their own self-interest. Architect Howard Roark, Rand's protagonist, explains to a court that he dynamited housing that he had designed for the poor because, as its creator, he owed it to no one:

It is believed that the poverty of the future tenants gave them a right to my work. That their need constituted a claim on my life. That it was my duty to contribute to anything demanded of me. . . . I came to say that I do not recognize anyone's right to one minute of my life. Nor to any part of my energy. Nor to any achievement of mine. No matter who makes the claim, no matter how large their number or how great their need. I came here to say that I am a man who does not exist for others (Rand 1961:100).

This self-interest-focused value scheme also leads people to accept even the harsh economic and social consequences of the market as the inevitable results of impersonal forces beyond anyone's control. If the market is impersonal, moreover, it can be neither just nor unjust. It is absurd, the argument goes, to demand justice of such a process because there is no answer to the question of who has been unjust. When bad things happen to people, they are misfortunes not injustices. As one distinguished economist put it, "'social justice' is simply quasi-religious superstition" (Hayek 1976:66).

The economic and social philosophy of *laissez faire* is, therefore, an elaborate and interconnected set of values in which freedom is the economic freedom of the entrepreneur; democracy is a government system that gives maximum protection to property rights; progress is economic growth; individualism means the right to use one's property as he or she desires and to compete with others; and society is a market society that promotes and does little to interfere with competition in which the fittest win out. None of the drafters of the UDHR believed that the unregulated market system would promote or protect human rights. Their core concept that every life is sacred is incompatible with notions that one is worth only what one has to sell or that, if one has nothing to sell, one is nothing (Goulet 2005). The drafters, therefore, included in the document not only civil rights, such as the right to liberty, freedom from discrimination, equality before the law, and due process, but also economic and social rights, including the right to social security, the right to work, protection against unemployment, just pay, the right to form trade unions, the right to rest and leisure, the right to a standard of living "adequate for the health and well-being of himself and of his family, including food, clothing, housing and medical care," and the right to an education "directed to the full development of the human personality." Some refer to these as "positive rights" because they require a government to provide and promote them—as if so-called "negative rights" (civil and political rights) do not require government action.

The case for including economic rights was rooted in the preamble to the UN Charter (Charter of the United Nations 1945), which states, among other things, that "we the peoples of the United Nations" are determined "to promote social progress and better standards of life in larger freedom," and in Article 55 of the charter, which commits the UN to promoting "higher standards of living, full employment, and conditions of economic and social progress and development." Until the UDHR, the conception of human rights in the Western tradition had been limited to those individual rights that need to be protected against abuse by the state, particularly the freedom from being coerced into doing things. The corresponding duty of the state and other individuals, therefore, is simply a duty of self-restraint. From that perspective the essential rights of humanity were "negative." There was a historically important affinity between this 18th-century negative rights theory and the emergent free market *laissez faire* economics of the time that led to the doctrine advocating the minimalist state. This tradition helps explain why civil and political rights have dominated human rights discussions.

The United States' position on the idea of economic human rights has fluctuated from the time of Franklin Roosevelt's Economic Bill of Rights in 1944 to the Reagan administration's rejection of claimed economic rights as rights of any sort. When the UDHR drafters included in the preamble that not only freedom of speech and belief but also freedom from fear and want had been proclaimed as people's highest aspiration, they were paying tribute to Roosevelt and his ideals (Morsink 1999). Roosevelt had asserted that true freedom could not exist without economic security and independence. He went on to specify in his Economic Bill of Rights what he affirmed had become self-evident truths: the right to a useful and remunerative job, the right "to earn enough to provide adequate food and clothing and recreation," the right of every farmer and his family to a decent living, the right of every businessman to trade free from unfair competition, the right "of every family to a decent home," the right "to adequate medical care, and the opportunity to achieve and enjoy good health," the right "to adequate protection from the economic fears of old age, sickness, accident and unemployment," and the right to a "good education." (See *Congressional Record* 1944, pp. 55–57.) Those rights became essential parts of the UDHR.

The drafters, as well as Roosevelt, recognized that as economic development had generated and been generated by powerful private economic organizations that it was not only the state that had the power to violate people's rights. As stated in Articles 22 and 26, these economic, social, and cultural rights are considered indispensable for the free and full development of the human personality mainly because a unity of civil, political, and economic, social, and cultural rights is necessary for a fully human life.

The drafters also believed in the fundamental unity of all the human rights set forth in the UDHR. Each article was to be interpreted in light of the others in the sense that all were implicated in each other. They had no sense of any ranking of rights in terms of their importance. There were no second-class citizens or second-class rights, but rather the declaration had an organic unity.

The drafters, under the direction of the Commission on Human Rights established by the UN's Economic and Social Council, had set out to create an international bill of rights that would have the treaty status of a convention or covenant. When the Third General Assembly adopted the declaration, it called for the completion of the covenant that the commission had been unable to finish. It was subsequently decided to have two covenants instead of one, and in 1966 the International Covenant on Civil and Political Rights (ICCPR; International Covenant on Civil and Political Rights 1966) and the International Covenant on Economic, Social and Cultural Rights (ICESCR; International Covenant on Economic, Social and Cultural Rights 1966) were opened for signature. The U.S. signed and ratified the ICCPR, but with so many reservations that the U.S. domestic law has never been changed to ensure compliance with this covenant's obligations. The U.S. has not ratified the ICESCR. Ironically, however, the preamble of the ICCPR, as well as the preamble of the ICESCR, states unequivocally that "in accordance with the Universal Declaration of Human Rights, the ideal of human beings enjoying civil and political freedom and freedom from fear and want can only be achieved if conditions are created whereby everyone may enjoy his civil and political rights as well as his economic, social and cultural rights."

Article 22 of the ICCPR also recognizes that "everyone shall have the right to freedom of association with others, including the right to form and join trade unions for the protection of his interests." Closely following the UDHR, the ICESCR recognizes, among others, these rights: to work (Article 6); to fair wages, a decent living, safe and healthful working conditions, and rest and leisure (Article 7); to form trade unions for the promotion and protection of economic and social interests and to strike (Article 8); to social security (Article 9); to protection and assistance to the family and protection of children from economic and social exploitation (Article 10); to adequate food, clothing, and housing and to be free from hunger (Article 11); to the highest attainable standard of physical and mental health (Article 12); and to education for the full development of the human personality (Article 13).

Although the impact of employer decisions on human life is much more direct than the impact of most political decisions, there has been a preoccupation, even among human rights organizations and advocates, with issues of state power and political democracy—while most people are subjected to economic forces and economic power over which they have little or no control. In addition, skepticism and in some quarters outright rejection persist in regard to whether there are economic and social human rights and whether corporations have any obligations to respect human rights.

Individual and Collective Rights

Ironically, whereas some see workers' human rights, particularly economic rights, threatening, if not destroying, the free enterprise system, others see the same rights as masking a selfish egoism (Henkin et al. 1999). Because of the traditional human rights focus on the rights of the individual and an alleged emphasis on rights and not responsibilities, some fear the possibility of human rights devolving "into something approximating libertarian individualism" or "atomistic individuals functioning according to the dictates of the market" with "little organizational payoff" for U.S. labor or even a subversion of union solidarity and collective action (Lichtenstein 2003:70–72).

Human rights are not left-wing or right-wing devices designed to advance some organizational or political interest. If human rights have only a pragmatic justification, their defenders will abandon them whenever they are no longer useful or when some other approach is more useful (Tushnet 1984). One should never underestimate, moreover, the ability of some people to twist even the most noble principle into a defense of the most ignoble action—for example, using the concept of the natural rights of man and Christian religious doctrines to justify slavery.

Workers' human rights, however, are inextricably connected to workers' coming together to exercise their right of freedom of association through organizational and collective bargaining. Only then can they exercise control over their workplace lives. Too many workers stand before their employers not as adult persons with rights but as powerless children or servants totally dependent on the will and interests of their employers (Gross 1998). The drafters of the UDHR recognized this, asserting in Article 23(4) that "everyone has the right to form and join trade unions for the protection of his interests."

Contrary to the claim that human rights are all about individual rights and not about duties, the drafters of the UDHR understood that the exercise of rights requires a responsibility to others and to the larger society. Article 29 of the UDHR affirms that everyone has duties to the community and the obligation to respect the rights of others and to meet the "just requirements of morality, public order, and the general welfare in a democratic society." The UDHR was addressed not to individuals as isolated and separate persons but to individual persons as members of the human family. The full development of the human personality that is a theme of the UDHR can occur only in collaboration with others in a community of persons interacting with each other in a society characterized by cooperation and co-responsibility that respects the personal dignity and equality of its members (Baum 1996).

Inspired by the atrocities of World War II, the UDHR was addressed to the vulnerable and exploited with the purpose of affirming human rights that were intended to eliminate or minimize the vulnerability that leaves people at the mercy of others who have the power to hurt them. It expressed a unity of rights to a unity of humankind. It was never intended to leave people alone and isolated or for the document to become another manifesto justifying the pursuit of selfishness. The vision and values expressed in the UDHR clash with the vision and values of the dominant free market doctrines. The realization of a new human rights vision will require a revolution of values—but more about that later.

Cultural Relativism: "Asian Values"

The idea of human rights forces not only critical reexamination of what it means to be fully human and how individuals relate to one another in a society but also challenges the purposes and authority of governments and private employers and institutions. Because the struggle for human rights has been a struggle against traditional public and private authority and privilege, it has inspired powerful resistance (as well as ridicule) throughout history (Lauren 2003). That resistance still comes in many forms (some already discussed), but chief among them are claims of national sovereignty, cultural relativism, national exceptionalism, and ethnocentrism, or "moral imperialism." The recent "Asian values" controversy raises many of those challenges.

In 1993, a group of Asian nations, in what has become known as the Bangkok Declaration, challenged the very basis of the UDHR. They asserted a form of cultural relativism in arguing that human rights must be considered in the context of national and regional "particularities" and different cultural and religious backgrounds. Underlying the delicate phraseology was the assertion that human rights are rooted in "Western values" different from "Asian values."

One key difference, this argument goes, is that the importance of community in Asian culture is incompatible with the primacy of the individual on which the Western notion of human rights is based—an individualistic value that is allegedly destructive of Asian social values. The

Asian-values position combines the cultural-relativism and community-values arguments in support of the claim that social and economic rights and the right to economic development take precedence over political and civil rights. It objects to Western states emphasizing political and civil rights over economic, social, and cultural rights. In other words, Western-style civil liberties need to be sacrificed in order to meet more basic material needs in the short run. The Asian-values position argues, moreover, that an authoritarian governance is necessary for economic development and that democracy is an impediment to economic development because it leads to inefficiency (Bell 1996).

After the World Conference on Human Rights in 1993 (subsequent to the Bangkok Declaration), the UN General Assembly adopted the Vienna Declaration, which reasserted the universal nature of human rights and their indivisible and interrelated nature. Without mentioning the Bangkok Declaration specifically, the Vienna Declaration also states, "While the significance of national and regional particularities and various historical, cultural and religious backgrounds must be borne in mind, it is the duty of States, regardless of their political, economic and cultural systems, to promote and protect all human rights and fundamental freedoms" (paragraph 5).

To reject the relativist challenge to the idea of human rights, as the Vienna Declaration does, is not to deny that there can be and are differences in traditions, cultures, and conceptions of what ought not to be done to any human being or what ought to be done for any human being. It does not follow from that acknowledgment, however, that no act or failure to act is bad for or that nothing is good for every human being. There has been significant transcultural agreement since the end of World War II, for example, about many human rights, evidenced, in part, by the fact that 162 countries have ratified the ICCPR and 159 the ICESCR. Few in any culture believe that slavery, murder, genocide, torture, rape, or decapitating a child in front of that child's mother is good for anyone subjected to those acts (Perry 1998).

Cultural relativism, moreover, ignores the disparity of beliefs among cultures or even within a single culture. The concept "Asian values" suggests (or maybe exploits) a western view ignorant of an Asia of large geographic areas with immense diversity and with people of drastically different cultures, historical traditions, religions, and values as well as unevenly developed economic and political systems (Li 1996). Even the allegations that human rights are of Western origin is too simplistic and too ahistorical a claim. The origin of an idea, moreover, has nothing to do with its validity. The attempt to disparage human rights on the basis of their alleged Western origin, therefore, seems to be motivated more by the history of West–East relations and the desire to resist Western hegemony than to the origins of human rights. For starters, the international human rights movement advocates some very non-Western conceptions of human rights, including the economic, social, and cultural rights set forth in the UDHR and ICESCR.

The lingering charge of Western ethnocentrism is also due in part to an ignorance of the UDHR drafting process (Morsink 1999). The key drafters understood the philosophical and cultural traditions of Asia, the Middle East, and Latin America as well as Europe. In addition to individual experts, agencies including the International Labour Organization (ILO), the UN Educational, Scientific and Cultural Organization (UNESCO), the World Health Organization (WHO), and the International Refugee Organization (IRO) contributed insights and assessments. UNESCO, for example, assembled a worldwide group of 50 experts on philosophy to submit written comments to the drafters on the issues raised by human rights (Lauren 2003). The UN delegates who approved the UDHR in 1948 "came from Asia, the Pacific, the Middle East, North Africa, Europe and Latin America and represented an incredibly wide range of religious, philosophical and cultural opinion" (Lauren 2003:226).

One can find ample evidence in the history of Western thought supporting slavery and inequality and intolerance of difference and freedom only for those who matter, as well as ample evidence in the history of Eastern and Asian thought supporting freedom, even the freedom to oppose a government, tolerance of diversity in social and religious behavior, and egalitarianism. Some of those Eastern pronouncements of religious tolerance, for example, were being made at the same time the Inquisition was in full force in Europe. Amartya Sen states it well:

> The point of discussing all this now is to demonstrate the presence of conscious theorizing about tolerance and freedom in substantial and important parts of the Asian traditions. . . . Again, the championing of democracy and political freedom in the modern sense cannot be found in pre-enlightenment tradition in any part of the world, West or East. What we have to investigate, instead, are the constituents, the components of this compound idea. It is the powerful presence of some of these elements—in non-Western as well as Western societies—that I have been emphasizing. It is hard to make sense of the view that the basic ideas underlying freedom and rights in a tolerant society are "Western" notions, and somehow alien to Asia, though that view has been championed by Asian authoritarians and Western chauvinists (Sen 1997:38–9).

In addition, all the major religions of the world have in one way or another expressed a vision of human rights in their teachings about the dignity of human beings, their obligations to humankind, and their concepts of duty.

Some find hypocrisy in the Asian-values contentions, seeing them as camouflage for authoritarian governments, where community means the state and the state means those in power, so that opposition to the regime becomes, conceptually at least, a crime against the state, the community and, therefore, the people. Repressive rulers, therefore, use cultural relativism as justification for their actions. As one critic put it, "Thus, rulers use cultural relativist arguments to justify limitations on speech, subjugation of women, female genital mutilation, amputation of limbs, and other cruel punishment, arbitrary use of power, and other violations of international human rights conventions. It is no wonder that the doctrine that human rights are contingent on cultural practice has been called the 'gift of cultural relativists to tyrants'" (Shestack 1998:231).

Other critics point out that leaders professing Asian values have no qualms about accepting and implementing Western capitalist market philosophies or consumerism cultures (Li 1996). Others with a more pragmatic bent maintain that there is no conclusive evidence that civil and political rights inhibit economic development. It needs to be said, however, that the hypocrisy of many nations purporting to adhere to human rights principles, particularly civil and political rights, does not help the human rights cause. In the U.S., for example, the commission of violent and destructive acts around the world supposedly to promote freedom; the subordination of human rights, including workers' rights, when they conflict with commercial considerations; and U.S. support of nations with abysmal human rights records opens this country to claims that these actions are the consequences of "excessive pursuit of individual rights at the cost of common social goods" (Bell 1996:654).

There is no good reason why human beings anywhere in this world should have to choose between starvation and oppression. It is a false dilemma: "to acknowledge that the prospects for effective implementation of human rights differ according to circumstances is not to legitimize violations under those unfavorable conditions, nor is it to deny the universal applicability or validity of human rights to all human beings no matter what circumstances they face" (Li 1996:5).

Human rights advocates do need to pay more attention to diversity within and among different cultures and, while pursuing the implementation of human rights through the development of an international legal system, to understand the limitations of the law in bringing about human rights changes within countries and cultures. Conversation needs to at least supplement confrontation to eliminate oversimplified and intellectually shallow generalizations about "Western civilization," "Asian values," and "African culture" that create unnecessary divisiveness; to understand the diversity within as well as among cultures; to develop approaches and attitudes based on mutual respect and sensitivity; and to develop as well as the local support needed to make human rights a reality where Eleanor Roosevelt said they began:

> Where, after all, do universal human rights begin? In small places, close to home—so close and so small they cannot be seen on any maps of the world. Yet they ARE the world of individual persons; the neighborhood . . . the school or college . . . , the factory, farm, or office. . . . Such are the places where every man, woman and child seeks equal justice, equal opportunity, equal dignity, without discrimination. Unless these rights have meaning there, they have little meaning anywhere. Without concerned citizen action to uphold them at home, we shall look in vain for progress in the larger world (Lauren 2003:288).

National Sovereignty

The human rights movement thus challenges and is challenged by traditional conceptions of the sources of rights, the philosophy and practice of the unregulated market, the long-standing opposition to even the idea of economic rights, the supposed unbridgeable conflict between individual and collective rights, and the wide-ranging consequences of cultural and moral relativism. Yet no doctrine has challenged the realization of international human rights more powerfully than the doctrine of national sovereignty. At the same time, however, human rights challenge national sovereignty because their realization often requires the international community to interfere with the allegedly internal affairs of sovereign states.

Emperors, kings, pharaohs, caesars, tsars, khans, sultans, and dictators of all sorts claimed sovereignty, meaning the right to do as they wished with those under their control, long before the emergence of nation-states and the codification of national sovereignty in international law. Human rights have yielded consistently to national sovereignty. Even in the midst of the abhorrence to the Holocaust, an overwhelming number of states were unwilling to accept any intervention into their "internal affairs," even for the sake of human rights. Many of those governments, including the U.S., were guilty of violating the human rights of many of their own people.

> The United States could speak eloquently about civil rights around the world, for example, but not if they exacerbated what Dulles called "the Negro problem in the South." The

British had no trouble supporting the principle of extending political rights for others, but not if it applied to their empire. The Soviets could support economic and social rights, but not if they threatened to impose any restrictions on Stalin's dictatorship. The Chinese could strongly advocate the right of self-determination in colonial possessions or racial equality, but not if they entailed drastic reforms at home. But this could not simply be laid at the doorstep of the Great Powers alone. The Australians and New Zealanders could endorse a broad extension of human rights for the globe, but not if this jeopardized control over their own immigration policies against Asians or their respective populations of Aborigines or Maori. Jan Smuts of South Africa could enthusiastically draft the language about rights for the preamble to the Charter, but not if it committed his country to giving equal treatment for blacks. The Indians could argue passionately for the rights of all people, but not if it required them to eliminate their caste system. The Iranians could declare their agreement with principles of equality and justice, but not if it forced them to modify their policies toward women. The Cubans had no trouble supporting an international declaration of the rights and duties of all individuals, but not if this in turn threatened the strong-armed rule of Fulgencio Batista (Lauren 2003:192).

How different was war criminal Hermann Goering's defense that it was for Germany alone to determine how to deal with its "Jewish Problem"— "But that was our right! We were a sovereign state and that was strictly our business" (Lauren 2003:203–4)—and the claim that it was for the U.S. alone to determine how to deal with its "Negro Problem"? Still, national sovereignty became part of the UN Charter in Article 2(7), with the statement that "[n]othing contained in the present Charter shall authorize the United Nations to intervene in matters which are essentially within the domestic jurisdiction of any state or shall require Members to submit such matters to settlement."

The human rights challenge to national sovereignty remains in the UN Charter, however. The first sentence of the preamble begins with references not to nation-state signatories but to "[w]e the peoples of the United Nations" who "reaffirm faith in fundamental human rights, in the dignity of the human person, [and] in the equal rights of men and women of nations large and small." Article 1 of the Charter, moreover, pledges signatories to new international responsibilities, including the promotion and encouragement of respect for human rights.

One consequence of the prevalence of national sovereignty is that there is no international body with the authority to compel compliance with international human rights standards or to remedy their violation. Although a serious impediment to the realization of human rights, the current absence of international enforcement power does not render human rights meaningless. In the words of the International Commission on Intervention and State Sovereignty, the problem for human rights continues to be "delivering practical protection for ordinary people, at risk of their lives, because their states are unwilling or unable to protect them" (Lauren 2003:275).

There has been a growing privatization of enforcement covering a wide range of approaches and philosophies that include a "Washington Consensus" that claims democracy and workers' rights are the automatic consequences of economic development, which in turn is the consequence of freeing the market of regulation and shrinking the government. Other types of private enforcement include employer-administered and employer-controlled human relations techniques that purport to respect employees' rights; employer-initiated Codes of Corporate Responsibility, some with monitoring systems, that are advanced as voluntary observances of labor standards; and various regional and bilateral trade agreements between and among nations that include what are touted as potentially strong sanctions for labor rights violations (Compa and Vogt 2001).

In 1998, the ILO adopted a "soft law" instrument—the Declaration on Fundamental Principles and Rights at Work (1998), which privileges four core labor standards: freedom of association, freedom from forced labor and child labor, and nondiscrimination in employment. The ILO's previous focus was on rights set forth in ratified ILO conventions ultimately enforced through public shaming of violators, supervisory mechanisms, reporting requirements, commissions of inquiry, and personal visits to countries supplemented by technical assistance to facilitate the implementation of rights. The new ILO approach is promotional, avoiding negative condemnations or confrontations, with enforcement being voluntary and in the hands of private actors.

The new emphasis is controversial. Proponents contend that the role of the ILO is not to block member states through "legalisms" from pursuing their individual self-interest but rather "to help them see where their self-interest actually lies and to assist them in getting there" (Langille 2005:420). Opponents respond:

> If the self-interest of governments truly matched the interests of workers around the world, we would not need an international system to promote respect for standards. They would have no problem ratifying the relevant ILO conventions, since

these would express their self interest. This they have not
done, of course. And expressing optimism that the Declaration
will bring about a reconceptualization of governmental self
interest does nothing to address the reasons why labour rights
violations are ubiquitous (Alston 2005:473).

One has only to look at successful social protest movements, such as
the civil rights and women's movements in the U.S., the Solidarity movement in Poland, and the anti-apartheid movement in South Africa, to
understand the crucial importance of bottom-up movements to secure
social justice and human rights. People whose rights are at stake are the
ultimate source of power for enforcement. Currently in the U.S., for
example, there are social movements of women, consumers, students,
religious communities, and environmentalists as well as human rights
nongovernmental organizations including Human Rights Watch,
Amnesty International, Oxfam International, American Rights at Work,
Interfaith Worker Justice, the National Employment Law Project, and
many others working to promote and protect the human rights of workers and others. Although not widely reported, organized labor, in this
and other countries, engages in transnational labor actions as a powerful
form of self-help enforcement (Atleson 2003).

The fight for workers' rights around the world "is a struggle that
never ends, and advocates take victories—and they hope defeats—in
small measures" (Compa & Vogt 2001). As an ILO official put it, "If you
have a short attention span don't get into the human rights business"
(Lee Swepston, then chief of the ILO's Equality and Employment
Branch, to my Workers' Rights as Human Rights class in 2004).

U.S. Labor Law and Standards

The persistence of national sovereignty means that national governments remain principal actors in the promotion and protection as well as
the violations of human rights. Despite the globalization that has
occurred, domestic labor laws continue to be major sources of rights
protection. It is commonly asserted that labor laws and standards in the
United States, for example, are equal or superior to international human
right standards. They are not, either in their substance or in their interpretation and application.

The objective should be to bring our labor laws into compliance with
international human rights standards, including those already discussed
but also others, such as ILO Conventions No. 87 (Freedom of Association and Protection of the Right to Organise 1948), No. 98 (Right to
Organise and Collective Bargaining 1949), No. 155 (Occupational Safety
and Health 1981), and No. 111 (Discrimination [Employment and
Occupation] Convention 1958). The United States has a legal obligation

under international laws as well as a moral obligation as a member of the UN and the ILO to commit itself to the realization of human rights principles espoused by these organizations. For example, the UDHR, for which the U.S. voted, calls on all nations to promote human rights and to take "progressive measures, national and international to secure their universal and effective recognition and observance." Among these human rights are the right to freedom of association (Article 20), the right to form and join unions (Article 23[4]), and the right "to just and favorable conditions of work" (Article 23[1]).

The ICCPR, which the U.S. has signed and ratified, commits each state party to ensure the rights set forth in the covenant to all persons (Article 2), including the freedom of association and the right to form and join trade unions for the protection of their interests. The ICESCR, which the U.S. has signed but not ratified, obliges each state party to "take steps" to achieve the "full realization" of rights recognized in the covenant, including "just and favorable conditions of work" in particular to "safe and healthy working conditions" (Article 7) and the right of everyone to join trade unions "for the promotion and protection of his economic and social interests" (Article 8). Although the U.S. has not ratified the ICESCR, as a signatory the U.S. is obliged by established international law to refrain from acts that would defeat the object and purpose of the covenant (Vienna Convention on the Law of Treaties 1969).

The Declaration of Philadelphia (Declaration Concerning the Aims and Purposes of the Interntional Labour Organization 1944), annexed to the ILO's constitution, recognizes the solemn obligation of the ILO (of which the U.S. is a member) "to further among the nations of the world programmes which would achieve," among other things, the "effective recognition of the right to collective bargaining," "adequate protection for the life and health of workers in all occupations," and human beings' right to material well-being and spiritual development. The ILO's Declaration on Fundamental Principles and Rights at Work (1998), which the U.S. has adopted, states that "in freely joining the ILO, all members have endorsed the principles and rights set out in the Constitution and in the Declaration of Philadelphia, and have undertaken to work towards attaining the overall objectives of the Organization and to the best of their resources and fully in line with their specific circumstances." That declaration also states that even those members that have not ratified the ILO conventions dealing with the freedom of association and the right to collective bargaining (among other rights) "have an obligation, arising from the very fact of membership in the [ILO] to respect, to promote and to realize, in good faith and in accordance with the [ILO] Constitution, the principles concerning the fundamental rights set forth in these conventions."

The U.S. government and too many U.S. employers are not in compliance with the human rights standards set forth in these internationally
accepted documents. The violations of workers' human rights in this
country are pervasive. These violations are the result of deliberate
choices by legislators, judges, government agencies, employers, unions,
and labor arbitrators, not choices dictated by some unalterable economic
laws.

White superiority in this country, for example, has not made life simply more difficult for African Americans; it has denied them even those
minimal things without which it is impossible to develop one's capacities
and to live life as a human being. It was and is a denial of humanity.
What better evidence is there that this suppression of the human spirit is
ongoing than the separate and unequal education given to children in
the most poverty-stricken and ghettoized "inner cities" 50 years after the
Supreme Court rejected separate educational facilities for white and
black children. Who would disagree "that the most deadly of all sins is
the mutilation of a child's spirit"? (Kozol 1967:vii). Both the UDHR and
the Convention on the Rights of the Child (1990) confirm that everyone
has the right to an education, which for children is to be for "the development of the child's personality, talents and mental and physical abilities to their fullest potential."

What black workers are experiencing today across the United States
has deep roots. This was no economic misfortune; it was the inevitable
consequence of human choices to violate the human rights of black people or to accommodate those violations or not to resist them in any way.
It was one piece from slavery to Jim Crow separation doctrines; to state-
sanctioned segregation in every aspect of human life; to separation
enforced by public lynchings and other means of physical and psychological intimidation; to the denial of adequate health care and even a basic
education; to consignment to "Negro jobs" and the denial of workplace
rights, dignity, and economic opportunity by corporations, other businesses, and even unions that professed to promote and protect workers'
rights; to the ghettoization of housing often enforced by violence, unsavory
real estate practices, and neighborhood associations of ethnic working-
class and middle-class whites who used "homeowners' rights" as a rallying cry to keep blacks out of their neighborhoods. The sanitation
workers striking in Memphis at the time of Martin Luther King, Jr.'s
assassination carried on their picket signs the powerful human rights
message "I AM A MAN." No human rights document has said it better.

Servility is incompatible with human rights. The Wagner Act of 1935
was intended to enable workers, through the exercise of their freedom of
association, to obtain sufficient power to make the claims of their human

rights both known and effective. Respect for their rights, therefore, would not be dependent on the interests of the state, their employers, or others. Neither the Wagner Act nor its successor, the Taft-Hartley Act, is neutral. Both statutes declare it to be the policy of the U.S to encourage collective bargaining and to protect workers in the exercise "of full freedom of association, self-organization, and designation of representatives of their own choosing for the purpose of negotiating the terms and conditions of employment or other mutual aid or protection" (Labor Management Relations Act 1947).

In its 2000 report on the state of workers' freedom of association in the U.S., Human Rights Watch found that freedom of association was "a right under severe, often buckling pressure when workers in the United States try to exercise it" and that the "government is often failing its responsibility under international human rights standards to deter such attacks and protect workers' rights" (Human Rights Watch 2000:7–8). This is not the place to detail judicial and administrative agency decisions, such as those protecting employer anti-union speech, including captive audience speech, or denying non-employee union organizers access to employer property and excluding from employers' obligation to bargain subjects at the so-called core of entrepreneurial control. The fact is that we in the U.S. have declared a national policy that encourages worker participation in the decisions that affect their workplace lives, but in practice we reject it.

My own study of Wagner-Taft-Hartley from 1947 to 1994, published in *Broken Promise* (Gross 1995), shows how a policy that encouraged the replacement of industrial autocracy with a democratic system of power sharing was turned into governmental protection of employers' unilateral decision-making authority over decisions that greatly affected wages, hours, and working conditions. More specifically it demonstrates how the statute and NLRB case law have come to legitimize employer opposition to the organization of employees, collective bargaining, and workplace democracy—in other words, to legitimize opposition to the exercise by employees of their human right of freedom of association. As one scholar noted, "Few advanced democratic societies condone open opposition by employers to unionization" (Adams 1992:94). The fact that the government simply permits private power to be exercised does not absolve the government of its responsibility to intervene when that private power is used to interfere with a human right, such as the right to the freedom of association.

Over 40 years before the UDHR, the ILO had incorporated into its constitution the right of freedom of association. Social justice for all countries and individuals has always been the stated prime objective of the ILO, and freedom of association holds a special place in the organization's standards as a basic fundamental human right necessary for social justice. The ILO's 1948 Convention Concerning Freedom of Association and Protection of the Right to Organize (No. 87) establishes and defines the right of workers (and employers) to set up and join organizations of their choosing. It calls upon states to take all necessary measures to ensure that workers (and employers) can exercise freely their right to organize. The ILO's 1949 Convention No. 98, Concerning the Application of the Principles of the Right to Organise and to Bargain Collectively, asserts the right of workers to be free of anti-union discrimination, to organize, and to engage in collective bargaining.

Because of the importance of the freedom of association, the ILO has established special machinery to deal with complaints of its violation. The Committee on Freedom of Association (CFA), which examines such complaints and makes recommendations to the governing body of the ILO, is a key component of that machinery. Over the years, the CFA has issued a series of decisions and established principles intended to promote and protect workers' right of association. The CFA does not distinguish between charges leveled against governments and those leveled against persons but in both cases seeks to determine if a government has ensured the free exercise of rights to freedom of association within its borders.

The CFA has found that, in many important respects, U.S. labor law and practice do not conform to international human rights principles. The committee, for example, has called on the U.S. to guarantee the access of union representatives to workplaces, has expressed concerns about the long-standing problem of delay in our labor law system, found that the National Labor Relations Act (NLRA) did not treat workers and employers "on a fully equal basis" (because it mandates that the National Labor Relations Board [NLRB] seek an injunction against certain union unfair labor practices but not any employer unfair labor practices), and ruled that the permanent replacement of economic strikers meant that the essential right to strike "was not fully guaranteed." In addition, the committee has pointed out that, in some states, public sector workers have no statutorily protected right to collective bargaining, while, in other states, collective bargaining is banned (Gross 1999:81–5).

Most recently, the CFA concluded that the Supreme Court's denial to undocumented workers of the NLRB's back-pay remedy for violations of the NLRA left the board with remedial measures that provide little protection to undocumented workers "who can be indiscriminately dismissed for exercising freedom of association rights without any direct penalty aimed at dissuading such action" (International Labour Organization

2003:paragraphs 609, 610). The CFA also found that states in the U.S. that ban public sector collective bargaining are in violation of ILO Conventions Nos. 87 and 98 and, in regard to one of those states, North Carolina, requested that it establish collective bargaining in the public sector (International Labour Organization 2007). In 2006, the CFA requested that the U.S. government engage in collective bargaining with workers' organizations over the terms and conditions of employment for the approximately 56,000 federal airport screeners in the Transportation Security Administration—except for matters "directly" related to national security issues (International Labour Organization 2006). In 2008, the CFA responded to the charge that the expansion of the definition of "supervisor" was depriving workers who are not supervisors of their collective bargaining rights. The CFA found that certain NLRB interpretations gave rise "to an overly wide definition of supervisory staff that would go beyond freedom of association principles" (International Labour Organization 2008a). Finally, in response to a complaint that a decision of the NLRB denying graduate teaching and research assistants at private universities the right to engage in collective bargaining, the CFA concluded that insofar as they were workers, these teaching and research assistants were entitled to the full protection of their right to bargain collectively over the terms and conditions of their employment—excluding academic requirements and policies (International Labour Organization 2008b).

Among workers' human rights, no aspect of work is more directly related to the sacredness of life than the safety and health of men, women, and children who labor. It is the right to live that demands workplace health and safety (Spieler 2003). The right to life is embedded in every human rights declaration; it places the highest value on a human life, an eye, an arm, a leg, or a hand; and it proclaims the absolute priority of human rights over economic and institutional interests. Yet workers' right to life has been sacrificed to economic development, the government has failed to enforce its workplace safety and health laws, and courts and arbitrators give preference to management interests and deny workers the right to protect their own lives by engaging in self-help actions.

An employee's right to refuse hazardous work without retaliation, for example, is indispensable if workers are to take control over their own lives in regard to workplace health and safety. In the U.S., however, in contrast to other countries, such as Canada and Sweden, the judicial standard that maximizes employer control of employee discipline minimizes employee interference with that control. There is no need to rehash here the particulars of how that is done. The major point is that this pro–employer authority, pro–employer property rights standard confronts workers with an inherently unfair dilemma: to follow orders and work, thereby risking life and limb, or to refuse to follow orders, thereby risking discharge or other serious discipline. No decent society would permit human beings to be put in that position, particularly when economic necessity pressures so many to choose jobs over their own health and safety, more often than not with no or insufficient information about the health and safety hazards involved in what they are ordered to do. Workers' humanity and human rights to a safe and healthful workplace are disrespected whichever choice they make.

In many ways, moreover, human resources is simply another approach to denying workers their freedom of association rights. The economic profitability standard or cost–benefit standard cannot be the ultimate determinant of whether human rights will be respected, promoted, and exercised at the workplace. Judged by a human rights standard, human resources personnel would be held accountable for manipulating human beings and subordinating them to the interests of the organization. It is a manipulation that induces workers to see the world through their employers' frame of reference in order to maintain and legitimize employer control at the workplace without changing the power relationships of superior employer and subordinate employee. Combined with employment at will, human resources techniques leave workers powerless.

It is also a manipulation that uses people as resources for economic ends. Human resources has always expressed an active anti-unionism. This anti-unionism, euphemistically termed union avoidance or staying union-free, violates one of the most fundamental human rights: the right of workers to participate in the decisions that affect their workplace lives. Regardless of the quality of management or an employer's good or bad employee relations, exercise of the freedom of association is necessary so that workers can eliminate the vulnerabilities that leave them at the mercy of others. Human resources cannot fill a freedom of association gap. Those who manipulate the behavior of others to ensure their servility, powerlessness, and subordination are complicit in using workers as disposable commodities or resources for others' gain.

The Challenges: Labor Law, Labor Policy and Research

The promotion and protection of human rights at U.S. workplaces pose challenges to some of the most fundamental principles on which the U.S. labor relations system is based. U.S. labor law provides good examples. Over the years, there have been many legislative proposals designed to correct deficiencies in our current labor laws. They include proposals to increase the effectiveness of NLRB remedies, to crack down on the anti-union consulting industry, to lift prohibitions on secondary activity to permit unions to exercise solidarity around the world, to minimize employer coercive involvement in representation campaigns by the use of union authorization card certifications, and to guarantee employees who vote for a union (at least when their chosen representative fails to negotiate a first contract) a grievance procedure with binding arbitration. None of these efforts have been successful. It will be a momentous task to bring U.S. labor law into conformity with established workers' rights as human rights principles. A few examples should suffice.

Although the UDHR, the ICCPR, the ICESCR, and the ILO Convention No. 87 all affirm that everyone has the right to freedom of association, the Taft-Hartley Act expressly excludes millions of workers from the laws' coverage. Exclusions include resident and immigrant agricultural workers, domestic service workers, and independent contractors and even low-level supervisors and managers. These workers can organize if they wish, but their employers have no legal obligation to recognize or deal with their organizations and may intimidate or discharge them if they do attempt to exercise their freedom of association because those excluded workers are not protected by law. These legislative exclusions openly conflict with international human rights law.

In a closely related interpretation of the NLRA, unless there is a union that has the support of a majority of the relevant employees, workers' human right to freedom of association is lost in what Clyde Summers has called the "black hole" of no union rights (Summers 1990). Bargaining collectively with a nonmajority union that bargains for its own members is protected widely in other countries with systems of collective bargaining. Charles Morris has asserted that without nonmajority unions, the right of association advanced by ILO Convention No. 87 would be meaningless for workers who want to exercise that right but are unable to persuade a majority of their co-workers to join them (Morris 1994). There is also a serious question whether the U.S. conception of exclusive representation also denies workers their association rights by denying them the choice of alternative representation.

It is also worth noting that the value of the NLRA's freedom of association depends in great part on the effectiveness of collective bargaining, which in turn depends in great part on where the line, if any, is drawn between exclusive management functions on one side and the subjects of joint management–union determination on the other. The Supreme Court and certain Republican-appointed NLRBs have taken the lead in freeing management from the constraints of the NLRA by promoting management rights and limiting worker participation. The

Kennedy–Johnson NLRB's understanding of the subjects of collective bargaining—"the scope of collective bargaining is confined to the range of employees' vital interests" (Gross 1995:174)—was most consistent with the human rights conception of freedom of association and collective bargaining. It was also most consistent with the stated purpose of the NLRA, which is supposed to be the encouragement of collective bargaining even when management decision making might be "encumbered" (Atleson 1983).

Human rights principles, particularly workers' rights as human rights, pose even more fundamental challenges to U.S. labor law and policy. One is whether employers should be permitted to resist workers' exercise of their right of freedom of association. That question goes beyond the obvious contradiction (hypocrisy) of legislating a commitment to collective bargaining and then, in the same statute, allowing and even facilitating employers' use of their power over workers' jobs to discourage workers from exercising their statutory right to organization and collective bargaining. This involves much more than a matter of conflicting interests between labor and management. This is a fundamental human rights issue.

Implementation of human rights at the workplace also challenges the still-dominant theory of industrial and labor relations commonly known as industrial pluralism, attributed to "Wisconsin School" pioneer John R. Commons. The institutional economists that helped develop industrial pluralism rooted their work in a philosophy of pragmatism without any grand design such as that propounded by classical market economics. Industrial pluralism posits collective bargaining as its main labor relations problem-solving device, which through compromise establishes systems of work rules set forth in contracts that become the constitutions at workplaces. These contract-constitutions provide governance regarding wages, hours, and working conditions as well as a grievance-arbitration procedure constituting employers' and unions' own private judicial system.

The negotiation process is presumed to be between parties of roughly equal bargaining power. Commons was concerned that the exercise of bargaining power be "reasonable." Work rules were reasonable if the conflicting economic interests mutually and voluntarily negotiated and accepted them. For Commons, "the essential thing was that the line between reasonable and unreasonable exercises of power was not drawn by any broad social philosophy or public principle but was hammered out on a case-by-case basis, in the resolution of particular disputes." (Chamberlain 1963:84). Limits can be set on unequal bargaining power by "judicial-like" decisions by arbitrators and ultimately by courts of law that will move these groups "into reasonable relations with each other"

(p. 84) so that agreements do not become merely "the surrender of the weak to the strong and unscrupulous" (p. 6).

The Wagner and Taft-Hartley acts were in the industrial pluralist mode. They set forth procedures for workers to organize and bargain collectively, but they do not confer substantive rights on workers. Neither act was a radical break with the well-rooted freedom-of-contract concept. The private process of negotiation and contracting backed up by bargaining power was the way to determine workplace rights and duties (Klare 1982).

Congress added Section 9(d) in Taft-Hartley, moreover, to affirm that the mutual obligation of employers and unions to bargaining in good faith did not compel either party to agree to a proposal or require the making of a concession. The Supreme Court has concluded that "allowing the [NLRB] to compel agreement when the parties themselves are unable to agree would violate the fundamental premise on which the Act is based—private bargaining under government supervision of the procedure alone, without any official compulsion over the actual terms of the contract. (*H. K. Porter Company, Inc.* v. *NLRB* 1970).

The basic conflict between freedom-of-contract industrial pluralists and those favoring workers' rights as human rights is that pluralists make human rights negotiable. Industrial pluralism makes the very existence of workers' human rights dependent on the relative power of employers and unions. Human rights are nonnegotiable. They are possessed by every person by virtue of being a human being and not by virtue of being a member of a union powerful enough to negotiate human rights into an enforceable collective bargaining contract. Human rights are rights that no government or employer or union or any other body has the moral authority to grant or deny. The only use of power that is legitimate is that which promotes and protects human rights.

The contractual provisions resulting from collective bargaining are not necessarily just simply because they are in accord with the objectives of the negotiators, in the same way that laws are not necessarily just simply because a majority approve of such laws. Given the imbalance of bargaining power, moreover, there is also the possibility that no contract will be reached. Does that mean workers have no human rights, or any rights at all, at such workplaces?

Concerning those courts, administrative agencies, and arbitrators who supposedly would redress the negative consequences of severe imbalances of power, none of them, including the Supreme Court, have utilized human rights standards in their decision making. This "legal isolationism" is yet another challenge (Ignatieff 2005:8). It is essential that human rights at the workplace be enforceable.

Finally, pursuing the challenges posed by the new workers' rights as human rights movement will broaden the industrial relations research agenda and require new approaches to that research. This could make industrial relations research truly interdisciplinary because it requires understanding and applying history, law, philosophy, ethics, economics, religion, and the international and comparative aspects of all these disciplines. This will also require broadening the methodology of industrial relations research beyond quantitative techniques and opening for examination subjects previously not considered because they were not quantifiable. It would reintroduce concepts such as justice and injustice to a field that has come to disparage the "normative" as unscientific and subjective—ill-befitting the objective, value-free social scientist (Gross 2006).

References

Adams, Roy J. 1992. "The Right to Participate." *Employee Responsibilities and Rights Journal,* Vol. 2, no. 2, pp. 91–9.
Alston, Philip. 2005. "Facing Up to the Complexities of the ILO's Core Labour Standards Agenda." *European Journal of International Law*, Vol. 16, no. 3, pp. 467–80.
Atleson, James. 1983. *Values and Assumptions in American Labor Law*. Amherst: University of Massachusetts Press.
Atleson, James. 2003. " 'An Injury to One . . .' Transnational Labor Solidarity and the Role of Domestic Law." In J. Gross, ed., *Workers' Rights as Human Rights*, Ithaca, NY: Cornell University Press, pp. 160–82.
Baum, Gregory. 1996. *Karl Polanyi on Ethics and Economics*. Montreal: McGill-Queen's University Press.
Bell, Daniel A. 1996. "The East Asian Challenge to Human Rights: Reflections on an East West Dialogue." *Human Rights Quarterly,* Vol. 18, no. 3, pp. 641–67.
Chamberlain, Neil W. 1963. "The Institutional Economics of John R. Commons." In Joseph Dorfman, C.E. Ayres, N.W. Chamberlain, S. Kuznets, and R.A. Gordon, eds., *Institutional Economics: Veblen, Commons, and Mitchell Reconsidered*. Berkeley: University of California Press, pp. 63–94.
Charter of the United Nations. 1945. G.A. Res. 1991 (XVIII).
Compa, Lance, and J. S. Vogt. 2001. "Labor Rights in the Generalized System of Preferences: A 20-Year Review." *Comparative Labor Law and Policy Journal*, Vol. 22, nos. 2 and 3, pp. 199–238.
Congressional Record. 1944. Vol. 90, pp. 55–57.
Convention on the Rights of the Child. 1990. 1577 U.N.T.S. 3.
Declaration Concerning the Aims and Purposes of the International Labour Organization (Declaration of Philadelphia). 1944. <http://www.ilo.org/ilolex/english/iloconst.htm>.
Declaration on Fundamental Principles and Rights at Work. 1998. International Labor Conference, 86th Session, Geneva. <http://www.ilo.org/public/english/standards/decl/declaration/index.htm>.
Delbanco, Andrew. 1995. *The Death of Satan: How Americans Have Lost the Sense of Evil*. New York: Farrar, Straus and Giroux.

Discrimination (Employment and Occupation) Convention. 1958. (No. 111). <http://www.ilo.org/ilolex/cgi-lex/convde.pl?c111.>. [February 28. 2008].

Donnelly, Jack. 1996. "International Human Rights: A Regime Analysis." In Henry J. Steiner and P. Alston, eds., *International Human Rights in Context: Law, Politics, Morals.* Oxford: Clarendon Press.

Freedom of Association and the Protection of the Right to Organise. 1948 (No. 87), 31st Session (1948).

Goulet, Denis. 2005. "On Culture, Religion, and Development." In Marguerite Mendell, ed., *Reclaiming Democracy: The Social Justice and Political Economy of Gregory Baum and Karl Polanyi Levitt.* Montreal: McGill-Queen's University Press, pp. 21–32.

Gross, James A. 1995. *Broken Promise: The Subversion of U.S. Labor Relations Policy, 1947–1994.* Philadelphia: Temple University Press.

Gross, James A. 1998. "The Broken Promises of the National Labor Relations Act and the Occupational Safety and Health Act: Conflicting Values and Conceptions of Rights and Justice." *Chicago-Kent Law Review,* Vol. 73, no. 1, pp. 351–87.

Gross, James A. 1999. "A Human Rights Perspective on United States Labor Relations Law: A Violation of the Right of Freedom of Association." *Employee Rights and Employment Policy Journal,* Vol. 3, no. 1, pp. 65–103.

Gross, James A. 2003. "A Long Overdue Beginning." In James A. Gross, ed., *Workers' Rights as Human Rights.* Ithaca, New York: Cornell University Press, pp. 1–22.

Gross, James A. 2006. "A Logical Extreme: Proposing Human Rights as the Foundation for Workers' Rights in the United States." In Richard Block, S. Friedman, M. Kaminski, and A. Levin, eds., *Justice on the Job: Perspectives on the Erosion of Collective Bargaining in the United States.* Kalamazoo, MI: W.E. Upjohn Institute for Employment Research, pp. 21–39.

Hayek, Friedrich. 1976. *The Mirage of Social Justice.* Chicago: University of Chicago Press.

Henkin, Louis, G.L. Neuman, D. E. Orentlicher, and D.W. Leebron, eds. 1999. *Human Rights.* New York: Foundation Press.

H.K. Porter Company, Inc. v. National Labor Relations Board, 397 U.S. 99 (1970), 108.

Human Rights Watch. 2000. *Unfair Advantage: Workers' Freedom of Association in the United States Under International Human Rights Standards.* New York: Human Rights Watch.

Ignatieff, Michael. 2005. "Introduction: American Exceptionalism and Human Rights." In Michael Ignatieff, ed., *American Exceptionalism and Human Rights.* Princeton, NJ: Princeton University Press, pp. 1–26.

International Covenant on Civil and Political Rights. 1966. 999 *United Nations Treaty Series* 171.

International Covenant on Economic, Social and Cultural Rights. 1966. 993 *United Nations Treaty Series* 3.

International Labour Organization. 2003. Committee on Freedom of Association Case No. 2227, Report No. 332-2003. Complaints against the Government of the United States presented by the American Federation of Labor and the Congress of Industrial Organizations and the Confederation of Mexican Workers.

International Labour Organization. 2006. Committee on Freedom of Association Case No. 2292, Report No. 343. Complaint against the Government of the United States presented by the American Federation of Government Employees, AFL-CIO, supported by Public Services International.

International Labour Organization. 2007. Committee on Freedom of Association Case No. 2460, Report No. 344. Complaint against the Government of the United States presented by the United Electrical Radio and Machine Workers of America, supported by Public Services International.

International Labour Organization. 2008a. Committee on Freedom of Association Case No. 2524, Report No. 349. Complaint against the Government of the United States presented by the American Federation of Labor and Congress of Industrial Organizations.

International Labour Organization. 2008b. Committee on Freedom of Association Case No. 2547, Report No. 350. Complaint against the Government of the United States presented by the United Automobile, Aerospace and Agricultural Implement Workers of America International Union and the American Federation of Labor and the Congress of Industrial Organizations.

Klare, Karl E. 1982. "The Public/Private Distinction in Labor Law." *University of Pennsylvania Law Review*, Vol. 130, no. 30, pp. 1358–422.

Kochan, Thomas A. 1998. "Back to Basics: Creating the Analytical Foundations for the Next Industrial Relations System." *Proceedings of the Fiftieth Annual Meeting* (Chicago, January 3–5, 1998). Madison, WI: Industrial Relations Research Association.

Kozol, Jonathan. 1967. *Death at an Early Age*. New York: Bantam Books.

Labor Management Relations Act. 1947. As amended by Public Law 86-257, 1959.

Langille, Biran. 2005. "Core Labour Rights—The True Story (Reply to Alston)." *The European Journal of International Law*, Vol. 16, no. 3, pp. 409–37.

Lauren, Paul Gordon. 2003. *The Evolution of International Human Rights: Visions Seen* (2nd ed.). Philadelphia: University of Pennsylvania Press.

Li, Xiaorong. 1996. " 'Asian Values' and the Universality of Human Rights." *Report from the Institute for Philosophy and Public Policy*, Vol. 16, no. 2, pp. 18–23. <http://www.publicpolicy.umd.edu/IPPP/li.htm>. [July 8, 2008.]

Lichtenstein, Nelson. 2003. "The Rights Revolution." *New Labor Forum*, Vol. 12, no. 1, pp. 61–73.

Miller, Arthur. 1976. *Death of a Salesman*. New York: Penguin Books.

Morris, Charles. 1994. "A Blueprint for Reform of the National Labor Relations Act." *The Administrative Law Journal of the American University*, Vol. 8, no. 3, pp. 461–565.

Morsink, Johannes. 1999. *The Universal Declaration of Human Rights: Origins, Drafting, and Intent*. Philadelphia: University of Pennsylvania Press.

Occupational Safety and Health Convention (No. 155). 1981. <http://www.ilo.org/ilolex/cgi-lex/convde.pl?C155.>. [February 28, 2008].

Perry, Michael J. 1998. *The Idea of Human Rights: Four Inquiries*. New York: Oxford University Press.

Rand, Ayn. 1961. *For the New Intellectual: The Philosophy of Ayn Rand*. New York: Random House.

Right to Organise and Collective Bargaining. 1949. (No. 98), 32nd Session.

Sen, Amartya. 1997. "Human Rights and Asian Values." *The New Republic*, July 14 and 21, pp. 33–40.

Shestack, Jerome J. 1998. "The Philosophical Foundations of Human Rights." *Human Rights Quarterly*, Vol. 20, no. 2, pp. 201–34.

Spieler, Emily A. 2003. "Risks and Rights: The Case for Occupational Safety and Health as a Core Worker Right." In James A. Gross, ed., *Workers' Rights as Human Rights*. Ithaca, NY: Cornell University Press, pp. 78–117.

Summers, Clyde. 1990. "Unions Without Majority—A Black Hole?" *Chicago-Kent Law Review*, Vol. 66, no. 3, pp. 531–48.

Tushnet, Mark. 1984. "An Essay on Rights." *Texas Law Review*, Vol. 62, no. 8, pp. 1363–403.

Universal Declaration of Human Rights. 1948. G.A. Res. 217 (III) of Dec. 10, 1948, UN General Assembly Official Records, 3rd Session, Resolutions, U.N. Doc. A/810.

Vienna Convention on the Law of Treaties. 1969. <http://www.oas.org/legal/english/docs/Vienna%20Convention%20Treaties.htm>. [April 16, 2009].

CHAPTER 3

A New Frontier for Industrial Relations: Workplace Health and Safety as a Human Right

JEFF HILGERT

Cornell University

Working conditions have been an ongoing topic of scholarship and government for more than a century, yet the understanding that workers' health and safety are human rights has a short history and has until recently not been a significant justification for industrial and labor relations policy. In this chapter, I respond to this gap, challenging industrial relations and labor economics to examine the scope and nature of the problem and articulate a framework of workers' health and safety as human rights concerns. The field of industrial relations has historically characterized workers' health and safety as less than fundamental human rights. This paper is an exploration of the human rights framework and a response to critics in an effort to establish a new foundation for industrial relations scholarship and in turn build the human rights foundation for labor policy.

Acknowledging that workers' health and safety are not only human rights problems but together constitute a major human rights crisis requires a specific understanding of the issue. Learning the situation on the ground is not easy because workers today have little freedom, voice, participation, or liberty to challenge hazards and report occupational injuries and illnesses. The U.S. public policy on occupational health and safety has been strategic workers' disempowerment, legal impunity for employer discrimination and hostility, and government promotion of mythical social progress through the collection and reporting of grossly inaccurate but official statistics on work-related illness, injury, and fatalities. Globally, working people throughout the developing world bear a disproportionate burden of all work-related illness and injury; reliable statistics are not as readily available, but estimates of work-related injury and illness indicate a staggering global problem.

Scholarship is far behind in providing this calamity the attention it deserves. While labor economics has criticized neoclassical economics and admits the need for labor institutions, it rarely extracts itself from the liberal market orthodoxy, including where alternative visions are the only way to protect workers from health and safety hazards. The inherent inefficiency of the labor market in terms of human consequences is lost on many scholars; this is true even where scholarship is highly critical of orthodox neoclassical economics and *laissez-faire* self-regulation. Underlying these problems is a historically strong culture of opposition to economic and social rights in the United States, often replicated internationally. Scholarship is not independent of its cultural context, and biases against economic and social rights must be examined directly and challenged if any progress is to be made recognizing human rights within industrial relations. I argue here that human rights can serve as the foundation for meaningful and objective industrial and labor relations scholarship.

Ongoing Statistical Inaccuracies

Despite what government officials of both political parties claim, the United States is no leader in protecting workers' health and safety. The late American reporter Tim Russert once described his working class town of Buffalo, New York, by explaining how the locals called their second job "the second front" ("Russert and Malloy: Two Guys from South Buffalo" 2008). This analogy is more insightful than are official statistics on health and safety, which fail to give workers' illnesses and injuries the careful attention they deserve and fail to account for the real scope of workers' illnesses and injuries.

The official line in the United States is as follows: The U.S. Bureau of Labor Statistics (BLS) announced that the number of fatal work injuries nationwide declined 6% between 2006 and 2007 to 5,488 deaths, the lowest number since the Census of Fatal Occupational Injuries (CFOI) began recording worker deaths (Bureau of Labor Statistics 2008). Secretary of Labor Elaine Chao attributed the decline in worker deaths to the government's new regulatory enforcement efforts:

> "This is continued evidence that the initiatives and programs to protect workers' safety and health, designed by and implemented in this administration, are indeed working. In addition to a decline in the overall number of fatalities, the rate for 2007 declined to 3.7 fatalities per 100,000 workers. This is the lowest fatality rate in recorded OSHA history" (Occupational Safety and Health Administration 2008).

The official line also reports declining nonfatal illness and injury data. Employer-maintained worker injury and illness logs are sampled by the BLS in the Survey of Occupational Illnesses and Injuries (SOII). According to the SOII, the U.S. witnessed an overall decline of occupational illnesses and injuries by 35.8% from 1992 to 2003 (Friedman & Forst 2007). The claim that work in the U.S. has become healthier and safer has also been heralded by Democrats, such as Clinton administration Secretary of Labor Alexis Herman:

> Workplace injury and illness rates declined in 1999 for the seventh straight year—nearly a 30% drop since 1992. This steady trend downward shows that employers and workers are making occupational safety and health a high priority. That's good news for business, workers, and all Americans. Injuries and illnesses dropped 4% in 1999 even though employment rose 2%. That means 200,000 more workers went home to their families without a job related injury or illness than in 1998 (Friedman and Forst 2007).

The official U.S. line indicates that no human rights crisis exists and that the market-friendly labor regulations piloted on the American worker over the last 30-plus years are now bearing fruit.

These assertions are more an indication of disconnection with the concerns of vulnerable workers than they are accurate explanations of tangible social progress. The official line and the statistics that support it are woefully erroneous and mislead the general public. The government knows it undercounts by large margins work-related illnesses, injuries, and fatalities. To begin an accounting of the inaccuracies of these official statistics, these figures ignore all fatalities from work-related diseases. Academic studies, media exposés, and human rights groups have reported the inaccuracy of injury and illness data provided by employers (Compa 2004; Leigh, Marcin, and Miller 2004; U.S. Congress 2008; "Worker Safety" 2008), and the medical literature is in agreement on the inaccuracy of the government figures that result from this data. If politicians and the regulatory community took action, they would find a human rights crisis divorced from the public discourse about the government's proper role in regulation of the labor market and working conditions.

Government and university researchers have estimated the magnitude of death, illness, and injury from work-related causes in the United States. Steenland et al. (2003) estimate mortality from occupational diseases to be as high as 49,000 deaths annually. When added to official traumatic death figures, the total number of work-related deaths in the

United States rises to 55,200 people. Others have argued this estimate is conservative (Schulte 2005), and with new questions raised about the traumatic fatality figure (*Hazards* 2008), the combined annual death toll may be over 60,000. As a guide to how comparatively significant this number is, consider that 58,195 deceased are honored on the Vietnam Veterans Memorial in Washington, although the names of those fallen soldiers span not one but 20 years. Imagine constructing a Fallen Workers' Memorial of equal size each and every year. Work in the U.S. is the eighth leading cause of death, between diabetes, which kills 64,751 people annually, and suicide, responsible for 30,575 deaths. A person in the United States is more likely to die from work than from either being killed in a motor vehicle accident (Steenland et al. 2003) or killed by another person's firearm (Bureau of Justice Statistics 2004).

The official undercount of work-related injuries and illnesses misses as much as 61% of illness and injury (Rosenman et al. 2006). The BLS survey fails to include broad categories of workers and occupational diseases. At least three categories of data are missing from the government's SOII injury and illness survey: occupational illnesses with long latency periods; illnesses and injuries suffered by out-of-scope workers, including public employees, the self-employed, and other groups; and the injuries and illnesses simply not counted by the statistical officialdom, even if work-related (Ruser 2008a).

Friedman and Forst (2007) studied changes in the regulations on record-keeping that employers must maintain on workers' illnesses and injuries. The authors look at two key changes in records regulations made in 1995 and 2001 and found that 83% of the reported decline in illness and injury between 1992 and 2003—a decline heralded by both the Clinton and the Bush administrations—was due to the changes in record-keeping requirements. The government not only undercounts illnesses and injuries, it has loosened employer record-keeping practices while making claims of major regulatory progress. Despite the resources of the U.S. government, no one knows the exact number of workers injured or made ill by work in the U.S. Evidence indicates it may be as high as 12.3 million workers each year (AFL-CIO 2008). These work injuries and illnesses are estimated to cost the U.S. an estimated $170 billion annually—"five times the cost of HIV/AIDS and three times the cost of Alzheimer's disease" (Rosenman 2008:1).

The failure to describe workers' health and safety as a human rights crisis is compounded by uncritical media reporting. *The New York Times* reported on workplace health and safety in 2007: "Government records show that in 2005, more than 6,800 workplace-related deaths occurred, along with 4.2 million injuries and illnesses" (Labaton 2007:A24). This confusion between "workplace-related deaths" and one category of work-related deaths, *fatal work injuries,* was certainly not lost on Mr. Eric Peoples, the injured worker profiled in the article. The 35-year-old worked at a microwave popcorn plant in Jasper, Missouri, where he and other employees were exposed to the chemical diacetyl, a food-flavoring agent. Over time, the workers were diagnosed with "a rare, life-threatening disease that was ravaging their lungs." Peoples's life expectancy was cut to ten years with a double lung transplant. The death of Eric Peoples will ironically not be counted in official U.S. workplace mortality figures. Fatality statistics do not include deaths from work-related disease, and there is no nationwide occupational disease mortality surveillance system in the United States. Mr. Peoples and tens of thousands of others dead from work-related diseases each year will simply not be counted when evaluating federal regulatory success (Labaton 2007).

Perhaps more frustrating than the triumphant news release by Republican and Democratic administrations is that regulators are fully aware of these data inaccuracies. The breadth of their knowledge about the inaccuracies was reported in *Hidden Tragedy* (U.S. Congress 2008), a report presented to the House Committee on Education and Labor by the congressional majority staff. These inaccuracies were all well known to regulatory officials, and their knowledge of the problem was evident. Regulating employment for the benefit of workers is the real third rail in American politics. Property rights are sanctified by government even where they are known to maim and kill workers, aka people.

A Labor Policy of Worker Disempowerment

The government is so offended by the notion of worker empowerment that it will not directly approach workers in survey efforts, instead relying exclusively on employer-provided data. BLS statisticians argue that "our focus is on employers because those are the entities that provide us with our data. . . . We are focusing on talking to employers. We have chosen not to talk to employees" (Ruser 2008b). That workers' health and safety regulations require the empowerment of workers to be effective has been known for a generation by health and safety activists. "The question becomes one of power," noted Tony Mazzocchi (1989:155) in securing worker health and safety protections.

> Ever since the Industrial Revolution we have vested the power to regulate with the producer. But I believe that you cannot solve occupational safety and health problems while those who produce are given the responsibility to regulate themselves. That system does not work, and we ought to examine a new

option. We ought to separate our responsibilities. . . . Those
workers who are the potential victims ought to regulate. . . . It
should be the worker who carries out the mandate of the law,
the right to inspect, the right to cite, the right to bring about
change based on what is known, the right to be notified, the
right to know. When we think about the subject in terms of
empowerment, we will truly make a difference (Mazzocchi
1989:155).

Empowerment is a critical element of labor policy on workers' health
and safety. In the U.S., the norm is the empowerment of employers over
workers. From collective bargaining policies to the right to refuse unsafe
work to reporting workplace injuries and illnesses and receiving the
proper medical attention and recovery time needed to heal when
injuries do happen, labor law and policy supports employers in their
efforts to disempower workers and maintain unilateral control.

Employers are said to have strong market "incentives" to underreport
injuries and illnesses, and this is cited as a major cause of underreporting.
Workplaces with fewer injuries and illnesses "are less likely to be
inspected by OSHA; they have lower workers' compensation insurance
premiums; and they have a better chance of winning government contracts and bonuses," according to recent testimony provided to Congress
(U.S. Congress 2008:2). The consequence of these "incentives" is a business atmosphere of employee intimidation, abuse, harassment, and discrimination for even the slightest move to report injuries and illnesses:

• Workers report widespread intimidation and harassment when
  reporting injuries and illnesses. Reports, testimony, and news
  accounts show that many employers have fired or disciplined workers who report injuries and illnesses or complain about safety hazards. Others have added "demerits" to an employee's record for
  reportable injuries or illnesses or for absenteeism that allegedly
  result from "safety violations" (U.S. Congress 2008).

• Employers have been reported to provide inadequate medical treatment and force workers back to work too soon after serious
  injuries—sometimes right after surgery—so that their injuries will
  not be properly recorded (U.S. Congress 2008).

The act of using a word like "incentive" to explain the underreporting of illnesses and injuries by employers has all the qualities of 1984
Newspeak. It suggests supernatural market forces are responsible for
consciously formulated business policy decisions to overpower worker
unrest on health and safety and to impede the fundamental human
rights of workers to health and safety.

One example of how employers "respond" to "incentives" was documented in a PBS *Frontline* report ("Dangerous Business" 2003). Marcos Lopez, a husband and father of three, had suffered a debilitating accident while employed at Tyler Pipe, a Texas foundry owned by the McWane Corporation. To the company, Mr. Lopez was "a malingerer," and his back injury was deserving of no more than a back brace provided by the employer's clinic. After 25 days of pain, Lopez sought proper medical treatment and was diagnosed with a spinal compression fracture. When asked why the management at Tyler Pipe refused to tell Mr. Lopez he had a broken back, the response was "because then he would know how injured he is." Marcos Lopez is partially disabled for life, according to Texas State Medical Examiners. The word "incentive" fails to capture the true barbarism of these conscious policy decisions. These inhumane decisions by employers are business policy choices and should not be pardoned-away as the responsibility of natural market forces.

Disempowerment and the regulation of workers' unrest is the United States labor policy on occupational safety and health. A survey conducted in 2006 by a group of business lawyers found workplace health and safety to be the #1 reason workers elect to form a union and seek collective bargaining protections, ranking higher than either benefits or wages (*Daily Labor Report* 2006). Workers face aggressive employers that are permitted to legally oppose workers' freedom of association rights well beyond norms established by international labor standards. The violation of workers' human rights by U.S. employers has been well documented by human rights groups (Compa 2000, 2004). Despite claims of a new era of business social responsibility, the union-avoidance industry in the U.S. has grown into a multi-billion-dollar enterprise (Logan 2006). Dismantled by employers and government over the last generation was a de facto nationwide system of worker-based occupational health and safety enforcement centered on trade union collective bargaining of working conditions. Individual employment protections have failed to fill this void in any systematic way. The mass of workers in the U.S. today have neither meaningful bargaining leverage nor the right to refuse unsafe work when hazards present themselves, leaving millions vulnerable and at risk of death or injury without legal recourse while being subjected to a humiliating self-censorship at work and a less than human existence.

The Occupational Safety and Health Administration has provided little solace as this calamity has unfolded. The number of OSHA inspectors for every worker is a fraction of the number required by international (ILO) labor standards—1:63,913 in the U.S. versus a target of 1:10,000 for industrialized economies (International Labour

Organization 2006). At OSHA's current rate, an inspection of each work-place will occur from once every 24 years in Oregon to once every 228 years in Florida (AFL-CIO 2008). OSHA inspectors are also not empowered to enter the employers' premises without a warrant (Lofgren 1989). Work safety and health standards-setting is bottlenecked nation-ally by a business-dominated OSHA lawyers' bar serving management interests by protecting the due process rights of corporations (Schmidt 2005). When OSHA inspectors do fine companies, an elaborate appeals process routinely lowers fines and consolidates citations. The top 25 OSHA fines of all time have been reduced on average 57% through appeals (Lewis and Kjellman 2008). OSHA mandates no worker partici-pation in management decision making where hazard concerns exist and provides little protection against discrimination for exercising the right to refuse unsafe work. This potent mix of labor policies on workers' health and safety has contributed to what Jordan Barab (2006) has called "the invisibility of workplace death" in the United States. This disem-powerment and invisibility has unfolded in the most developed and advanced economy of the world. Employer property rights are respected and protected in U.S. labor policy, making the protection and respect of workers' health and safety secondary and causing a major human rights crisis at workplaces nationwide.

The Disproportionate Burden Worldwide

Workers' health and safety globally demonstrate the extent of the challenge facing labor advocates. More than 80% of the world's workforce lives in the developing world. These workers bear a disproportionate bur-den of the world's hazardous work, raising questions about the nature of what has unfolded in a generation of economic globalization and world-wide shifts in production. Is the search for cheap labor by the world's multinationals better characterized as a search for disposable labor and an unspoken license to kill workers when production demands?

The ILO estimates that 2.2 million workers are killed by work-related injuries and illnesses annually (Takala 2005), and these figures are rising (International Labour Organization 2008). Another 270 mil-lion nonfatal work-related accidents occur annually, and 160 million new cases of work-related diseases are estimated to develop each year (Inter-national Labour Organization 2008). Occupational safety and health, in addition to the humanitarian toll, exact incredible costs on society, esti-mated in some regions to range between 2% and 11% of gross domestic product, figures that if halved would in some countries eliminate all for-eign debt (Giuffrida, Iunes, and Savedoff 2002; Pan American Health Organization 1999). Occupational illnesses and injuries suffered by unprotected workers in unregulated work are a leading cause of morbidity among adults in many countries of the global south (Giuffrida, Iunes, and Savedoff 2001).

Agriculture remains the largest global employer, employing half of the world's labor force; the ILO reports 1.3 billion people are active in the agriculture sector worldwide (International Labour Organization 1999). Pesticides and other agrochemicals are major occupational hazards for agricultural workers, and the United States remains a major exporter of dangerous pesticides, including ones banned domestically after successful campaigning by U.S. trade unionists and health advocates a generation ago. One analysis of U.S. Customs Service records over three years found the quantity of pesticides exported by the U.S. was over a billion pounds annually:

> Analysis of U.S. Custom Service records for 2001–2003 indicates that nearly 1.7 billion pounds of pesticide products were exported from U.S. ports, a rate greater than 32 tons per hour. Exports included greater than 27 million pounds of pesticides whose use is forbidden in the United States. . . . Pesticide exports included more than 500,000 pounds of known or suspected carcinogens, with most going to developing countries; pesticides associated with endocrine disruption were exported at an average rate of greater than 100 tons per day. . . . These products pose unacceptable risks in countries where unsafe use and storage practices are prevalent (Smith, Kerr, and Sadripour 2008).

The export of agricultural hazards from the developed world to the global south is consistent with a broader pattern of exporting industrial hazards to poor countries. All the old problems of workers' safety and health, which were the source of aggressive struggle by U.S. trade unionists in the generation past, have resurfaced as the occupational health tragedies of the developing world today.

> Workers in the developing world are being exposed when wide-spread knowledge is available about the risks and effective preventive measures. . . . [T]hese workers are forced to replay history, despite the availability of information and knowledge transfer unthinkable just a generation ago (Rosenstock, Cullen, and Fingerhut 2006:1128). . . . The burden of occupational health problems is staggering in both human and economic costs, and workers in the developing world bear this burden disproportionately. Moreover, the most vulnerable—children and the poor—are also disproportionately at risk (Rosenstock, Cullen, and Fingerhut 2006:1143).

Working conditions remain a widespread social concern amid more than a half century of ongoing economic integration and globalization. The many problems of workers' safety and health, from cotton dust to brown and black lung, known since the 1970s in the world's industrialized nations, have resurfaced in geographies with few regulations. These have unfolded in the wake of an explosion of new synthetic organic chemicals and their worldwide trade. Whereas hazards like asbestos, lead, and white phosphorus were once the main cause for alarm outside safety hazards, 1,000 new chemicals—2 to 3 per day—are introduced in the global marketplace every year, bringing the number of synthetic chemicals in use throughout the economy to over 100,000 and growing. Emerging hazards and the absence of the regulatory state that protects human rights over employer property rights means workers in the global south bear a disproportionate burden of the world's dangerous work.

Developing a Human Rights Analysis

Human rights have a short history as a justification for labor policy, especially workers' health and safety policy. This poses the question, how is the human rights worldview different from other schools of thought? The hostility toward protective labor policies by human resource management leaves little space for reconciliation with the human rights framework. Yet is a human rights analysis distinct from that of institutional labor economics, the other historically dominant school of thought and scholarship in the industrial and labor relations field?

Since taking shape as an academic discipline in the early 20th century, industrial relations adopted institutional labor economics (ILE) as a midrange theory, and both fields shared scholars, concepts, and values. Institutional labor economists originated as a group of economists in dissent against orthodox neoclassical economics early in the 20th century. ILE describes itself as problem-focused and concerned about social justice. Given this claimed focus on social justice, would adopting a human rights analysis differ in any material way from ILE? If human rights can be realized in ILE policy frameworks, the need for any independent human rights analysis would be limited. If the converse is true, then a distinct human rights analysis school in industrial relations must be recognized, defined, and constructed to replace or at least rival ILE policy frameworks and establish a scholarship that does not render worker deaths invisible.

Workplace health and safety are considered economic and social rights by international human rights law. The issue of worker health and safety is identified in the Universal Declaration of Human Rights and the International Covenant on Economic, Social and Cultural Rights

(ICESCR). The declaration states that everyone has the right "to just and favorable conditions of work" and "the right to rest and leisure, including reasonable limitation of working hours" and "the right to a standard of living adequate for the health and well-being of himself and his family." Article 7 of the ICESCR holds governments responsible to protect "just and favorable conditions of work" and "safe and healthy working conditions."

Institutional labor economists have asserted that human rights do not provide a deeply rooted critique of orthodox neoclassical economics (McIntyre 2008) and are thus an inadequate substitute to replace ILE as the primary voice of opposition to the known ravages of free market economic policies. ILE argues that the negotiation of market conditions between groups like labor unions and employers is the best framework to achieve social justice. John Commons advocated this in his theory of reasonable value (Commons 1913) and suggested that a voluntarist-style arrangement would better improve working conditions, as it opened the door for groups of workers to organize and band together to negotiate. Unions were not always hostile to ILE, because it recognized the role of labor as an institution, although in a framework of voluntarist collective bargaining policy. In the U.S., the National Labor Relations Board has no authority to order collective bargaining agreements, not even when employers commit unfair labor practices. Confusion about this authority has been settled by the Supreme Court in favor of the protection of employer property rights (*H.K. Porter Co. v. NLRB* 1970; Gross 1995).

Workers' health and safety illustrate the contrasts between institutional labor economics and human rights. The long history of policy debates on the regulation of working conditions in industrial relations shows that the human rights worldview offers a fundamentally different perspective than ILE. The logic of human rights necessitates a more radical departure from contemporary political thought and policy than indicated by much writing on workers' rights as human rights. Human rights philosophy in no way precludes strong trade union rights, provides a stronger critique of orthodox neoclassical economics than ILE, and challenges many of the assumptions behind ILE. A human rights analysis raises different questions and provides different answers than these market-oriented labor scholarships. The key characteristics of a human rights analysis that stands in contrast to ILE include policy evaluation in reference to fundamental human rights standards, a complex analysis of all government policy and labor institutions, and the understanding that human rights are realized within their social context and in relationship to other human rights.

Evaluation under Human Rights Standards

Normative values are brought into a human rights analysis through concrete human rights claims, standards, and principles. These claims may or may not be defined in traditional human rights declarations or documents, but they at least articulate some inalienable social duty owed to a person simply by his or her being a human being. Human rights have had an uneasy relationship with social scientists fearful of bringing unwanted normative values into what they perceive as values-free research. The human rights view is needed, however, to maintain basic objectivity in industrial relations scholarship. Human rights analysis does not adopt theoretical biases like those that have historically surrounded conceptions of the state and labor markets in industrial relations. The normative framework is explicit and is known from the outset of research, and while it does frame studies, it does not allow preexisting theory frameworks to cloud how reality is interpreted. This approach contrasts with economic scholarship where preconceived ideas about the market and vague assertions of what is possible preclude certain understandings and policy alternatives. Normative values in a human rights analysis present themselves explicitly, while economics often presents itself as objective despite a highly normative framework that impacts its research dramatically.

The disposition of the labor economists can be explained by their "high theory" and the way it structures their specific normative judgments. Michael Piore described this theory well:

> The high theory is structured around the notion of Pareto optimality, which defines normative criteria in a very precise way. Applied economic research is directed at the solution of a set of specific, and in the end well-specified, social problems. The theory itself is built around the idea of rational individuals pursuing their self-interest in a competitive market, where they interact indirectly with each other through price signals. The theory seeks to produce as its outcome a stable equilibrium; normative judgments are derived by comparing alternative equilibrium (Piore 2006:149).

The focus on achieving humane market equilibrium in employment relations today is described as a "balancing imperative" between enterprise *efficiency* and employment *equity* (Budd 2004). The difference between the values of a human rights analysis and the values of a labor economist is that the values framework of the economist extends through the theoretical explanations and in turn shapes how she or he views the empirical world. In the human rights analysis, values are used to fix the object of study but do not impose any comparable preexisting theory framework that in practice impacts how scholarship theorizes and interprets the real struggles of workers' lives.

A human rights analysis adopts no other philosophical or theoretical disposition beyond the definition of human rights. Researchers may desire the realization of human rights much like a labor economist seeks well-functioning labor markets, but for the human rights researcher no bias is held about the role of government in the economy or any other policy matter such as the value of free trade or the privatization of services. A human rights analyst is focused only on the impact of policy choices on the realization of human rights. Where policies and actions impede human rights, it is implicit that people who care about human rights would encourage change, but it is otherwise not worthwhile to burden a specific research project with constraints from preexisting theories that may cloud the complexity of what is happening on the ground. A human rights analysis provides a much more objective disposition capable of a deeper understanding of the institutional origins and underlying causes of contemporary human rights problems at work.

Complex Analysis of Government and Labor Institutions

"Human rights and fundamental freedoms are the birthright of all human beings; their protection and promotion is the first responsibility of Governments" (Vienna Declaration and Programme of Action 1993). This statement was written as the world was reflecting on the role of government and the prospect for human rights at the end of the Cold War. Representatives from 171 countries and over 800 civil society groups attended the World Conference on Human Rights in 1993 to reflect on the Universal Declaration of Human Rights at a critical period in history. The Vienna Declaration provides a universal definition of government's purpose: It is the *first responsibility* of government to protect human rights and fundamental freedoms, and this includes protecting economic and social rights, like the right to a safe and healthy workplace.

Political theorists have traditionally divided government policy related to human rights into two general categories, positive and negative state action. Human rights that are said to require negative "action" require only government forbearance, tolerance, and self-restraint. Human rights said to require positive action require government effort, materials, services, or action. This dichotomy has been discredited (Donnelly 2003; Shue 1979, 1980).

> All human rights require both positive action and restraint on the part of the state. . . . [W]hether a right is relatively positive or negative usually depends on historically contingent circumstances.

For example, the right of food is more of negative right in the wheat fields of Kansas than in Watts or East Los Angeles. Equal protection of the law is somewhat more positive in South Bronx than in Stockholm (Donnelly 2003:30).

The traditional idea that certain rights could be protected by government inaction alone no longer stands. As a consequence of this emergent understanding, the analysis of all government policies becomes critical and moves front and center in importance on questions of human rights at work. Protecting human rights is the first responsibility of government. Understanding how to protect human rights requires understanding all dimensions of government policy—not only macroeconomic policy choices, but choices that directly impact worker health and safety, including those that have become part of the unspoken operation of society. The human rights analysis on workplace health and safety requires an assessment that can encompass all institutional policy choices. This includes choices like injured-worker legal exemptions from civil tort remedies and maintaining employer due process rights for business corporations in the process of formulating and establishing nationwide workplace health and safety standards, in addition to broader questions about sweeping constitutional grants of authority to corporations by nation-states and the impact of these decisions on the protection of workers' rights.

Institutional labor economics limits its analysis to groups involved in establishing reasonable market values or rules. Often these values or rules may not address issues like occupational safety and health. ILE, despite a focus on labor institutions, ignores many nonmarket policy decisions that impact the environment within which the abstract *reasonable value* is negotiated. A human rights analysis understands the state in all its forms and does not restrict its analysis to a narrow definition of labor institutionalism in a market context.

Such a focus on institutions might seem obsolete in an era of international labor activism, transnational solidarity networks, and global social movement research. Without this analysis of institutions, however, labor scholars may be imitating the dominant market orthodoxy that argues that labor market actors exist in a stateless marketplace independent of nonmarket forces. A human rights analysis does not mysticize labor markets; it questions how legal institutions constitute and construct the market. Economic theory, in contrast, frequently limits analysis of the state outside a market efficiency framework. Worker health and safety is understood only by understanding all of society's institutional complexity. This includes an analysis of the powers and privileges granted by governments to various actors in an economic setting and in an employment relationship. Even where governance seems weak and there appears on first glance to be a stateless marketplace, a comparative historical analysis reveals real policy choices that impact workers.

Understanding Human Rights in a Social Context

If we leave our worldview to be shaped by the "existing world of institutional templates" (Hall and Taylor 1996:953) like those created by the Occupational Safety and Health Act (1970), we might see workers' safety and health as only an individual human rights concern best ameliorated through a centralized labor inspectorate. Collective questions would appear moot points on safety and health, lending support to claims of an individualist era in employment relations (Piore and Safford 2006). Collective protections cannot be separated, however, from the issue of workplace safety and health given the strategic advantage collective representation holds for protecting precarious workers' health and safety.

ILE is often presented as the only theory capable of recognizing collective labor protections. Other labor scholars have expressed concern that unions and other workers' organizations are adopting human rights as a mobilizing principle (Brody 2005; Lichtenstein 2003). The basis of concern is that human rights promote individualism and this individualism is an impediment to the collective solidarity important to securing industrial relations protections throughout history. Institutional labor economists also sound the alarm regarding human rights.

> "Human rights" are problematic as a basis for worker rights because they deal with what the individual is entitled to rather that what is in the interest of the community, solidarity, or civic virtue. This was the conclusion of the most incisive conservative, liberal, and socialist nineteenth-century writers on rights (McIntyre 2008:56).

These good faith criticisms raise interesting critiques. They are not, however, damning critiques to workers' rights as human rights. The notion that human rights are individualistic and impede the idea of community, solidarity, civic virtue, and, in our context, the goals of collective bargaining is a misunderstanding of them, and it commits the sin of omission from human rights history.

Human rights philosophy explicitly argues that human rights exist in a social world. Human rights constitute an interconnected and often clashing mix of claims and social duties that each when realized meets some desired social obligation. Where human rights directly clash, the focus of the analysis is comparative social obligations and preferencing the social obligations meeting the higher social need. This does not mean abstractly preferencing fundamental human rights, as did the Declaration on Fundamental Principles and Rights at Work (International Labour Organization 1998). Ranking human rights is not possible given their indivisible, universal, interdependent, and interrelated character. Human rights analysis sees the inherently bounded human condition and recognizes that human rights do not exist as isolated rights and thus cannot be understood outside their social context.

The relationship between human rights and social obligations was a subject of significant debate among the drafters of the Universal Declaration of Human Rights. The debate revolved around the location and prominence given to Article 29. Declaration drafters came to an agreement on the language but not the prominence of Article 29. Some said the words should be placed first among all articles. A vote passed by 8 to 7 with 1 abstention to move the article to the end of the declaration, where it now sits, not because of any philosophical fight, but because some drafters thought it more logical to discuss duties and the social context of human rights after articulating a list of human rights. The inclusion of Article 29 indicates that human rights should not be taken as a "mere offshoot of the eighteenth-century tree of rights," which the declaration drafters were taking pains to avoid (Morsink 1999:245):

> Article 29. (1) Everyone has duties to the community in which alone the free and full development of his personality is possible. (2) In the exercise of his rights and freedoms, everyone shall be subject only to such limitations as are determined by law solely for the purpose of securing due recognition and respect for the rights and freedoms of others.

These were not the rights pronounced by "the men of 1789" (Weil 1952:4). Article 29 explains that human rights exist within a social context. This moves universal human rights to the center of the discourse on collective social obligations. Human rights may be limited only where rights clash as clearly evidenced by the "subject only to such limitations as" phrase in Article 29 (2).

It is important to know this hidden history of the social fabric of human rights. To claim that human rights are merely isolated individual rights that confound collective protections misinterprets the modern human rights philosophy. Human rights are not a rabid rights individualism incapable of any deference to collective laws on workers' rights. They are rights rooted in the social world. As Simone Weil argued forcefully at the time of the negotiation of the Universal Declaration of Human Rights, collectivities are due the respect and protection of government and society based on how they satisfy social obligations.

> We owe our respect to a collectivity, of whatever kind—country, family or any other—not for itself, but because it is food for a certain number of human souls. The degree of respect owing to human collectivities is a very high one. . . . The first thing to be investigated is what are those needs which are for the life of the soul what the needs in the way of food, sleep and warmth are for the life of the body. We must try to enumerate and define them. . . . The lack of any such investigation forces governments, even when their intentions are honest, to act sporadically and at random (Weil 1952:8–10).

There is no inconsistency between workers' rights as human rights as a strategy to protect the collective voice of labor. The human rights analyst recognizes this and works to reclaim this human rights history and philosophy so that the social formula of human rights becomes known.

Overall, these three characteristics of a human rights analysis—the introduction of values through specific human rights, a complex analysis of government and labor institutions, and the recognition that human rights exist in a social world—illustrate that the human rights worldview poses a much more significant challenge to the orthodoxy of neoclassical economics than does any other market-based economic philosophy, including the institutional labor economics school.

Institutional Labor Economics and Workers' Health and Safety

Some historical background is needed to explain how institutional labor economics has viewed workers' health and safety. In this section, I describe how working conditions were viewed by the early industrial relations scholars, focusing on Sidney and Beatrice Webb as influential Fabian socialists in England and on John Commons of the Wisconsin School of industrial relations. The objective is to illustrate how the foundations of ILE have been inconsistent with the notion of protecting workers' health and safety as universal human rights.

Sidney and Beatrice Webb "effectively laid the foundation for the new field of industrial relations" (Kaufman 2004:9) before it became institutionalized in the U.S. alongside the work of John Commons, institutional labor economist and advocate of injured workers' compensation systems. The philosophic foundations of industrial relations developed early in the life of the field and have impacted the regulatory perspectives of labor scholars ever since. The impact of industrial relations has especially been felt on the topic of occupational health and safety policy.

Investigating occupational sanitation and safety, Sidney and Beatrice Webb questioned the role of government in the regulation of English industrial hazards. In *Industrial Democracy* (1897), they noted the effectiveness of social regulation to prevent worker death. Despite the new protections of workers' freedom of association granted by Parliament, wrote the Webbs, "neither Mutual Insurance nor Collective Bargaining availed to put down the evil among the worst employers" and as a result "the union then turned to the law" (Webb and Webb 1897:359), which the Webbs called the Method of Legal Enactment. They described how this social regulation of the labor market was, pragmatically speaking, the line of least political resistance given the broad-based and cross-class coalitions that often supported worker health and safety.

> Scarcely a session of Parliament now passes without new . . . protection of the health or safety of one or another class of operatives being, amid general public approval, added to our Labor Code. We attribute the rapid development of this side of Trade Unionism to the discovery by the Trade Union leaders that it is the line of least resistance. Middle-class public opinion . . . cordially approves any proposal for preventing accidents or improving the sanitation of workplaces. . . . Something, we think, is to be attributed to the general fear of infectious disease. Along with this fear of infection there goes a real sympathy for the sufferers, ill-health and accidents being calamities common to rich and poor. More, perhaps, is due to the half conscious admission that, as regards Sanitation and Safety at any rate, the Trade Union argument is borne out by facts, and that it is impracticable for the individual operative to bargain about the conditions of his labor (Webb and Webb 1897:359–62).

Yet upon admission of the effectiveness of the legal enactment, the Webbs quickly changed heart. After recognizing the strength of policing employment relations with social regulations, they questioned such policies as the mass of work injuries and illnesses as unforeseen "acts of God."

> [A]n accident is as likely as not to be nobody's fault. It is necessary to emphasize this, because most accidents are, to use the traditional phrase of the bill landing, "the act of God." In the great majority of industrial casualties—probably in three cases out of four—it is impossible to prove that the calamity has been due to neglect on any one's part. A flash of lightning or a storm at sea, a flood or a tornado, irresponsibility claim their victims. The greatest possible care in buying materials or plant will leave undiscovered hidden flaws which one day result in a calamity. In other cases, the accident itself destroys all trace of its own cause. In many, perhaps in most, of the casualties of

the ocean or the mine, the shunting yard or the mill, the diffi-
culties in the way of bringing home actual negligence to any
particular person are insuperable (Webb and Webb 1897:380).

One explanation for this mysterious religious awakening is that if
worker death were deemed preventable by legal enactment, common
law tort liability for industrial accidents would thus immediately follow.
The Webbs understood the magnitude of common law tort liability facing employers and argued against holding any employers liable, even in
cases deemed avoidable.

A new formula was needed to remedy these inconsistencies between
human rights and employer control. Scholarship responded: full
employer protection from liability for workplace safety and health violations. The injured and dead must be barred from remedy at common
law.

Despite the efficacy of social enactments in protecting against dangerous industrial hazards, the Webbs then offered what can only be
described as a reprehensible prescription. The solution was outright
restriction of effective state action through a strong preventive labor
inspectorate.

[T]he necessary regimentation of employers and their control
by rigid rules would be extremely distasteful to English capitalists, whilst there would be real difficulty in adapting any such
organization to the remarkable variety, complexity, and mobil-
ity of English industry. . . . [C]ompensation avoids all these dif-
ficulties, and requires no more regimentation or registration
than is already submitted to by every mine or factory
owner. . . . [Compensation] might count on the powerful support of the great capitalists in the coal, iron, and railway industries, who would find themselves relieved of the special and
exceptional burden now cast upon them (Webb and Webb
1897:391).

To say nothing of the "special and exceptional burden" placed upon
widows and orphans of the dead and the misery that availed the survivors of industrial accidents. The Webbs' consolation would be payment
upon injury or death and a weakened preventive labor inspectorate.
Anything otherwise would be "distasteful to English capitalists" and
must be avoided. This was written as the frequency of worker death was
remarkable in England and Wales: "between 1868 and 1919 a miner was
killed every six hours, seriously injured every two hours and injured
badly . . . every two or three minutes. Mining was not always, as is often
assumed, the most dangerous occupation of the time. General laborers

in England and Wales had mortality rates nearly three times the rate of coal miners between 1900 and 1902" (Church 1986).

The earliest industrial relations scholars preferred the protection of capital to protection of workers' human right not to be killed on the job. Thus, from the earliest foundations, human rights were marginalized ideas and took a backseat to what became the constructed vision of the labor market and its acceptable regulation. The consolation prize for workers was blood money upon injury and death. Would this shameful situation improve as industrial relations scholarship developed with John R. Commons and the institutional labor economists across the Atlantic?

Institutional labor economists were "the principal architects of the policy response to neoclassical rejection of labor standards legislation during the Progressive Era and the Great Depression." Their diagnosis of the problems of modern society was "market imperfections":

> Their empirical study and observation led them to support regulatory laws on grounds widespread employment and poverty wages resulted from market imperfections and externalities originating in social institutions rather than as the inevitable price of overall progress. Such socially determined conditions included too little or too much competition in labor markets, either of which could be devastating in the absence of institutional protections. Market imperfections generated market externalities absorbed by individual workers, working-class households and industrial communities in the form of low wages, bad working conditions, and social welfare experiments (Craypo 1997:232).

Commons railed against "the menace of competition," yet at the same time constructed rationales that allowed state power to back industrial negligence on health and safety. The state thus had an integral role in reinforcing the capitalist labor market despite the market often being cast by both neoclassical and institutional labor economics as a stateless, naturalistic social institution. These views developed at the exact time states were moving to hold employers responsible for hazards.

> Many states passed statutory modifications of the common law. These statutes, known as employer's liability laws, frequently modified or completely abolished the fellow-servant rule and other employer defenses. The laws also frequently made an employer's failure to comply with government safety codes a basis for negligence (Chelius 1977:20).

As employers were facing increasing tort liability for worker deaths and injuries, Commons argued that the regulation of occupational safety and health was subject not to a human rights regulatory standard but to what he enthusiastically called the business "reasonableness" standard.

> The doctrine which the court applies to this function of [health and safety] investigation is both the noblest and the most practical of legal doctrines—"reasonableness." By this doctrine the court applies its philosophy to the particular facts, but requires that all of the facts be taken into account. . . . When the commission began its work of selecting its staff, it had entertained the idea that it should place at the head of its safety and sanitation work engineering and medical experts. But after interviewing a number of these experts it was discovered that they considered their problem to be that of drawing up ideal or standard specifications, which the commission, going out then with a "big stick," should compel employers to adopt. . . . [B]ut a democratic country would not consent to be ruled by those whose ideal standards might be removed from the everyday conditions of business. This decision of the [Wisconsin Industrial Commission] also conforms to the doctrine of reasonableness, which requires practicability adapted to existing conditions (Commons 1913:398).

The protection of workplace health and safety as a human right was for John R. Commons an impractical affront to "the everyday condition of business." Despite evidence that strong social enactments were the best policy strategy to protect against illness and injury, workplace health and safety was to be the sacrificial lamb of industrial relations scholarship, courtesy of strong state protection of business in what became perhaps the queerest lexical juxtaposition of all labor policy—a system known as "voluntarist" labor relations. Regulation to protect against worker deaths and injuries would occur only where output and "the everyday condition of business" was first safeguarded by the state. The state would provide employers immunity from torts when brought by aggrieved workers and instead pay a fraction of profits upon the injury or death of any employee. The workers' compensation idea was not first deduced from a concern about hazard prevention. It was derived from the fear that the state was challenging property rights, business production, and the constructed and fictitious vision of the capitalist labor market as a natural, stateless social institution that operates in a realm removed from government regulation. Industrial relations scholars justified and legitimized market-based labor policies accordingly.

Workers' safety and health highlight a contradiction of the institutional labor economists. On the one hand, their criticism of neoclassical economists characterized them as progressive social reformers; on the other hand, their constructed vision of the labor market existed alongside a ceaseless justification of state protection of capital's right to kill and maim workers in those labor markets. Despite the expressed need for better labor institutions, government's role was highly proscribed to prevent only those tragedies capable of protection within a framework of alternative labor market efficiencies. Protecting workers' health and safety as fundamental human rights was a secondary concern to justifying state safeguards on business property rights.

This allegedly voluntarist trajectory set early by industrial relations scholars would be largely unchanged through the 20th century. Bruce Kaufman, in his impressive historical account of the industrial relations field, identified the "core ethical and ideological premises" in early U.S. industrial relations scholarship. To these scholars, labor was not a commodity and "human rights should have precedence over property rights in the employment relationship" (Kaufman 2004:128). Yet if human rights include the right to health and safety, as the global community agrees they should, this human rights claim lacks evidence. The constructed vision of the labor market by industrial relations pluralists made them endorse policy strategies not for their effectiveness at protecting workers but for their management of the state and regulatory noninterference with business output and thus capitalist property rights. These predetermined theories served to marginalize strong protections for workers' health and safety. Industrial relations scholars gave preeminent priority to the "free" labor market, uninterrupted business production, and employer property rights, even as the state was called on to make this possible. This history disqualifies the institutional labor economists from claiming the banner of universal human rights advocacy and illustrates the need for a distinct human rights analysis in industrial relations scholarship.

Examining Today's Market-Oriented Labor Scholarship

Bringing the focus on market-oriented labor scholarship to the present, we find that labor economists continue to challenge occupational safety and health protections as human rights concerns. Unlike a hundred years ago, today's policy debates are global in scope. Among the policies advocated today is the negotiated labor standards approach (Piore and Schrank 2008; Schrank and Piore 2007). As with the earliest ILE scholars, a human rights analysis can help with understanding this approach and its implications on the ground for the protection of workers' health and safety.

As is common with many market-oriented labor economic ideas, the negotiated labor standards approach begins with the assumption of the stateless market and conceptualizes regulations as being "singularly inflexible impediments to job creation" and a challenge to "the kind of rapid adjustment in the productive structure that is required to compete effectively in the international marketplace" (Piore and Schrank 2008:3). Piore and Schrank argue for the negotiation of labor standards, where rank-and-file regulatory authorities "adjust their efforts to prevailing economic conditions" by "systematizing what is at present a largely unspoken understanding of the relationship between labor standards and business practice" (2008:2). The task of negotiating labor standards rests on the labor inspector in the Franco–Latin Model, given this model's flexible design that bestows on the inspector a strong authority to decide law enforcement. The goal is to "make compliance good for business and thereby minimize resistance to regulation" and "regulation with economic flexibility" in a way that transforms "inspectors into the shock troops of a campaign for decent work." (Piore and Schrank 2008:2) From the viewpoint of the negotiated labor standards approach, the ILO Decent Work agenda becomes a seamless continuation of institutional labor economics.

Piore and Schrank argue that inspectors "play the role of business consultant by transferring best practices from leading to lagging enterprises" and adopt the mantra "compliance is good business" (2008:7). What is unclear about the negotiated labor standards approach is why it is prescribed as an exclusive regulatory model. The idea that businesses be taught balance sheet arguments for the regulations they must implement is not new and supplements strong regulatory states in other countries. When used as an exclusive regulatory remedy, however, serious problems unfold. Developing a complete regulatory regime based on negotiation with employers appears very ill conceived, a recipe for institutionalizing the employer's ability to game the regulatory system. Negotiated labor standards make legal the very real political problems of traditional regulation such as clientelism, nepotism, and favoritism and would most likely lead to weaker governance of the labor market, not to the improved governance and social advancement its advocates suggest.

Piore and Schrank, like ILE scholars, hold static understandings of "employer hostility and resistance to the regulatory process" (Piore and Schrank 2008:17) and cast the labor market as a collection of natural stateless phenomena and forces. A human rights analysis would not adopt this deterministic and static view, and it would not advocate handing over the regulatory state to the perpetrators of what in some countries would be criminal acts. Piore and Schrank are correct when they say that their prescriptions are "overtly and explicitly normative" (2008:20). Negotiated labor standards, they argue, pose "an ideological

challenge to neoliberalism, to be sure, but not an operational one"
(2008:20). Human rights, unlike the market-oriented economics that
seek all solutions in a framework of alternative market efficiencies, pose
an explicit operational challenge to neoclassical economics.

Perhaps the most troubling aspect of negotiated labor standards is
that they are proscribed with the help of U.S. government aid in Central
America, a region where business negligence on occupational safety and
health is stunning amid a political–historical backdrop of violence that
has not been so easily forgotten by many people who live there. Making
the business case for safety was promoted by grants to Central American
labor ministries during the negotiation of the contested Central American
Free Trade Agreement. The *Centro Regional de Seguridad y Salud Ocu-
pacional* (CERSSO) has trained over 600 inspectors and technicians in
this method of regulatory negotiation. Piore and Schrank (2008) argue
that these investments have paid off, citing two reports based on garment factories in El Salvador, Guatemala, and Nicaragua where the
return for the business after making health and safety improvements was
four to eight times the investment costs. These claims, if true, are good
news for those workers, but what about the working conditions where
the business case for safety is not strong or is a net negative for the bottom line? It is in these workplaces, not in cherry-picked sites, where an
exclusivist regulatory formula must be judged. The human rights analysis
argues all workers have a right to return home from work as alive as
when they punched in, regardless of the business cost estimate. Even
modern-day incarnations of the institutional labor economics framework
of old continue to clash with the fundamental human rights philosophy
and worldview.

Building a Culture of Human Rights in Scholarship

The historically strong culture of opposition to economic and social
rights in the United States has been replicated internationally. Scholarship is not independent of its cultural setting, and it behooves people to
question the theories and frameworks that bias the idea of economic and
social rights. Industrial relations has rested on a midrange theory framework constructed within a narrow vision of alternative market efficiencies. This view fails to see the complex institutional environment that
shapes the labor market and fails to recognize universal human rights,
especially workers' health and safety as human rights. New foundations
in the study of labor and employment relations are needed that are capable of encompassing fundamental human rights ideas and advancing an
academic culture respectful of human rights. The human rights analysis
outlined here is one step in moving toward this goal in articulating an

alternative framework. Given the complexity of globalization and the role of the state in constructing and maintaining labor markets, a human rights analysis helps industrial relations maintain a basic distance from these preconceived theories and explanations that serve to marginalize the real-world experience faced by workers. In turn, the human rights worldview makes industrial relations a more objective and rigorous endeavor with much more honesty paid to the empirical world the academic field is said to study and be passionate about.

Economic rights as human rights are challenged by marginalization in scholarship, and ideation remains critical to making policy choices. Virginia Bras Gomes (2005:104) has argued that "the insufficient implementation of economic, social and cultural rights is not only due to the lack of resources but also and above all to the development of domestic priorities that do not attribute sufficient relevance to economic, social and cultural rights." As economic rights are increasingly expressed with clarity and subject to justicability standards like those of many civil and political human rights, scholarship should no longer be used to justify economic policies that ignore human rights and advocate the regulation of workers versus the regulation of work.

The culture of opposition to economic and social rights has deep roots in U.S. political culture. As the Universal Declaration of Human Rights was being drafted, the idea of including economic and social rights was opposed by the United States legal community. The American Bar Association recommended against the declaration. After it was passed in 1948, a uniquely U.S. political movement sprouted and was organized to fight against incorporating economic and social human rights into domestic law. Senator John W. Bricker, a Republican from Ohio, mobilized against the Universal Declaration amid Cold War hysteria and caused one of the major constitutional struggles of the century (Tananbaum 1988). While some historians argue that these 20th-century movements were manifestations of a conservative desire for states' rights or an isolationist foreign policy after engagement in two world wars, the argument has been made convincingly that they are more accurately understood as a groundswell of opposition within the U.S. political culture to the prospect of realizing social and economic rights in the nation's domestic constitutional legal order (Tananbaum 1988).

This history of contested politics is important because the most powerful ideological opposition to social and economic rights originated from this period, and these arguments have been repackaged and repackaged ever since. Economic and social rights, said Jeane Kirkpatrick, a self-described "A.F.L.-C.I.O. Democrat" (Allen 2006) and UN ambassador under Ronald Reagan, claimed economic and social rights were nothing but letters to Santa Claus (Kirkpatrick 1981), and today the argument remains ensconced in popular economic lore that economic and social rights serve "no useful purpose" (*Economist* 2007:76). These ideas are created fictions, deserving relegation to the status of children's holiday fairy tale. Workers' health and safety are fundamental human rights, economic and social rights that today constitute a major crisis worldwide. Labor scholarship of any variety that fails to recognize this phenomenon and preferences the study of frameworks that disappear workers' death and disease as a critical human rights issue should be challenged. Protecting and realizing the human rights of workers is unlikely without first recognizing these misconceptions. Scholarship must catch up with the reality of suffering that many millions of workers worldwide wish they had never come to know.

References

AFL-CIO. 2008. *Death on the Job: The Toll of Neglect. A National and State-by-State Profile of Health and Safety in the United States.* Washington, DC: AFL-CIO.

Allen, R.V. 2006. "Jeane Kirkpatrick and the Great Democratic Defection." *New York Times.* December 16, 2006, opinion page.

Barab, J. 2006. "Acts of God, Acts of Man: The Invisibility of Workplace Death." In V. Mogensen, ed., *Worker Safety Under Siege: Labor, Capital, and the Politics of Workplace Safety in a Deregulated World.* Armonk, NY: M.E. Sharpe, pp. 3–16.

Brody, D. 2005. *Labor Embattled: History, Power, Rights.* Urbana, IL: University of Illinois Press.

Budd, J.W. 2004. *Employment with a Human Face: Balancing Efficiency, Equity, and Voice.* Ithaca, NY: Cornell University Press.

Bureau of Justice Statistics. 2004. July 15. "Firearm Deaths by Intent, 1991–2001." Key Facts at a Glance. <http://www.ojp.usdoj.gov/bjs/glance/tables/frmdth.htm>. [September 15, 2008].

Bureau of Labor Statistics. 2008. *National Census of Fatal Occupational Injuries in 2007.* Washington, DC: U.S. Department of Labor.

Chelius, J.R. 1977. *Workplace Safety and Health: The Role of Workers' Compensation.* Washington, DC: American Enterprise Institute for Public Policy Research.

Church, R. 1986. *The History of the British Coal Industry, Volume 3, 1830–1913: Victorian Pre-eminence.* Oxford: Clarendon Press.

Commons, J.R. 1913. *Labor and Administration.* New York: Macmillan.

Compa, L. 2000. *Unfair Advantage: Workers' Freedom of Association in the United States Under International Human Rights Standards.* Ithaca, NY: ILR Press.

Compa, L. 2004. *Blood, Sweat, and Fear: Workers' Rights in U.S. Meat and Poultry Plants.* New York: Human Rights Watch.

Craypo, C. 1997. "Alternative Perspectives on the Purpose and Effects of Labor Standards Legislation." In Bruce E. Kaufman, ed., *Government Regulation of the Employment Relationship.* Ithaca, NY: Cornell University Press, pp. 221–52.

Daily Labor Report. 2006. "Workplace Safety Is Key Issue In Union Organizing, Poll Finds." Washington, DC: Bureau of National Affairs. 174, p. A-3.

"Dangerous Business." 2003. *Frontline.* PBS. January 9.

Donnelly, J. 2003. *Universal Human Rights in Theory and Practice.* Ithaca, NY: Cornell University Press.

Economist. 2007. "Stand Up for Your Rights—Human Rights." March 22.

Friedman, L.S., and L. Forst 2007. "The Impact of OSHA Recordkeeping Regulation Changes on Occupational Injury and Illness Trends in the US: A Time-Series Analysis." *British Medical Journal,* Vol. 64, no. 7, pp. 454–60.

Giuffrida, A., R.F. Iunes, and W.D. Savedoff. 2001. *Economic and Health Effects of Occupational Hazards in Latin America and the Caribbean.* No. SOC-121. Washington, DC: Inter-American Development Bank.

Giuffrida, A., R.F. Iunes, and W.D. Savedoff. 2002. "Occupational Risks in Latin America and the Caribbean: Economic and Health Dimensions." *Health Policy and Planning,* Vol. 17, no. 3, pp. 235–46.

Gomes, V.B. 2005. "The Future of Economic, Social and Cultural Rights." In R.K.M. Smith and C.v.d. Anker, eds., *The Essentials of Human Rights.* New York: Hodder Arnold, pp. 103–5.

Gross, J.A. 1995. *Broken Promise: The Subversion of U.S. Labor Relations Policy, 1947–1994.* Philadelphia: Temple University Press.

Hall, P.A., and R.C.R. Taylor. 1996. "Political Science and the Three New Institutionalisms." *Political Studies,* Vol. 44, no. 5, pp. 936–57.

Hazards. 2008. "USA: OSHA Fiddles While Workers Die." *Hazards Magazine: Trade Union Health & Safety,* no. 371, August 30. Online edition. <http://www.tuc.org.uk/h_and_s/tuc-15254-f0.cfm#tuc-15254-22>. [April 17, 2009].

H. K. Porter Co. v. National Labor Relations Board, 397 U.S. 99 (1970).

International Labour Organization. 1998. *Declaration on Fundamental Principles and Rights at Work.* Geneva: International Labour Organization.

International Labour Organization. 1999. *SafeWork: The ILO Programme on Occupational Safety and Health in Agriculture.* <http://www.ilo.org/public/english/protection/safework/agriculture/agrivf01.htm>. [April 17, 2009].

International Labour Organization. 2006. *General Survey of Labor Inspection.* International Labor Conference, 95th Session, Report III, Part 1B. Geneva, May 31–June 16.

International Labour Organization. 2008. *My Life, My Work, My Safe Work: Managing Risk in the Work Environment.* Geneva: International Labor Organization and the International Social Security Association.

Kaufman, B. 2004. *The Global Evolution of Industrial Relations: Events, Ideas and the IIRA.* Geneva: International Labour Organization.

Kirkpatrick, J.J. 1981. "Establishing a Viable Human Rights Policy." *World Affairs,* Vol. 143, no. 4, p. 323.

Labaton, S. 2007. "OSHA Leaves Worker Safety in Hands of Industry." *New York Times.* April 25, pp. A1, A24.

Leigh, J.P., J.P. Marcin, and T.R. Miller. 2004. "An Estimate of the U.S. Government's Undercount of Nonfatal Occupational Injuries." *Journal of Occupational and Environmental Medicine,* Vol. 46, no. 1, pp. 10–18.

Lewis, R., and K. Kjellman. 2008. *Top OSHA Issued Penalties.* September 17. <http://www.propublica.org/special/osha-fines>. [October 15, 2008].

Lichtenstein, N. 2003. *State of the Union: A Century of American Labor.* Princeton, NJ: Princeton University Press.

Lofgren, D.J. 1989. *Dangerous Premises: An Insider's View of OSHA Enforcement.* Ithaca, NY: ILR Press.

Logan, J. 2006. "The Union Avoidance Industry in the United States." *British Journal of Industrial Relations,* Vol. 44, no. 4, pp. 651–75.

Mazzocchi, A. 1989. "The Workers' Place in Enforcing OSHA." *Annals of the New York Academy of Sciences,* Vol. 572, December, pp. 155–6.

McIntyre, R.P. 2008. *Are Worker Rights Human Rights?* Ann Arbor: University of Michigan Press.

Morsink, J. 1999. *The Universal Declaration of Human Rights: Origins, Drafting and Intent.* Philadelphia: University of Pennsylvania Press.

Occupational Safety and Health Administration. 2008. *U.S. Labor Secretary Elaine L. Chao Applauds Census of Fatal Occupational Injuries Report Showing Decline in Worker Fatalities.* Washington, DC: Occupational Safety and Health Administration.

Pan American Health Organization. 1999. *Workers' Health in the Region of the Americas.* 41st Directing Council (CD 41/15). Washington, DC: Pan American Health Organization.

Piore, M.J. 2006. "Qualitative Research: Does It Fit in Economics?" In E. Perecman and S. R. Curran, eds., *A Handbook for Social Science Field Research: Essays and Bibliographic Sources on Research Design and Methods.* Thousand Oaks, CA: Sage, pp. 143–57.

Piore, M.J., and S. Safford. 2006. "Changing Regimes of Workplace Governance, Shifting Axes of Social Mobilization, and the Challenge to Industrial Relations Theory." *Industrial Relations,* Vol. 45, no. 3, pp. 299–325.

Piore, M.J., and A. Schrank. 2008. "Toward Managed Flexibility: The Revival of Labour Inspection in the Latin World." *International Labour Review,* Vol. 147, no. 1, pp. 1–23.

Rosenman, K.D. 2008. *Testimony to the Full Committee Hearing "Hidden Tragedy: Underreporting of Workplace Injuries and Illnesses."* Washington, DC: House Committee on Education and Labor.

Rosenman, K.D., A. Kalush, M.J. Reilly, J.C. Gardiner, M. Reeves, and Z. Luo. 2006. "How Much Work-Related Injury and Illness Is Missed by the Current National Surveillance System?" *Journal of Occupational and Environmental Medicine,* Vol. 48, no. 4, pp. 357–65.

Rosenstock, L., M. Cullen, and M. Fingerhut. 2006. "Disease Control Priorities in Developing Countries." In Dean T. Jamison et al., eds., *Occupational Health.* New York: Oxford University Press, pp. 1127–45.

Ruser, J.W. 2008a. "Examining Evidence on Whether BLS Undercounts Workplace Injuries and Illnesses." *Monthly Labor Review,* Vol. 131, no. 8, pp. 20–32.

Ruser, J.W. 2008b. *Testimony to the Full Committee Hearing "Hidden Tragedy: Underreporting of Workplace Injuries and Illnesses."* Washington, DC: House Committee on Education and Labor.

"Russert and Malloy: Two Guys from South Buffalo." 2008. StoryCorps. NPR. *Morning Edition,* June 18.

Schmidt, P. 2005. *Lawyers and Regulation: The Politics of the Administrative Process.* Cambridge: Cambridge University Press.

Schrank, A., and M. Piore. 2007. "Norms, Regulations and Labor Standards in Central America." *Estudios y Perspectivas,* no. 77 (February). Mexico City: United Nations.

Schulte, P. 2005. "Characterizing the Burden of Occupational Injury and Disease." *Journal of Occupational and Environmental Medicine,* Vol. 47, no. 6, pp. 607–22.

Shue, H. 1979. "Rights in the Light of Duties." In P.G. Brown and D. Maclean, eds., *Human Rights and U.S. Foreign Policy.* Lexington, MA: Lexington Books, pp. 65–81.

Shue, H. 1980. *Basic Rights: Subsistence, Affluence, and U.S. Foreign Policy*. Princeton, NJ: Princeton University Press.
Smith, C., K. Kerr, and A. Sadripour. 2008. "Pesticide Exports from U.S. Ports, 2001–2003." *International Journal of Occupational and Environmental Health*, Vol. 14, no. 3, pp. 176–86.
Steenland, K., C. Burnett, N. Lalich, E. Ward, and J. Hurrell. 2003. "Dying for Work: The Magnitude of US Mortality from Selected Causes of Death Associated with Occupation." *American Journal of Industrial Medicine*, Vol. 43, no. 5, pp. 461–82.
Takala, J. 2005. *Decent Work – Safe Work: Introductory Report to the XVIIth World Congress on Safety and Health at Work*. Orlando, FL: International Labour Organization.
Tananbaum, D. 1988. *The Bricker Amendment Controversy: A Test of Eisenhower's Political Leadership*. Ithaca, NY: Cornell University Press.
U.S. Congress. 2008. *Hidden Tragedy: Underreporting of Workplace Injuries and Illnesses*. Majority staff report. Washington, DC: Committee on Education and Labor of the U.S. House of Representatives, June.
Vienna Declaration and Programme of Action, 1993. World Conference of Human Rights. Vienna, June 14–25. Adopted by the U.N. General Assembly A/Conf.157/23 July 12, 1993.
Webb, S., and B.P. Webb. 1897. *Industrial Democracy*. London, New York, Bombay: Longmans Green.
Weil, S. 1952, 2001. *The Need for Roots: Prelude to a Declaration of Duties Towards Mankind* (2nd ed.). London: Routledge.
"Worker Safety." 2008. *Bill Moyers Journal*. PBS. June 27.

CHAPTER 4

Child Labor in Human Rights Law and Policy Perspective

BURNS H. WESTON
The University of Iowa

It is indisputable. Child labor is a human rights problem, and increasingly recognized as such the world over (Weston 2005a).[1] According to the latest published estimates of the International Labour Organization (ILO), some 218 million children between ages 5 and 17 were engaged in "child labor" worldwide as of 2004, 126 million or 58% of them in "hazardous work" (International Labour Organization 2006). Large though uncertain numbers toil in appalling conditions, are ruthlessly exploited to perform dangerous jobs with little or no pay, and thus are made often to suffer severe physical and emotional abuse.

They can be found in brick factories, carpet weaving centers, fishing platforms, leather tanning shops, mines, and other hazardous places, often as cogs in the global economy. They can be found—most abundantly—in domestic service, vulnerable to sexual and other indignities that escape public scrutiny and accountability. They can be found on the streets as prostitutes, forced to trade in sex against their will. They can be found as soldiers in life-threatening conflicts. Working long hours under exploitative conditions, often beaten or otherwise abused, and commonly trafficked from one country to another, they are unable to obtain the education that can liberate and improve their lives; their health is severely threatened from years of exposure to hazardous material; many, if they survive, are deformed and disabled before they can mature physically, mentally, or emotionally. Such are the brute facts (Cullen 2007; International Labour Organization 2004, 2006; Weston 2005a).

Before the 1989 United Nations Convention on the Rights of the Child (CRC),[2] however, the issue of child labor, even in its worst forms, was seldom addressed as a human rights problem.[3] The practice of the ILO over the years, though the organization has been long sensitive and attentive to the needs and wants of immediate importance to most people, is illustrative. Reflecting the ILO's traditional labor market perspective, no ILO convention addressing child labor prior to the 1989 CRC couched its provisions in the language of rights to define its mission or achieve its goals—not Convention (No. 29) Concerning Forced or Compulsory Labour, not Convention (No. 105) Concerning the Abolition of Forced Labour, not Convention (No. 138) Concerning Minimum Age for Admission to Employment. The first of these key initiatives may perhaps be excused for having been concluded in 1930, before human rights law began to be taken seriously in world affairs—before the 1945 Charter of the United Nations[4] and the 1948 Universal Declaration of Human Rights (UDHR).[5] But not so the other two treaties, concluded in 1957 and 1973; they joined a long list of ILO conventions concerning worker issues without engaging human rights discourse (Grimsrud 2002; Gross 2003, Leary 1996).

The reason seems clear. Although the idea of human rights can be traced to antiquity, it is relatively new on the world stage[6]; and, as everyone knows, social change—especially progressive social change—ordinarily takes place slowly, the more so when, nationally and internationally, command and enforcement mechanisms familiar to mature legal systems are relatively lacking.

Even today a human rights understanding of child labor is not widespread. Yet there are prices to be paid—often steep prices—for human rights myopia or quiescence. As James Gross has observed regarding worker rights specifically: "This lack of [human rights] attention has contributed to workers being seen as expendable in worldwide economic development and their needs and concerns not being represented at conferences on the world economy dominated by bankers, finance ministers, and multinational corporations" (Gross 2003:3).

It is important to acknowledge, however, that, since the adoption of the 1989 CRC and particularly the 1999 ILO Convention (No. 182) Concerning the Prohibition and Immediate Elimination of the Worst Forms of Child Labour[7], a commitment to the abolition of child labor as a human rights imperative has taken hold and begun to spread. Key intergovernmental organizations (IGOs) working in the field now actively affirm the link between child labor and human rights—most prominently, even if sometimes equivocally, the ILO (International Labour Organization 2006; Röselaers 2002) and the United Nations Children's Fund, known as UNICEF (Beigbeder 2001; UNICEF 2001). Also committed to a rights-based approach to child labor is the World Health Organization (WHO), whose Department of Child and Adolescent Health and Development (CAH) recognizes that the basic health needs of children and adolescents are fundamental human rights dependent for their protection and fulfillment on the realization of other rights such as "freedom from all forms of exploitation."[8]

Human rights orientations to child labor are now found also, even more conspicuously, among nongovernmental organizations (NGOs) working in this field—for example, Anti-Slavery International (formerly the Anti-Slavery Society), the London-based International Save the Children Alliance, and Global March Against Child Labour. Also noteworthy are Amnesty International (relative to child soldiering), the Children's Rights Division of Human Rights Watch (largely focused on forced and bonded child labor), and Defence for Children International. Certain regional and local NGOs, too, have become well known for combating child labor from a rights-based perspective—Child Workers in Asia is just one example.[9] The same is true of some national governments as well.[10]

Thus, both alone and in growing combination, variously specialized IGOs and NGOs, increasingly in collaboration with national governments, have in recent years placed child labor, especially its worst forms, high among their concerns and in the process have confirmed its human rights standing. Perhaps not coincidentally, these organizations also have begun to show some discernible progress.

But not nearly enough. However hopeful the ILO's reported 2000 to 2004 decline in child labor worldwide, the circumstance of abused and exploited children remains huge and grotesque, and oftentimes seemingly intractable. Why?

A primary explanation resides in the array of economic and political forces worldwide—mostly though not exclusively nationally based—whose various interests are served not by the elimination or reduction of child labor but by its perpetuation and proliferation. Child labor exists also because, except for a valiant few, the world's governing elites have yet to discover not just the political and economic will that is needed to surmount the problem, but also the comprehensive understanding of it upon which solutions adequate to its abolition depend. Such understanding is essential for the vision that is needed to energize the grand will that so far is lacking.

This chapter, intended to help offset this deficit, is therefore premised on five interrelated propositions:

- *First,* that child labor—work done by children that is harmful to them for being abusive, exploitative, hazardous, or otherwise contrary to their best interests—constitutes a major blight on human civility and welfare worldwide.

- *Second,* that it therefore begs to be abolished by all who profess ethical–moral conscience and/or pragmatic self-interest in the well-being of present and future generations.

- *Third,* that it manifests itself in complex and diverse ways and thus requires both multidimensional and singly focused approaches and techniques to achieve its eradication in whole or in part.
- *Fourth,* that these approaches and techniques must be informed by frank recognition that no form or level of social organization can claim "business as usual"—i.e., exemption from meaningful, even fundamental change—if the goal of abolition is genuinely to succeed in situations large or small over time.
- *Fifth,* that such change and the benefits to human dignity that can flow from it are not likely to be achieved except episodically without a dedicated and ongoing commitment to the contextual application of human rights law and policy, including the right of children to have a say about their own lives.

The time is long overdue when, from the most local to the most global circumstance, the rights of working children—not just their needs—must be taken seriously in the making and shaping of agendas pertinent to their lives, and especially, of course, when such agendas affect them directly.

Rethinking Child Labor: A Multidimensional Human Rights Problem

It is not just the brute facts that substantiate the problem of child labor as a human rights problem. So does the law.

Consider, for starters, the 1966 International Covenant on Economic, Social and Cultural Rights (ICESCR),[11] Article 10(3) of which provides in part as follows:

> Children and young persons should be protected from economic and social exploitation. Their employment in work harmful to their morals or health or dangerous to life or likely to hamper their normal development should be punishable by law. States should also set age limits below which the paid employment of child labour should be prohibited and punishable by law.

Consider also the 1989 CRC, more widely adopted than any other human rights compact in history. Article 32(1) of the convention is explicit:

> States Parties recognize the right of the child to be protected from economic exploitation and from performing any work that is likely to be hazardous or to interfere with the child's education, or to be harmful to the child's health or physical, mental, spiritual, moral or social development.

Article 32(2), requiring the states parties to take "legislative, administrative, social and educational measures" in respect of the foregoing, gives formal muscle to this human rights injunction. Also to the point, albeit less explicitly, is 1999 ILO Convention No. 182. In its preamble, it recalls, among other things, the 1989 CRC, the 1998 ILO Declaration on Fundamental Principles and Rights at Work, and the 1956 United Nations Supplementary Convention on the Abolition of Slavery, the Slave Trade, and Institutions and Practices Similar to Slavery. Thus it predicates its prohibitions of child labor's "worst forms" on a human rights framework, at least in part.

But particularly instructive, especially when accounting for the most egregious forms of child labor, are multiple additional provisions of the CRC, among them these:

- Article 3, requiring the states parties, "in all actions concerning children," to ensure "the best interests of the child," including "such protection and care as is necessary for his or her well-being"
- Article 6, requiring the states parties to ensure "to the maximum extent possible the survival and development of the child"
- Article 8, requiring the states parties to respect "the right of the child to preserve his or her identity, including . . . name and family relations"
- Article 9, requiring the states parties to ensure that, unless otherwise provided by law, "a child shall not be separated from his or her parents against their will"
- Article 11, requiring the states parties "to combat the illicit transfer and non-return of children abroad"
- Article 12, requiring the states parties to assure that "the child who is capable of forming his or her own views the right to express those views freely in all matters affecting the child," including "in any judicial and administrative proceedings affecting the child"
- Article 13, safeguarding the right of children to "freedom of expression," including "freedom to seek, receive, and impart information and ideas of all kinds"
- Article 15, recognizing the right of children to "freedom of association" and "peaceful assembly"
- Article 16, protecting children against "arbitrary or unlawful interference with his or her privacy, family, home or correspondence"
- Article 18, requiring parents to assume "common" and "primary" responsibility for "the upbringing and development of the child," guided by "the best interests of the child"

- Article 19, requiring the states parties "to protect the child from all forms of physical or mental violence, injury or abuse, neglect or negligent treatment, maltreatment or exploitation, including sexual abuse"
- Article 24, recognizing "the right of the child to the enjoyment of the highest attainable standard of health"
- Article 26, recognizing "for every child the right to benefit from social security"
- Article 27, recognizing "the right of every child to a standard of living adequate for the child's physical, mental, spiritual, moral and social development"
- Article 28, recognizing "the right of the child to education"
- Article 31, recognizing "the right of the child to rest and leisure"
- Article 34, requiring the states parties "to protect the child from all forms of sexual exploitation and sexual abuse"
- Article 35, requiring the states parties "to prevent the abduction of, the sale of or traffic in children for any purpose or in any form"
- Article 36, requiring the states parties to protect the child "against all other forms of exploitation prejudicial to any aspect of the child's welfare"
- Article 37, protecting children against "cruel, inhuman or degrading treatment"
- Article 38, requiring the states parties "to ensure that persons who have not attained the age of fifteen years do not take direct part in hostilities" and to "refrain from recruiting any person who has not attained the age of fifteen years into their armed forces"

The 1989 CRC thus recognizes the factual truth: child labor is not only a human rights problem simply put, but a human rights problem that is multidisciplinary, multifaceted, and multisectoral—in a word, multidimensional. It recognizes child labor to involve practices that violate children's rights directly (e.g., slavery), that abridge them indirectly (e.g., compulsory labor that results in denial of the right to education), and, indeed, that implicate the whole broad panoply of entitlements beyond children's rights per se, that span the entire spectrum of rights with which, at least in theory, *all* members of the human family are endowed (children obviously included)—that is, the three "generations" of rights that have evolved since at least the English Bill of Rights of 1689 to the present day: "first generation" civil and political rights; "second generation" economic, social, and cultural rights; and, most recently, "third generation" community (or "solidarity") group rights.[12] Each has its own historical roots that track the evolution of modern industrial society, including the development of a labor class (Cunningham and Stromquist 2005). Each is thus linked to the problem of child labor in one or more of its manifestations, including such third-generation rights as the right to peace,[13] the right to development,[14] and the right to a clean and healthy environment.[15]

The exploitative employment of trafficked children for commercial sexual acts, for example, flouts the right to the security of one's person, ergo first-generation civil and political rights. The exposure of working children to toxic and otherwise hazardous substances infringes directly upon the human right to health, ergo "second-generation" economic, social, and cultural rights. Child soldiering subverts not only the first-generation right to security of one's person but, likewise, the group right to peace, ergo third-generation community (or solidarity) rights.

Indeed, few provisions of the three historic instruments that constitute the "International Bill of Human Rights"—the 1948 UDHR, the 1966 ICESCR, and the 1966 ICCPR—are untouched by the problem of child labor. This is particularly apparent when one looks upon human rights from a "human capabilities" perspective, in the manner of Martha Nussbaum and Amartya Sen—that is, by reference less to abstract wants (policy objectives) than to concrete and measurable needs (life functions), such as life itself; bodily health and bodily integrity; senses, imagination, and thought; emotions; conscience; affiliation as friendship and respect; and political and material control over one's environment (Nussbaum 1997; Sen 1985). It is impossible to disassociate the problem of child labor, especially its worst forms, from any one of these most central of human capabilities and therefore, as well, from any of their human rights correlatives. A mere glance at the UDHR proves the comparative point.[16]

But it is not only the multidimensionality of the child labor problem that reveals its human rights linkages. Also highly relevant is its interrelatedness with the human rights of the parents or guardians of working children—a point well understood by, for example, UNICEF, which works to advance the rights of children and of women (as mothers) in tandem (UNICEF 1999b). The safeguarding of children's rights depends not merely on the promotion and protection of their rights, but on the promotion and protection of the fundamental human rights of their parents or guardians as well, and under UDHR Article 2 "without distinction of any kind, such as race, colour, sex, language, religion, political or other opinion, national or social origin, property, birth or other status." Denying parents or guardians their human rights contributes to the propagation or perpetuation of child labor and thereby denials of the rights of children.

In sum, the nexus between child labor and human rights is broad and deep. That a number of states, intergovernmental institutions, and nongovernmental organizations engaged in the struggle against child labor have adopted or begun to adopt rights-based policies to prosecute its abolition is thus not surprising.

Still, a commitment to a rights-based approach to child labor is not yet common in official policy or practice. Skeptics assert that rights-based approaches to social ills such as child labor lack pragmatism because, it is sometimes said, they focus on unrealistic, aspirational norms that have little or no connection to the "real world." Indeed, in respect of child labor at least, some suggest that human rights approaches tend to be counterproductive (O'Neill 1992) and, more generally, that the international human rights movement is part of the problem, not the solution (Kennedy 2002, 2004).

I demur and contest these claims in the section "Contesting Resistance to Human Rights Strategy." While the skeptics certainly have some valid points (the human rights movement is, after all, a human—ergo imperfect—project), there is no denying that a rights-based approach to child labor, especially when conceived and executed from a holistic, multidimensional perspective, has strong pragmatic underpinnings and thus can have substantial beneficial results. One can point to numerous instances in which human rights discourse and strategy have had real impact (Cassel 2001; Slye 2001), including in the area of child labor.[17] Given the continued skepticism, however, it behooves us to explain why, and to explain also why the skeptics are mistaken.

The Utility of a Human Rights Approach to Child Labor

Why is it important to think and act upon the problem of child labor as a human rights problem? What purposes are served by such an approach?

Human rights as "trumps." In his germinal book, *Taking Rights Seriously,* legal philosopher Ronald Dworkin asserts unequivocally—and correctly—that when a claimed value or good is categorized as a "right" it "trumps" most if not all other claimed values or goods (Dworkin 1977). Rights discourse confers a status of special importance on claimed entitlements, juridically more elevated than commonplace "standards" or "laws," which in contrast to "human rights" are subject to everyday revision and recision for lack of such ordination. A proximate analogy is the distinction between a contractual or statutory claim and a constitutional one.

Thus, when child labor is designated a condition from which children have a *right* to be free, not merely an option for which regulating (but easily revocable) *standards* must be devised, there results an opportunity for empowerment and mobilization that otherwise is lacking. A rights-based approach to child labor elevates the "needs" and "interests" of children in this context to societal needs and interests, with associated claims of legal and political legitimacy. As UNICEF's 1997 *State of the World's Children* report characterized the organization's strategic decision to use rights to reduce child labor: "The idea that children have special needs has given way to the conviction that children have rights, the same full spectrum of rights as adults: civil and political, social, cultural and economic" (UNICEF 1997:8). Or as UNICEF put it two years later in its 1999 *State of the World's Children* report: "What were once seen as the needs of children have been elevated to something far harder to ignore: their rights" (UNICEF 1999a).

In sum, rights are not matters of charity, a question of favor or kindness to be bestowed or taken away at will (Santos Pais 1999). They are high-level public order values or goods that carry with them a sense of entitlement on the part of the rights-holder and obligatory implementation on the part of the rights-protector—intergovernmental institutions, the state, society, the family. They are values or goods deemed fundamental and universal; and while not absolute, they nonetheless are judged superior to other claimed values or goods. To assert a *right* of a child to be free from abusive, exploitative, and hazardous work is, thus, to strengthen a child's possibility for a life of dignity and well-being. It bespeaks duty, not optional—often capricious—benevolence.

Human rights as interdependent agents of human dignity. Central to the concept of human rights is the notion of a "public order of human dignity," a public order *(ordre publique)* "in which values are shaped and shared more by persuasion than by coercion, and which seeks to promote the greatest production and widest possible sharing, without discriminations irrelevant of merit, of all values among all human beings" (McDougal 1960:987). This notion of public order, encapsulating "the basic policies of an international law of human dignity" (McDougal, Lasswell, and Chen 1980) is embedded in the 1948 UDHR. Its preamble proclaims the concept of human rights to grow out of "recognition of the inherent dignity . . . of all members of the human family" as "the foundation of freedom, justice and peace in the world."

In the struggle against child labor, thus, a rights-based approach signals more than the alleviation of child abuse and exploitation per se. It signals also that norms of nondiscrimination, justice, and dignity must be central in all aspects of a working child's life, including provision for her or his education, health, and spiritual, moral, or social development— precisely as the 1989 CRC envisions. A rights-based approach to the child labor problem is part of a complex web of interdependent rights that extends protection beyond one domain to many others in a child's life. Most if not all human rights depend on the satisfaction of other human rights for their fulfillment. Treating freedom from abusive, exploitative, and hazardous child work as a human right thus raises the stakes against those who would put children in harm's way. It transforms the struggle *against* child labor into a struggle *for* human dignity and thus better captures responsible attention and heightened pressure in the search for enduring solutions.

Human rights as a mobilizing challenge to statist and elitist agendas. Because they trump lesser societal values or goods and because they are agents of human dignity, human rights challenge and make demands upon state sovereignty. Scores of human rights conventions entered into force since World War II require states to cede bits of sovereignty in the name of human rights. Legal obligations of great solemnity, the 1989 CRC and 1999 ILO Convention No. 182 are among them.

Proof that human rights challenge and make demands upon state sovereignty is found, too, in the many occasions in which states, intergovernmental institutions, NGOs, professional associations, corporations, trade unions, churches, and others have relied successfully on this *"corpus juris* of social justice" (Van Boven 1982:88) to measure and curb state behavior. The legitimacy of political regimes—hence their capacity to govern noncoercively or at all—is today judged by criteria informed and refined by human rights.

All of this is well known. Keenly aware of their interdependencies, most states, however much they may resist human rights pressures from within and without, are mindful that their national interests and desired self-image depend on their willingness to play by the rules, especially those that weigh heavily on the scales of social and political morality. Even the most powerful states are vulnerable to what has come to be called "the mobilization of shame" in defense of human rights (Drinan 2001). The case of apartheid South Africa is perhaps the best-known example in this regard. There is no reason why states that encourage or tolerate abusive, exploitative, and hazardous child work cannot or should not be similarly targeted and shamed. Robert Mugabe's Zimbabwe comes presently to mind.

But not only states. Human rights challenge and make demands upon the particularist agendas of private elites as well. Why? Because human rights have as their core value that of respect, by definition possessed equally by all human beings everywhere; they insist upon equality of treatment across the board.[18] "Equality or non-discrimination," writes Virginia Leary, "is a leitmotif running through all of international human rights law" (Leary 1994:37). True, no observant person would dispute the widespread disregard of these principles. Still, there is no denying the potential of human rights discourse and strategy to dare and defy the special interests, private as well as public, that, usually for selfish reasons, dismiss the equal treatment of all human beings and thus contribute to such social ills as child labor.

In sum, ordinary norms, institutions, and procedures are not typically defined by the language of human rights and therefore do not have the same gravitas as their human rights counterparts. They do not carry with them the same moral authority upon which, in democratic societies at least, governing elites depend to exercise and retain legitimacy and power. The potential of human rights norms to dislodge or seriously burden those private exclusive interests that help to perpetuate child labor is likewise manifest.

Human rights as empowerment for children. Human rights carry with them not only a sense of entitlement on the part of the rights-holder. They embrace also "the right of the individual to know and act upon his [sic] rights,"[19] hence a sense of duty and redress on the part of the state and other actors. The essence of rights discourse (or human rights law) is that, in Michael Freeman's pointed alert, "if you have a right to x, and you do not get x, this is not only a wrong, but it is a wrong against *you*" (Freeman 2002:61). This extends inexorably to children as rights-holders. CRC Article 12(1) expressly requires that states parties "assure to the child . . . the right to express [her or his] views freely in all matters affecting the child" and that "the views of the child [be] given due weight."

At least four specific ways have been identified by which human rights accomplish this empowerment.[20] Each bears obvious relevance to children and others who seek the abolition of child labor.

- First, human rights provide a level of accountability that transcends that of other legal obligations. Like those obligations, human rights provide victims of rights violations with the authority to hold violators accountable, even to the point of criminal liability. However, because human rights entail fundamental values of "superior" moral order, their violation correspondingly entails greater moral condemnation than other wrongs. This is what distinguishes "rights" from "benefits" or from being the beneficiary of another's obligation (Donnelly 1985, 1989). It is what makes possible, for example, "the mobilization of shame" and the condemnation of the international community, commonly without even having to go to formal court. The "truth and reconciliation" processes of Argentina, Chile, El Salvador, Ghana,

Guatemala, Haiti, Malawi, Nepal, Nigeria, The Philippines, Serbia and Montenegro, South Africa, South Korea, and elsewhere are proof enough.[21] On occasion, they can be more effective than their more formal legal counterparts in overcoming impunity (Dugard 1999; Minow 1999; Rotberg and Thompson 2000).

- Second, human rights provide access to international institutions dedicated specifically to their promotion and vindication, including the human rights mechanisms of the United Nations (Marks 1999) and of the regional human rights regimes of Europe, the Americas, and Africa (Shelton 1999). The effectiveness of these institutions as enforcement mechanisms is not consistent and often cumbersome and time-consuming, particularly at the global level. Nevertheless, they confirm that human suffering is and can be taken seriously, providing formal legal tools to remedy or otherwise mitigate abuses and thereby help to prevent future abuse. Like less formal techniques (e.g., a civil society mobilization of shame), their use can result in both specific and general deterrence, potentially ensuring individual and group rights.

- Third, human rights generate legal grounds for political activity and expression because, as already noted, they entail greater moral force than ordinary legal obligations. This is abundantly seen in the many global and regional conferences and other gatherings commonly called under the auspices of the United Nations (including the UN's former Commission on Human Rights, now the UN Human Rights Council following a 2006 restructuring)[22] and such regional organizations as the Council of Europe, the Organization of American States, and the African Union, each providing a forum in which the voices of human rights victims and advocates can be heard. The history of the anti-apartheid movement is replete with examples. Also illustrative are the annual conferences of the ILO and the high-level meetings of UNICEF and other intergovernmental organizations. All contribute to political empowerment, from the adoption of new resolutions and treaties to the recommendation of new norms and mechanisms to the reinterpretation of existing international and domestic norms and procedures—according to which "[t]he more fortunate are called upon to assist the less fortunate as an internationally recognized responsibility" (Robinson 1999:v). In turn, the resulting rights vocabulary and action plans help to refine the theoretical and operational foundations for all varieties of human rights projects, reinforced by the authority with which the sponsoring organizations and attending participants are regarded.

- Finally, human rights discourse and strategy, which exist to promote and protect human capabilities of all sorts, encourage the creation of initiatives both within and beyond civil society that are designed to facilitate the meeting of "basic needs." Except for the 1975 Helsinki Accords, such initiatives were not easy to find before the fall of the Berlin Wall in 1989, when tensions sacrificed these concerns on the altar of Cold War rivalries. But since then, they have proliferated, especially in the human rights advocacy and scholarly communities (Wiseberg 2005), which is of profound importance because the provision of basic needs provides the material basis for people to act on their rights—the very definition of empowerment.

Despite the relevance of these (and possibly other) forms of empowerment to children and others who seek child labor's abolition, however, some scholars question whether they can in fact extend to children. Onora O'Neill, for one, is skeptical because "[y]ounger children are completely and unavoidably dependent on those [adults] who have power over their lives" (O'Neill 1992:42).[23] Beyond perhaps the first six to eight years of childhood, I respectfully disagree, as would also most modern anthropologists, historians, and sociologists of childhood. While usually dependent on adults when very young, children are no longer "completely and unavoidably" dependent as they mature in age and experience. In fact, they may exhibit considerable independence and self-initiative well before adolescence, particularly in our brave new world of cyberspace. What is more, their growing independence may be collective as well as individual. As Michael Freeman has argued, "there are prototypes or at least germs of children's movements already in existence" (Freeman 2002:57). Indeed, children's movements have long been noted among working children. In early-20th-century American cities, for example, the self-organization of child newspaper vendors to defend their interests and rights attracted much public attention, and in some places it even was supported by enlightened city officials who linked it to public child protection mechanisms (Nasaw 1986).

Present-day working children's organizations and movements in Africa, Asia, and Latin America have been amply noted and discussed in the literature (Black 2004; Miljeteig 2000; Swift 1999; Tolfree 1998), among them organizations linked in an international children's movement (the World Movement of Working Children and Adolescents), which maintains contact between countries and periodically holds international "summit" conferences. A "Final Declaration" from a summit in Berlin in April and May 2004, in which the assembled working children reaffirmed their commitment to "practice protagonism" and fight for "recognition as social actors so that our voices be heard in the whole world," is noteworthy: "We value our work and view it as an important human right for our personal development. We oppose every kind of exploitation and reject everything that hurts our moral and physical integrity. . . . [W]e reaffirm our will to continue constructing a world movement that not only fights for, defends and promotes the rights of working children, but of children in general."[24]

In addition, *non*working children have organized specifically to combat child labor. A prominent example is the Free the Children network founded by Canadian youth Craig Kielburger, the work and motto of which ("Often assumed to be the leaders of tomorrow, our generation must be the leaders of today") also challenge skepticism of the sort expressed by O'Neill (Kielburger 1998). Another is the Global March Against Child Labour. While an adult-led initiative to mobilize international opinion against child labor, it affords ample opportunity for the participation of both working and nonworking children to make their views known.[25]

To be sure, there is room for debate over the extent to which children can or should be self-empowered, as evidenced by the manner in which the above-noted Berlin and Florence gatherings were organized and conducted—the first primarily by working children, the second primarily by adults. The fact remains, however, that children—including working children—are today demonstrating increasing resolve to assert their own interests and to do so as self-conscious expression of their universal civil and political rights to access and participate in the decision- and policy-making processes that affect their lives. Indeed, direct involvement by children in defense of their interests and rights often is key to the validity and vitality of their claims. They are themselves often the best witnesses to the harm that results from violations of their rights and thus are uniquely well positioned to provide the most compelling evidence of the need for redress. Which is why, of course, the 1989 CRC and human rights values generally mandate the right of children to express their views freely and where it counts. Empowerment of children is not only a result of a rights-based approach to child labor, it is, subject to their evolving capacities, a virtual requirement of it.

Contesting Resistance to Human Rights Strategy

However manifest the premise and virtues of a human rights approach to the problem of child labor, advocacy of it would be incomplete were one not to confront the conceptual, psychosocial barriers that all too commonly are mounted to resist human rights agendas and thwart their potential—often from the start (testimony, of course, to the potential of human rights law and policy in the first place). In the ensuing subsections, I respond to these conceptual barriers and to the vested interests that cluster behind them. Also, believing that there is nothing as practical as a good theory except for the debunking of bad theory, I urge that human rights vis-à-vis child labor be taken seriously and actualized in everyday planning and programming. This may seem an obvious or even redundant thing to say, but it is important to appreciate completely the artfulness of one's detractors in order to weigh in confidently with a human rights orientation to child labor and thereby reap fully its benefits in the making of daily decision and policy. Much hangs in the balance.

Contesting the Claimed Immutability of State Sovereignty

There is no disputing that the state has diminished in relative influence in the last half century. Nevertheless, the classical international law doctrine of territorial sovereignty and its corollary of nonintervention remain the central props of our inherited state-centric system of world order. The values associated with these doctrines, however—a legal license to "do your own thing" and an injunction to "mind your own business"—resist the values associated with human rights, which tell us that "you are your brothers' and sisters' keeper" and therefore invite international scrutiny and outside interference in what otherwise would be internal matters (Claude and Weston 2006).

In short, human rights qualify state sovereignty and power, and as a consequence, governments naturally are resistant to embracing the language of human rights, let alone rights-based agendas. Even governments that have voluntarily consented to human rights treaties are inclined to demur when it comes to implementation. However, it is disingenuous of them to tarry when they have committed officially to these legal promises. More importantly, after more than a half-century of mounting international rejection of the claim that "the king can do no wrong," it is no longer tenable for them to delay—least of all when, as in the case of the 1989 CRC and 1999 ILO C182, the treaty obligations command the support of the vast majority of the world's states.

In short, a sovereignty defense against human rights violations, particularly of the worst sort, is now, at least theoretically, a thing of the past. To be sure, the radical foundation upon which the scaffolding of contemporary international human rights law and policy has been erected is yet new and fragile. But, as evidenced by at least the formal agendas of most international institutions and foreign offices, the agendas of global civil society aside, the world no longer deems impunity from human rights wrongs acceptable.

Contesting the Claimed Sanctity of Corporate Sovereignty

Also explaining resistance to a rights-based approach to child labor is what may be called "corporate sovereignty" (I coin the term to cover a multitude of private business formations, not to single out corporations per se). Just as states seek to control the territory and populations of their claimed jurisdictions, so business enterprises, in pursuit of profits and market shares, seek sovereignty over the means of production that principally define their more or less private jurisdictions (including, of course, their labor forces). Human rights agendas, however, tend to be costly and otherwise inconvenient to this fundamental objective and thus are often downplayed or ignored (Jennings and Entine 1998; Mock 2000). Not infrequently, business enterprises actively resist human rights agendas—as when, for example, to curry favor with host governments, they break sanctions against repressive regimes, cooperate with these regimes economically, or lend them internal political support of some kind (Lippman 1985; Monshipouri, Welch, and Kennedy 2003). In these circumstances especially, human rights discourse itself is avoided lest it encourage outside scrutiny, possibly intervention. True, many—perhaps most—business enterprises strive to be "good corporate citizens," to accept if not actually promote human rights agendas when called upon to do so.[26] True also, corrupt governmental practices often force business enterprises to comply with discriminatory and otherwise repressive legislation. Still, the impulse of corporate sovereignty remains a powerful deterrent to a rights-based strategy opposed to abusive, exploitative, and hazardous child work, especially when large-scale enterprises with great influence are involved.[27]

Corporate sovereignty, however, is an impulse to which public policy need not and should not always defer. Throughout the world, governments adopt and enforce laws to limit factory emissions, regulate product content and safety, set minimum wages, establish occupational workplace standards, and the like. Indeed, labor conditions may be the most heavily regulated of business matters. Business enterprises should not therefore expect that a grotesque problem such as child labor should be subject to any less scrutiny and control. Nor should they, in their own self-interest, want such an outcome. Most business enterprises care more about respected and stable production and marketing climates than they do about ideology, and the surest way to guarantee that such climates prevail is to help safeguard the fundamental rights of the populations on which they depend for economic reward (Jennings and Entine 1998).

Contesting the Claimed Irrelevance of Public International Law to Private Actors

Closely related to notions of state and corporate sovereignty as explanations for resistance to a rights-based approach to child labor—indeed supportive of them—is the orthodox theory that, by definition, public international law applies only to public, not private, actors.[28] Given that the vast majority of the world's working children labor on behalf of private, not public, actors, this theory is of no small consequence to the present discussion. Public international law (which includes international human rights law) simply does not apply, so the argument goes, to private business associations, including ones that employ children.

Of course, theories are but intellectual paradigms, prototypes of thought that define not only what we look at but also how we go about looking at what we look at. They do not necessarily mirror reality. So when the facts of life no longer fit the theory, it is time, as Copernicus taught us, to change the theory. In recent years, feminist scholars have urged this kind of rethinking regarding the theoretical structure of international law, particularly in relation to the status of women internationally (Charlesworth and Chinkin 2000). There is no reason why the same cannot be done relative to the status of working children in private business enterprises, making such enterprises directly accountable to international human rights norms relevant to them.

In any event, there is UDHR Article 30: "Nothing in this Declaration may be interpreted as implying for any State, *group or person* any right to engage in any activity or to perform any act aimed at the destruction of any of the rights and freedoms set forth herein" (emphasis added). Additionally, reflecting an emerging consensus that the large economic and political power of at least multinational corporations must be subjected to heightened international accountability, the UN Global Compact launched by UN Secretary-General Kofi Annan in 1999, the former UN Commission on Human Rights, and the UN High Commissioner for Human Rights as well as growing numbers of legal scholars now urge theories of international transparency and responsibility that rewrite the relationship between international law and the private sector, including in relation to human rights.[29] As key beneficiaries of the new economic world order created by international law (e.g., the World Trade Organization, the North American Free Trade Agreement, etc.), private business enterprises have no standing, it is appropriately argued, to claim immunity from the corresponding obligations established by international law;

and trends in actual decision, both national and international, suggest that human rights responsibilities on the part of private persons are increasingly recognized and enforced (Shelton 2002; UN High Commissioner for Human Rights 2000).[30] Expressly or by implication, many of the most fundamental human rights instruments recognize human rights obligations on the part of private actors per se,[31] while others and cognate treaties require states parties to ensure and enforce the rights enumerated against violations by private perpetrators. Labor treaties that have emerged from the ILO, for example, have long required governments to enact domestic legislation affecting private businesses.

States often adopt laws giving domestic effect to human rights norms and standing to seek redress for their violation by private actors as well.[32] Also, with increasing frequency, corporations commit themselves at least morally to human rights obligations via voluntary "codes of conduct" (Schrage 2004), while consumers and other members of civil society invoke nonjuridical mechanisms to hold private actors accountable by voting with their pocketbooks and otherwise mobilizing shame against private human rights violators.[33]

True, legal scholars differ over the extent to which developments such as these confer "international legal personality" upon corporations and other nonstate actors. Moreover, old canons die hard. But resistance to a rights-based approach to child labor can no longer be justified on the basis of orthodox theory about the "subjects" and "objects" of international law. The world is now far too interpenetrating a place for that.

Contesting the Claimed Indeterminacy of Human Rights

Some scholars criticize the language of human rights as lacking conceptual clarity, noting that there are conflicting schools of thought as to what constitutes a right and how to define human rights (Gewirth 1996). For this reason, they claim the concept to be "indeterminate" and therefore distrust its capacity to address "real world" social ills effectively or at all.[34] They observe that there are many unresolved theoretical questions about rights: "whether the individual is the only bearer of rights" (in contradistinction to such entities as families; groups of common ethnicity, religion, or language; communities; and nations); "whether rights are to be regarded as . . . constraints on goal-seeking action or as parts of a goal that is to be promoted"; "whether rights— thought of as justified entitlements—are correlated with duties"; and, not least, "what rights are understood to be rights to" (Nussbaum 1999:26–27)—a certain level of well-being? A certain access to certain resources in one's life pursuit? A certain quality of opportunity in that pursuit? The recent debate over "Asian values" and its underlying tension between cultural relativist and universalist approaches to human rights make clear that all this questioning is no idle intellectual chatter. It is very much present in the political arena as well, and thus serves as another possible explanation for resistance to a rights-based approach to child labor.

The claimed indeterminacy of "human rights," however, is less problematic than perceived. The core of the human rights concept is as well defined and clearly articulated as any social or legal norm, a fact proven by the numerous widely accepted—and increasingly enforced—human rights norms already noted. Moreover, even conceding that unresolved theoretical issues relating to human rights remain, this fact should not distract from the broadest and most effective actualization of the fundamental principles and values on which there is virtually universal agreement—for example, the right of children to be free from abusive, exploitative, and hazardous labor.

Thus, while the concept or language of rights, like most legal language, sometimes suffers ambiguity, it is not to be discarded in the anti–child labor struggle (or any other) simply for this reason. Rather, as with any human—incomplete and imperfect—system, one must make use of those elements that are established and effective while working to finalize and perfect those that remain vague or incomplete, just as we do all other legal norms as a matter of course all the time.

Contesting the Claimed Absence of Human Rights Theory

Perhaps the most confounding of the alleged unresolved theoretical issues about human rights is the claimed absence of a theory to justify human rights (Rorty 1993). In the presence of ongoing philosophical and political controversy about the existence, nature, and application of human rights in a multicultured world, a world in which Christian natural law justifications for human rights are now widely deemed obsolete, one must exercise caution when adopting a human rights approach to social policy lest one be accused of cultural imperialism. It is not enough to say, argues Michael Freeman, that human beings possess human rights simply for being human, as does, for example, the 1993 Vienna Declaration and Programme of Action, which proclaims that "[h]uman rights and fundamental freedoms are the birthright of all human beings."[35] Writes Freeman: "It is not clear why one has *any* rights simply because one is a human being" (Freeman 2002:60–61).

I do not disagree. But neither do I accept that there exists no theory to justify human rights in our secular times, ergo no theory to justify a human rights approach to child labor. The concept of human rights is or can be firmly established on sound theoretical ground.

First, there is the proposition, formally proclaimed in both the 1948 UDHR and the yet more widely adopted and revalidating 1993 Vienna Declaration, that human rights derive from "the inherent dignity . . . of all members of the human family" or, alternatively, from "the dignity and worth inherent in the human person."[36] While this proposition informs us little more than the assertion that human rights extend to human beings simply for being human, it does point the way. Unless one subscribes to nihilism, it is the human being's inherent dignity and worth that justifies human rights. Of course, the obvious question remains: how does one determine the human being's inherent dignity and worth?

Noteworthy in this regard is the previously cited work of Nussbaum and Sen on "capabilities and human functioning." In their search for a theory that answers at least some of the questions raised by rights talk, they have pioneered the language of "human capabilities" as a way to speak about, and act upon, what fundamentally is required to be human—"life," "bodily health," "bodily integrity," "senses, imagination, and thought," "emotions," "affiliation" ("friendship" and "respect"), "other species," "play," and "control over one's environment" ("political" and "material") (Nussbaum 1999; Sen 1985; Williams 1987). While Nussbaum and Sen do not reject the concept of human rights as such[37]— indeed, they see it working hand in hand with their concept of capabilities, jointly signaling the central goals of public policy—they propose emphasis on human capabilities as the theoretical means by which to restore "the obligation of result" and thereby move the discussion from the abstract to the concrete without having to rely on controversial transempirical metaphysics to cut across human differences. There remains, however, the question of how to distinguish those capabilities that are central to human existence—hence worthy of the title "human rights"—and those that are not. Control over one's political and/or material environment, for example, can lead to some very nasty results.[38]

The work of the late John Rawls (1971) points the way. Rawls proposed a thought experiment, akin to Kant's "categorical imperative," in which a group of thinking men and women of diverse characteristics (race, class, creed, etc.) come together in their private capacity (i.e., not as state representatives) in some "original position" to construct a just society with their personal self-interests in mind, but without knowing their own position in it (economic, social, racial, etc.). Behind this "veil of ignorance," these "original position" decision makers, rationally contemplating their own self-interest, freely choose a society that is fair to all, one in which benefits (rights) and burdens (duties) are distributed equally and in which a core of fundamental liberties (freedom of conscience, speech, movement, religion, etc.) and equality of opportunity are protected. This social constructionism, however, need not be restricted to Rawls's historically Western core values favoring individual civil and political rights. Accounting for *all* the voices assembled, the "original position" decision makers, transcending personal self-interest even while accounting for it, could equally well choose a set of basic but diverse values (rights and/or capabilities) that would win the general assent of human beings *everywhere*—a set of universal basic values of human dignity that, grounded in principles of reciprocal tolerance and mutual forbearance, define the human rights society. It is such a society that can most guarantee the fairest distribution of basic wants (rights) and needs (capabilities) among all human beings and thereby ensure that all will benefit as much as possible and, by the same token, suffer the least possible disadvantage.

And therein lies, I submit, the theoretical justification for human rights in our secular age: a kind of share-and-share-alike Golden Rule that, in an "original position" behind a "veil of ignorance" and as rational human beings contemplating our own self-interest, we would choose for ordering a society in which all of us would want to live. However interpreted and applied in real world conflict and contestation, human rights are theoretically justified because they satisfy the fundamental requirements of socioeconomic and political justice. In the words of former UN High Commissioner for Human Rights Louise Arbour before a working group on economic, social, and cultural rights of the Commission on Human Rights in January 2005, "[h]uman rights are not a utopian ideal. They embody an international consensus on the minimum conditions for a life of dignity." When joined to the struggle against abusive, exploitative, and hazardous child work, they can be a uniquely powerful tool.

Abolishing Child Labor: A Multifaceted Human Rights Strategy

In the preceding section, I challenged a palpable if diminishing reluctance to use human rights to combat child labor: first, by calling attention to the multidimensional human rights nature of the problem; next, by detailing the virtues of human rights discourse and strategy to combat it; and finally, by contesting claims that would prevent or curtail resort to such rights talk and maneuver. These latter claims, I submit, are as unconvincing as the virtues of human rights law and policy are convincing. And thus I am driven to conclude that the core questions demanding responsible attention are not why or whether to bring human rights to the prosecution of child labor, but how and how quickly.

These core questions demand urgent as well as responsible attention. Economic globalization, which can no more be arrested than the transition from agrarian to industrial society (Howard-Hassmann 2005; Sen 2000), is proceeding apace, and while it has its bright sides, it has also its dark sides that threaten human rights generally and the rights of working children in particular. A human rights approach to child labor, one that foresees a true culture of respect for children's rights, can help to offset these darker forces if it is urgently as well as responsibly embraced and pursued.

In this section, therefore, using an established typology of decision-making functions to facilitate coverage and coherence, I recommend a more-or-less comprehensive series of concrete policies and courses of action that, in various combinations especially, can be effective in combating child labor in general and from a human rights perspective in particular. Without disparaging smaller, incremental approaches when circumstance and opportunity permit—indeed, I wholeheartedly support them when such instances arise—I nevertheless proceed on the belief that a hugely multidimensional human rights problem such as child labor begs for a coextensively multifaceted human rights strategy for its solution, in whole or in major part. Once the human rights of working children are recognized and their legal content understood, such a strategy can translate into effective policies, programs, and projects that promote, it bears repeating, a true culture of respect for the rights of children. Of course, space limitations require that much of this "nuts-and-bolts" discussion be restricted to descriptive outline, leaving it to other occasions to fill in the gaps and flesh out the details. Moreover, such recommendations as I do offer here are tendered more in tentative than definitive spirit. Making human rights work for the abolition of child labor must be understood as a continuing process of reflection and debate, open to reappraisal and redirection as time and experience dictate. It is risky to be categorical. At the same time, it is irresponsible to rest content with expressions of theoretical commitment only. Once human rights are recognized and their legal content understood, their formal expressions must be made operational.

Before engaging this nuts-and-bolts discussion, however, it is important to revisit the two central injunctions made earlier:

- *first, to accept—self-consciously and proactively—the premise and virtues of human rights law and policy on all topical and tactical fronts* (because such acceptance of human rights as child labor's moral and legal reference point can effectively counter practices that contradict children's best interests and, at the same time, promote those practices that facilitate their human dignity, including their rights to a reasonable standard of living, to education, even to the right to work in ways that are not abusive, exploitative, hazardous, or otherwise contrary to their best interests)

- *second, to reject—again self-consciously and proactively—the psychosocial (conceptual) barriers that all too commonly are mounted to resist human rights initiatives and thus thwart their potential from the start* (because such rejection of the conceptual barriers to human rights thought and action in the child labor context unleashes the contributions that states, intergovernmental organizations, NGOs, and others can and must make toward the solution of this complex and pervasive problem)

These injunctions—essentially to take children's human rights *seriously*—are critical "nuts and bolts" in their own right, necessary first steps in any human rights strategy worthy of child labor's abolition and of the social transformations required to make that happen. As Marta Santos Pais has put it relative to the operationalization of UNICEF's approach to development, "[t]he expression of a solemn commitment to human rights legitimizes our work and constitutes a catalyst for our actions" (Santos Pais 1999:15).

Taking Working Children's Human Rights Seriously

Although there exists today an emerging commitment to a rights-based approach to child labor (as in the case of UNICEF), the fact is that, as previously noted, it is not common in official policy or practice, especially on the national plane. Nor is it a conspicuous feature on the international plane, not even of official rhetoric. The ILO's most recent major report on child labor, *Global Report 2006*, suggested a possible shift in this regard, and not an insignificant one considering the ILO's prominence in the anti–child labor struggle.[39] But a palpable hesitancy at the idea of human rights discourse and strategy as an effective tool in this struggle lingers all the same, even among well-wishers. Doubtless this uncertainty is a function, at least in part, of bureaucratic inertia or even general disinterest—and surely, as well, of incomplete understanding of the virtues of human rights discourse and strategy in the first place. It probably is a function, too, of strongly held beliefs in the minimum age/labor market approach to children's work represented by 1973 ILO Convention No. 138. I believe, however, that it is also—perhaps even primarily—a function of the statist, elitist, patriarchal, and paternalistic logics that shape our worldviews and lives. Through many years of psychosocial acculturation, these logics have come to define not only

what specifically we see to be possible but also, more generally, how we
go about seeing what is possible.

As long as we continue in this way, however, we never will achieve
the social transformations that are needed to abolish the abuse and
exploitation of working children on an enduring basis (in whole or in
part). The time is overdue when we must champion the rights of children not simply as *children's* rights, so labeled at risk of marginalization,
but as *human* rights which, at their core, evince concern for the alleviation of *all* human suffering—and therefore also, in Costas Douzinas'
evocative phrase, "concern for the unfinished person of the future for
whom justice matters" (Douzinas 2000:15). UNICEF's Innocenti
Research Centre comes close in its call for "a new global ethic for children."[40] But not, I think, close enough. Needed is a wholesale paradigm
shift not only in the way we think about children specifically, but also—
guided by an ethos of species identity—in the way we think about social
governance generally, a shift away from the statist, elitist, patriarchal,
and paternalistic logics that stand in the way of the genuine alleviation of
child and other human suffering. Needed is an internalized worldview
that, on behalf of working children and in continuously persevering
ways, actively embraces the premise and virtues of human rights discourse and strategy, consistently contests the psychosocial (conceptual)
barriers that impede their operation and systematically mainstreams the
full human rights agenda (civil, political, economic, social, cultural, and
communitarian) in each and every policy that is devised and in each and
every measure that is taken. The need is for a culture of respect for children's human rights, a culture of human rights as a way of life.

It is this kind of rethinking that appears to have shaped the Declaration and Programme of Action of the 1993 Vienna World Conference on
Human Rights; that later, in 1997, guided UN Secretary-General Kofi
Annan to summons all UN entities to mainstream human rights into the
activities and programs that fell within their mandates; and that, as a
consequence, in May 2003, found expression in a Statement of Common
Understanding (SCU) of a UN "Inter-Agency Workshop" outlining a
human rights–based approach to the development planning and programming of UN agencies.[41] While intended for UN development agencies specifically, this 2003 SCU points the way for *all* who would seek to
abolish child labor via human rights discourse and strategy.

First, it identifies several key "human rights principles" to "guide all
programming in all phases of the programming process"—which itself is
defined to include "assessment and analysis, programme planning and
design (including setting of goals, objectives and strategies); implementation, monitoring and evaluation" (p. 91 of the SCU). Specifically, it

articulates and explains the following principles: "universality and inalienability; indivisibility; interdependence and interrelatedness; non-discrimination and equality; participation and inclusion; accountability and the rule of law" (p. 91 of the SCU).

Next, but first cautioning that "the application of good programming practices does not by itself constitute a human rights-based approach," the SCU cites four "required additional elements" deemed by the May 2003 UN Inter-Agency Workshop to be "necessary, specific, and unique to a human rights-based approach":

1. Assessment and analysis [to] identify the human rights claims of rights-holders and the corresponding human rights obligations of duty-bearers, as well as the immediate, underlying, and structural causes when rights are not realized.

2. Programmes [to] assess the capacity of rights-holders to claim their rights, and of duty-bearers to fulfill their obligations, [and the development of] strategies to build these capacities.

3. Programmes [to] monitor and evaluate both outcomes and processes guided by human rights standards and principles.

4. Programming [that] is informed by the recommendations of international human rights bodies and mechanisms.

Finally, the SCU lists 13 other elements deemed essential for a human rights–based approach to development planning and programming. I quote them in full, modestly amended to demonstrate their especial relevance to the struggle against child labor:

1. People *[including all working children]* are recognized as key actors in their own development, rather than passive recipients of commodities and services.

2. Participation is both a means and a goal.

3. Strategies are empowering.

4. Both outcomes and processes are monitored and evaluated.

5. Analysis includes all stakeholders.

6. Programmes focus on marginalized, disadvantaged, and excluded groups *[including among working children]*.

7. The development process *[relative to working children]* is locally owned.

8. Programmes aim to reduce disparity *[between working and non-working children and others]*.

9. Both top-down and bottom-up approaches are used in synergy.

10. Situation analysis is used to identity immediate, underlying, and basic causes of development problems [*including the causes of child labor*].

11. Measurable goals and targets are important in programming.

12. Strategic partnerships are developed and sustained.

13. Programmes support accountability to all stakeholders.

All of the foregoing "required" and "essential" elements of the May 2003 SCU can and should be understood to be part of the human rights discourse and strategy that can and should be directed against child labor. At a minimum, a human rights approach to the abolition of child labor requires:

1. Reliance upon human rights criteria and norms when selecting and establishing anti–child labor program priorities, standards, tactics, and strategies

2. The identification of child labor claims-holders and whether they have the capacity to articulate and advocate for their rights and participate in the process

3. The identification of duty-bearers and their capacity to meet their anti–child labor obligations as well as constraints on their ability to perform

4. The establishment of mechanisms for monitoring, assessing, and redressing child labor situations with human rights norms all the while in mind, shaping one's outlook and purpose.

Proceeding according to this or like-minded designs, anti–child labor programs and projects, even if not conceived initially in human rights terms, become, ipso facto, human rights programs and projects by virtue of their deliberate conceptual reorientation. To the extent that the strategic design is adhered to, and regardless of the substantive measures implemented, it works naturally to protect, promote, and fulfill children's human rights, including those of working children.

In sum, an ethos of species identity that takes working children's suffering seriously, unaffected by considerations irrelevant of merit, is what is needed if the abolition of child labor is to succeed—a primary even if evolutionary first step in any human rights strategy worthy of child labor's abolition and of the social transformations that are required to make that happen. It is children's human *rights* we are defending, not just their human *needs*. And we must do so not only in matters of substance but, as well, in matters of procedure—in the invention, design, implementation, monitoring, and evaluation of policies and programs directed against child labor, giving particular consideration to such core human rights values as transparency, accountability, participation, and nondiscrimination.[42] If the abolition of child labor is truly the goal, nothing less will do. Even incremental measures, if they are to succeed enduringly, benefit from such human rights outlook and strategy.

Invoking and Inventing Legal and "Extra-Legal" Means to Promote and Protect Working Children's Rights

Due to the global nature of the child labor problem, much of what follows focuses on the promotion and protection of the rights of working children largely on the international plane. It is essential to appreciate, however, that all that has been said up to now and much of what has yet to be said applies as well to national policy making and decision making. Indeed, the implementation of human rights doctrines, principles, and rules on behalf of working children is, generally speaking, probably most efficiently and effectively achieved at the national or even subnational level through the institutions and procedures of each country's own legal-political order—broadly defined to include both the formal and informal mechanisms that avail human rights in this setting. Where there is effective will, a domestic legal–political order that provides formal and informal "remedies" for violations of human rights—internationally as well as nationally prescribed—can serve richly the promotion and protection of human rights worldwide. This is as true for working (and nonworking) children's human rights as it is for any other category of human rights. And the examples abound: in the formulation and execution of national strategies and agendas for the implementation in the 1989 CRC and 1999 ILO Convention No. 182; in efforts at national and subnational policy and law reform based on these same and cognate human rights instruments; in the development of independent governmental institutions at the national level for promoting and protecting the rights of working (and nonworking) children[43]; and so forth. It bears emphasis, however, that the majority and probably most effective enforcement strategies are "extra-legal" (quasi-legal and nonlegal) in kind.

The same is true on the international plane, and much of it at the hands of nongovernmental organizations (NGOs) and other civil society associations rather than states. Nevertheless, to facilitate necessary perspective, it is beneficial to account first, if only briefly, for the formal international legal mechanisms that in recent decades have been established to promote and protect human rights globally and regionally. Regrettably, space limitations prohibit extended discussion here. Readers interested in the details are invited to consult my earlier works from which this essay is drawn—and, of course, noteworthy studies published before and since (Cullen 2007; Weston 2005a).

Implementing children's human rights via formal international legal processes. Few of the formal international legal mechanisms and procedures established to promote and protect human rights have been pressed into serious anti–child labor service. Certainly this is due in major part to the vast number of human rights violations that, worldwide, compete for the attention of already overburdened officials. Possibly fear of duplication among them and even insufficient knowledge about them play a role as well. Whatever the explanation, however, there appears to be no good reason why in theory more of these mechanisms and procedures cannot or should not be enlisted or improved to assist in child labor's abolition in fact—and potentially to genuine profit. While resorting to formal legal processes may seem inconsistent with goals of social transformation because they represent established officialdom, they should not therefore be dismissed. If used wisely and with tolerance for quasi-legal and nonlegal mechanisms and procedures, they can assist the anti–child labor struggle nobly, both as change agents in their own right and as catalysts for change. Indeed, resorting to them even only occasionally among the many elements that comprise a human rights approach to child labor's abolition can send a much needed signal that the anti–child labor movement means to be taken seriously, sending ripples of persuasion that cut across all forms of resistance in the world system, from the most global to the most local.

Within the United Nations system, UNICEF is the chief systemwide advocate of children's rights and well-being. It has played an important role in *promoting* the abolition and reduction of child labor, including, as previously noted, from a human rights perspective.

Only two UN institutions established specifically to *enforce* human rights, however, have played a significant direct role in this regard: the Committee on the Rights of the Child, a creature of the 1989 CRC charged to monitor its implementation, and the ILO relative to the implementation of 1973 ILO Convention No. 138 and 1999 ILO Convention No. 182 (as well as other ILO conventions), though largely without resort to the language of rights. And while not without difficulty and legitimate criticism, they have done so, it must be acknowledged, with notable success, primarily though not exclusively via periodic reports from states communicating their progress in fulfilling their CRC or ILO treaty obligations, followed by review and, if need be, investigation and recommendation (by the CRC Committee and a Committee of Experts in the case of the ILO).[44] With modest exception vis-à-vis the ILO, neither has a mandate to receive and consider in quasi-judicial manner "communications" (i.e., complaints, applications, or cases) from individuals or groups who claim to be victims of violations of the human rights norms they are charged to promote and uphold.[45]

At the same time, however, the CRC Committee may refer such claims, where substantive jurisdiction permits, to UN "treaty bodies" having such competence—the Committee on the Elimination of All Forms of Racial Discrimination; the Human Rights Committee; the Committee against Torture and Other Cruel, Inhuman or Degrading Treatment or Punishment; or the Committee on the Elimination of Discrimination against Women.[46] It also may invite "competent bodies" to provide expert advice or recommend that the General Assembly request the Secretary-General to study "specific issues relating to the rights of the child" and "make suggestions and general recommendations based on the information received."[47]

For its part, the ILO can also boast its complementary International Programme on the Elimination of Child Labour (IPEC), an innovative technical assistance initiative established in 1992 and active in 88 countries worldwide as of this writing. Working to eliminate child labor through a phased, multisectoral strategy of technical cooperation that includes a legal unit for monitoring and evaluating ILO conventions, IPEC reinforces the ILO's essentially supervisory system (International Labour Organization 2008). When it comes to the enforcement of ILO Conventions No. 138 and 182, indeed, IPEC must be given the lion's share of credit. Also pertinent, however, are three essentially adjudicative processes of enforcement involving the ILO's governing body.[48] Though seldom used generally and seemingly never in respect of child labor (including an opportunity to appeal to the International Court of Justice), they do afford further means for direct enforcement of child labor rights and standards.

Finally, it bears emphasis that, for all the good that the CRC Committee and the ILO have done and of which they are capable in respect of child labor, there is no apparent reason why responsibility for this critical issue should not extend to other UN human rights enforcement mechanisms and procedures where appropriate, including ones yet to be invented. The following among many possible examples come immediately to mind:

- The preparation and issuance by the Committee on Economic, Social and Cultural Rights (established by the Economic and Social Council [ECOSOC] in 1987 to interpret the 1966 International Covenant on Economic, Social and Cultural Rights [ICESCR] and monitor its implementation) of a "general comment" on ICESCR

Article 10, arguably the most important ICESCR provision pertinent to child labor but an initiative the committee has yet to take,
though authorized to do so since 1988

- The invocation and application by the UN Human Rights Council
  and its Sub-Commission on the Promotion and Protection of
  Human Rights of their special "country situations" and "thematic
  issues" procedures (or "mandates") relative to specific violations
  (actual and threatened) of the rights of working children (Rodley
  and Weissbrodt 2004)—possibly as well the so-called "1503 procedure" (after 1970 ECOSOC Resolution 1503)[49] relative to such
  "worst forms" of child labor as reflect "consistent patterns of gross
  violations of human rights" (the substantive jurisdiction of the
  Council and Sub-Commission per Resolution 1503)[50]

- The creation of a working children's ombudsperson in the form of,
  say, a new UN High Commissioner for Children (analogous to Norway's Cabinet-appointed Ombudsman for Children).[51]

Indeed, given the multidimensionality, interrelatedness, and interdependencies of the worldwide child labor problem, the entire UN human
rights system, especially at the treaty-body level, should be brought to
bear upon it, and in a comprehensive and coordinated way that invites
the active participation of interested governments and civil society as
well. It is this kind and degree of reordering and mobilization that is
needed to ensure child labor's abolition. UNICEF, the Committee on
the Rights of the Child, and the ILO are indispensable, of course. But
they alone cannot win the day. Needed is a kind and degree of reordering and mobilization within the UN system that can raise the stakes dramatically higher on the scales of moral and legal aspiration and
endeavor.

In addition to the United Nations on the intergovernmental plane,
there exist today three regional human rights systems: *in Europe,* pur-
suant to the 1950 European Convention for the Protection of Human
Rights and Fundamental Freedom and its protocols, the 1961 European
Social Charter, and the 1996 European Social Charter (Revised); *in the
Americas,* pursuant to the 1948 Charter of the Organization of American
States (OAS), complemented by the 1948 American Declaration on the
Rights and Duties of Man and the 1969 American Convention on
Human Rights and its additional protocols; and *in Africa,* pursuant to
the 1981 African Charter on Human and Peoples Rights (or "Banjul
Charter") and the 1990 Charter on the Rights and Welfare of the Child.
Each of these regional systems possesses state-to-state and individual
complaints procedures for judicial or quasi-judicial redress of violations

of their founding human rights treaties and amending instruments (Shelton 1999).

Only the European system, under the aegis of the Council of Europe, however, has addressed the issue of child labor to any significant degree, generally successfully. A full-time European Court of Human Rights (ECHR) interprets and enforces the 1950 European Convention and its many protocols, with procedural jurisdiction extending to both interstate and private petitions alleging convention violations. A European Committee on Social Rights (ECSR), echoing somewhat the ILO, oversees a report–review–investigation–recommendation process relative to the two European social charters and a complementary process of collective complaints that is available to national trade union federations and employer organizations[52] (potentially also to NGOs with Council of Europe consultative status once an amending protocol enters into force).[53]

While the ECHR's substantive jurisdiction is defined by the European Convention's primary emphasis on "first generation" civil and political rights, convention provisions pertinent to child labor afford the court opportunity to influence European law in this regard—for example, "right to life" (article 2), "prohibition of slavery and forced labor" (article 4), and "freedom of assembly and association" (article 11). It is, however, the ECSR with its substantive ("second generation") jurisdiction defined by the 1961 and 1996 European social charters that is the most involved with working children and their many issues (Cullen 2007). While neither charter has been ratified by all 47 member states of the Council of Europe as yet, the trend favors the 1996 charter, which provides for comprehensive recognition of economic and social rights, with an emphasis on employment-related rights and, like 1999 ILO Convention No. 182, a concern for the protection of children from severe physical and moral hazards.[54]

As for the inter-American and African human rights systems, excepting a few studies by appointed special rapporteurs, little or no effort appears to have been made to focus on child labor in an explicit, sustained way. This need not be the case, however. Both systems are substantively and procedurally competent to address the issue, each partly by adjudicative processes comparable to the ECHR in the European system and partly by report–review–investigate–recommend procedures reminiscent of the European system's ECSR. It is not unreasonable to expect that the inter-American system, arising out of a more economically advanced and politically stable environment than the African system, should be able to take on the child labor problem more aggressively. Given the genocidal conflicts, political corruption, poverty, pandemic disease, climate change harms, and other rank indignities that Africa has had to endure (some of them legacies of a not-too-distant colonial past), it is not unreasonable to expect that the African system will take longer.

It must be emphasized, however, that all three systems have at one time or another been criticized, and correctly so, for failing to protect human rights effectively or efficiently. In the case of the European system, for instance, huge backlogs and insufficient resources caused cases to drag out over years—providing impetus for reforming the system with a single, full-time human rights court. Similar criticism, coupled with charges of ineffectiveness, propelled the Organization of African Unity (now the African Union) to establish the African Court of Human and Peoples' Rights. Despite the well-founded criticisms, however, and despite also the present absence of vigorous and sustained action against child labor in the Inter-American and African human rights systems, it is clear that, for reasons of cultural and geographic propinquity, regional systems have a positive effect on human rights promotion and protection in their respective regions. Indeed, it is fair to say that the enforcement of human rights has proven generally more effective at the regional level than the global level. On the whole, states have responded cooperatively to the judgments of the regional tribunals, complying with their orders and changing their laws and practices as a result. Moreover, the regional systems collectively encourage further development and improvement of the global human rights system via interaction and collaboration. The regional human rights systems are thus another potentially useful tool for addressing abusive, exploitative, or hazardous labor practices affecting children. Their enforcement or implementing potential in the anti–child labor struggle must be actively supported, both for their direct impact and their catalytic ripple or demonstration effect.

Implementing human rights via "extra-legal" means. Though formal legal institutions and procedures created specifically to promote and protect human rights are indispensable components of a comprehensive strategy for the abolition of child labor, they are by no means the only components—indeed, not even the most effective or important in many instances. As previously stated, the abolition of child labor requires broad and deep social change, and for this is needed far more than the formal legal establishment, even when dedicated specifically to the promotion and protection of human rights. Legal solutions tend frequently to be "top-down" or "elitist," often suspect because they are inclined to overlook disparities in power—especially at points of conflict—between those who prescribe solutions and those who, typically less powerful, are on the receiving end of them. Though indispensable, they are not likely to make much headway against abusive and exploitative child work without calling into collaborative service a host of more or less informal approaches to the problem. Many of these are "bottom-up" or "grass roots" approaches. Generally they are of an "extra-legal" (quasi- and nonlegal) sort that interface closely with education, international trade, and other such societal infrastructures—and commonly, too, with those who daily fight in the trenches on behalf of working and nonworking children: intergovernmental organizations such as the ILO and UNICEF; NGOs such as Anti-Slavery International, Save the Children, and Global March; and a host of others from civil society—trade unions, business enterprises, consumer groups, children's service providers, working children's groups/organizations, faith-based groups, women's organizations, academic institutions, and so forth.

Increasingly, scholars and activists expert in these "extra-legal" realms are bringing their expertise publicly to bear on the problem of child labor (Bachman 2005; Cullen 2007; Garcia and Jun 2005; Wiseberg 2005). For this reason (in addition to space limitations), I limit myself here to outlining a *multifaceted problem-solving/policy-implementing typology* whose individual elements hold out, I believe, the potential for child labor's true abolition, especially when they are (a) conceived in human rights terms and (b) acted upon as fully and with as much coherence and coordination as possible, likewise in human rights terms. And this is so even if these elements are not perceived by their owners as components of a comprehensive human rights strategy against child labor. If this be the case, it is simply that their owners have not yet fully understood or internalized the power of a human rights outlook on child labor, in which event human rights education becomes the first imperative. Indeed, given the necessity of social transformation in the child labor context, human rights education—particularly that kind of human rights education that, from the nuclear family to the cosmopolitan state, impels all levels of social organization and action to view human rights as *a way of* life[55]—may be the single most important thing that anyone can do at this time. To each facet of each function recorded or capable of being recorded in our problem-solving/policy-implementing typology must be brought all of the conceptual and tactical elements I noted earlier that define what I mean by a human rights approach to the abolition and reduction of child labor.

It is, at any rate, from this perspective that I here identify in summary fashion the problem-solving/policy-implementing functions and their principal components that must be pursued if child labor is ever to be abolished or significantly reduced. The child labor problem being a polychromatic problem that insists upon polychromatic solutions, they include both formal institutions and procedures and quasi-legal approaches. In no way, however, do I presume to have exhausted the options. Nor do I presume that my cataloguing of them reflects an always precise, exclusive fit. What follows is meant to be heuristic, suggestive, *not* definitive—and to provoke discussion.

1. *Information-retrieval and dissemination* on behalf of working children's rights:
   - Improved methodologies (case studies, correlation studies, experimental studies, prototypes, etc.) for the systematic gathering, analyzing, and processing of data about child labor and its impact on the child laborers, their families, and their communities, including increased reliance for such data upon working children themselves
   - Expanded/strengthened NGO "watchdog" monitoring and trade union surveillance initiatives competent to retrieve, process, and disseminate accurate child labor data
   - Enhanced methods of social accounting/auditing
   - Improved/broadened curricular initiatives for K–12 and college level courses
   - Improved/broadened adult education programs, particularly for trade unions and business enterprises
   - Improved/broadened mass media programming (including, for example, documentary films)
   - Improved/broadened artistic and other intuitive programming (such as "art" films, popular theater, photographic exhibits, etc.)

2. *Promotion/advocacy* on behalf of working children's rights:
   - Improved coordination of anti–child labor agendas, definitions, and procedures, *among other things,* the UN, the ILO, UNICEF, the International Monetary Fund (IMF), the World Bank, free trade agreements (FTAs), and regional human rights systems
   - Enhanced coordination/competition among long-standing and emerging NGO lobbies working to eradicate child labor
   - Expanded/strengthened private sector lobbies specialized to particular child labor practices
   - Expanded/strengthened trade union capacity to campaign against child labor
   - Enhanced mechanisms and opportunities for working children to speak and act in their own defense (including trade union organizing)

3. *Prescription* on behalf of working children's rights:
   - Broadened/strengthened domestic (national and local) plans and legislation prohibiting child labor and related abusive practices, coupled with the creation of permanent governmental institutions

competent to ensure the effective implementation of human rights norms applicable to working children

- Expanded insinuation of "core labor standards" social clauses (prohibiting abusive/exploitative/hazardous children's work) in IMF/World Bank/World Trade Organization/FTA rules and regulations
- Broadened/strengthened corporate codes of conduct prohibiting abusive/exploitative child labor
- Broadened/strengthened industry codes of conduct prohibiting abusive/exploitative child labor

4. *Invocation* on behalf of working children's rights:
   - Strengthened national and international (global and regional) complaint procedures (including shareholder and tort actions)
   - Expanded NGO "watchdog" monitoring groups, such as the U.S.-based Fair Labor Association (FLA) and Worker Rights Consortium (WRC), competent to challenge violations of the rights of working children
   - Enhanced mechanisms and opportunities for working children and others to protest when norms for their protection are violated

5. *Application/enforcement* on behalf of working children's rights:
   - Expanded ratification and enforcement by states of international law-making instruments directed at the elimination of child labor
   - Strengthened enforcement mechanisms and procedures among the UN, the ILO, UNICEF, the IMF, the World Bank, FTAs, regional human rights systems, and other relevant IGOs
   - Strengthened domestic law enforcement mechanisms and procedures, including the effective coordination of governmental institutions charged with implementing human rights norms applicable to working children
   - Enhanced economic strategies such as consumer boycotts, economic embargoes, and trade sanctions
   - Improved/expanded product/social labeling or certification schemes

6. *Termination* on behalf of working children's rights:
   - Broadened/strengthened national and international initiatives directed at the repeal of public laws and policies that encourage, support, or otherwise tolerate child labor
   - Enhanced interception and cancellation of private contractual and other social arrangements that encourage, support, or otherwise tolerate child labor

7. *Appraisal/recommendation* on behalf of working children's rights: Strengthened evaluation of the short- and long-term effectiveness of anti–child labor norms, institutions, and procedures (local, national, and international) and revision or repeal of those proven misguided or unsuccessful, accompanied by concrete recommendations, both reformist and transformist in character, for enhanced performance in this regard and including the two sets of recommendations that follow:

a. *Reformist recommendations* on behalf of working children's rights:
   - Strengthened developmental strategies (including debt relief and foreign assistance) that facilitate the rehabilitation and social integration (including education) of working children and their families
   - Expanded/enhanced training of parents, teachers, social workers, medical authorities, police officials, and others responsible for protecting working children's best interests
   - Income substitution via public subsidies targeted for families of working children
   - Improved educational cost/opportunity/quality for children and enhanced support of them through education of families, employers, and communities
   - Provision of real economic and social advancement opportunities for children and their families
   - Broadened beneficial/nonexploitative work alternatives for children in need of income
   - Expanded/enhanced training of abused/exploited children to facilitate their social reintegration consistent with their individual dignity and potential

b. *Transformist recommendations* on behalf of working children's rights:
   - Expanded strategies of humane governance that seek persuasively, both within and outside households, to change the myths and values that affect the way people think and act relative to abusive/exploitative/hazardous children's work and that therefore commonly extend beyond the capacity of traditional enforcement means and mechanisms (e.g., innovative educational and work strategies that help children in their own efforts to change their life conditions, that help whole communities comprehend child labor in holistic public health terms, etc.)

- Broad and deep human rights education—both "top-down" and "bottom-up"—to encourage human rights as a way of life and thereby nurture a culture of respect for children's rights

I repeat: a strategy worthy of child labor's abolition requires a multitude of mechanisms and techniques—from systematic research and documentation to education and schooling to domestic legislative programs to national and international enforcement measures to long-term initiatives of social transformation—at all levels, from the most local to the most global, and on all fronts. It also must engage all elements of society (individuals, families, communities, academic institutions, trade unions, business enterprises, faith-based groups, NGOs and associations, government agencies, intergovernmental organizations). Perhaps most importantly, it must proceed always self-consciously and proactively in the knowledge and determination that all the imagination and energy required to succeed must be applied in service to children's human rights as well as their human needs.

Conclusion

On final analysis, the abolition of child labor requires broad and deep initiatives at social transformation. A human rights understanding and approach to the problem of child labor, presupposing a holistic and multifaceted orientation to the individual child and society, is therefore indispensable. Conceptualizing child labor as a human rights issue alone "raises the stakes"; it changes the dynamic in positive ways and gives claims of abuse and exploitation greater legal and moral force.

However, reorienting one's worldview, while essential, is not sufficient to bring about the broad-based change I believe is required to eradicate the workplace abuse and exploitation of children. Thus, I have sought to identify a wide range of practical mechanisms and measures, both legal and "extra-legal," that may be adopted or adapted in the planning, creation, implementation, assessment, and improvement of anti–child labor initiatives. Some of these mechanisms and measures draw on the human rights vocabulary and vocation; others do not, though with appropriate imagination and will they can be made to do so by reconceptualization of the task at hand and its solutions. Diverse mechanisms and measures drawn from multiple disciplines, founded on core human rights principles, maximally fine-tuned and coordinated, and guided by the values of transparency, accountability, participation, and nondiscrimination offer humankind's best hope, I believe, for righting the wrong of child labor. And when

one contemplates the brute statistics, and especially when one puts a
child's face on them—imagine, for example, a little Cambodian boy or
girl scavenging barefoot atop the huge Stung Meanchey garbage
dump on the outskirts of Phnom Penh—it becomes eminently clear
that the time is long past due to take children's human rights seriously
and abolish child labor without further delay. Nobel laureate Seamus
Heaney says it just right:

> Two sides to every question, yes, yes, yes . . .
> But every now and then, just weighing in
> Is what it must come down to . . .[56]

Acknowledgments

Copyright © 2009 by Burns H. Weston. This chapter is revised from
Burns H. Weston and Mark B. Teerink, 2006, *Child Labor through a
Human Rights Glass Brightly* (Human Rights and Human Welfare; Work-
ing Paper No. 35, October 2006; available at http://www.du.edu/
gsis/hrhw/working/2006/35-weston_teerink-2006.pdf), in turn consolidated
and revised from chapters 1 and 10 in *Child Labor and Human Rights:
Making Children Matter,* edited by Burns H. Weston. Copyright © 2005 by
Burns H. Weston. Reprinted with permission of Lynne Rienner Publishers,
Inc. I acknowledge with gratitude the contributions of my former student
and collaborator, Mark B. Teerink, to those works.

Endnotes

[1] I define "child labor" here as I did in *Child Labor and Human Rights: Making
Children Matter* (Weston 2005a), to wit, as work done by children that is harmful to
them because it is abusive, exploitative, hazardous, or otherwise contrary to their best
interests—a subset of a larger class of children's work, some of which may be compat-
ible with children's best interests (variously expressed as "beneficial," "benign," or
"harmless" children's work). This definition is derived in major part from Judith
Ennew, William E. Myers, and Dominique Pierre Plateau, "Defining Child Labor As
If Human Rights Really Matter," chapter 2 in Weston 2005a.

[2] U.N. Convention on the Rights of the Child (hereinafter "1989 CRC" or
"CRC"), November 20, 1989, 1577 *United Nations Treaty Series* 3, reprinted in 3
International Law and World Order: Basic Documents III.D.3 (Burns H. Weston
and Jonathan C. Carlson, eds., 5 vols., 1994–; hereinafter "Weston and Carlson").
See also Optional Protocol to the Convention on the Rights of the Child on the
Involvement of Children in Armed Conflict, May 25, 2000, General Assembly Reso-
lutions 54/263 (Annex I), *U.N. General Assembly Official Records,* 54th Session,
Supplement No. 49, p. 7, U.N. Doc. A/RES/54/263 (2000), reprinted in 3 Weston
and Carlson III.D.5; *Optional Protocol to the Convention on the Rights of the Child
on the Sale of Children, Child Prostitution and Child Pornography,* May 25, 2000,
General Assembly Resolutions 54/263 (Annex II), *U.N. General Assembly Official*

Records, 54th Session, Supplement No 49, p. 6, U.N. Doc. A/RES/54/263 (2000), reprinted in 3 Weston and Carlson III.D.6.

[3] An early exception is the 1924 Declaration of Geneva on the Rights of the Child, adopted by the Council of the League of Nations Assembly, Fifth Assembly, September 26, 1924, Official Journal–5, League of Nations O.J. Spec. Supplement 23, p. 177 (1924), reprinted in 3 Weston and Carlson III.D.1. Paragraph IV of the declaration, reflecting a former concerned era, provides "[t]he child must be put in a position to earn a livelihood and must be protected against every form of exploitation."

[4] Charter of the United Nations, 1976 *Yearbook of the United Nations* 1043 (1945), reprinted in 1 Weston and Carlson I.A.1.

[5] Universal Declaration of Human Rights, June 10, 1948, General Assembly Resolutions 217A, *U.N. General Assembly Official Records,* 3d Session, Pt. I, Resolutions, p. 71, U.N. Doc. A/810 (1948), reprinted in 3 Weston and Carlson III.A.1 (hereinafter "1948 UDHR" or "UDHR").

[6] On the history as well as the meaning and scope of human rights, see Burns H. Weston, *Human Rights,* in 20 *Encyclopædia Britannica* 656 (15th ed., 2005), available online at *Encyclopædia Britannica Online* (http://www.britannica.com/eb/article?tocId= 219350); also on the website of The University of Iowa Center for Human Rights (http://www.uichr.org).

[7] Convention (No. 182) Concerning the Prohibition and Immediate Elimination of the Worst Forms of Child Labour, June 17, 1999, reprinted in 38 *International Legal Materials* 1207 (1999) and 3 Weston and Carlson III.D.4 (hereinafter "1999 ILO C182" or "ILO C182"). The expression "the worst forms of child labour" is defined by ILO C182 in Article 3.

[8] UNICEF has worked closely with the ILO in this realm and is now known for putting rights at the center of its child labor advocacy and fieldwork. See, for example, UNICEF 2001 (http://www.unicef.org/publications/index_4302.html) and UNICEF 1999b (http://www.unicef.org/publications/index_5587.html). See also Beigbeder 2001.

[9] See the Child Workers in Asia website (http://www.cwa.tnet.co.hth/whatiscwa/whatiscwa.htm).

[10] See, for example, the country studies by Donald Mmari (Tanzania), Victoria Rialp (Philippines), and Benedito Rodrigues dos Santos (Brazil) in Weston 2005a, 169–231.

[11] International Covenant on Economic, Social and Cultural Rights (hereinafter "1966 ICESCR" or "ICESCR"), December 16, 1966, 993 *United Nations Treaty Series* 3, reprinted in 3 Weston and Carlson III.A.2.

[12] The notion of three "generations" of human rights is the brainchild of French jurist and former UNESCO legal advisor Karel Vasak, inspired by the three themes of the French Revolution: *liberté* (civil and political rights), *égalité* (economic, social, and cultural rights), and *fraternité* (community, group, or "solidarity" rights). See *"Pour une troisième génération des droits de l'homme,"* in *Studies and Essays on International Humanitarian Law and Red Cross Principles* (C. Swinarski, ed., 1984). For extensive explication, see Stephen P. Marks, "Emerging Human Rights: A New Generation for the 1980s?" 33 *Rutgers Law Review* 435 (1981). See also Burns

H. Weston, *Human Rights* (2005), *supra* note 6: "Vasak's model is, of course, a simpli-
fied expression of an extremely complex historical record, and is not intended to suggest a linear process in which each generation gives birth to the next and then dies
away. Nor is it to imply that one generation is more important than another. The
three generations are understood as cumulative, overlapping, and, it is important to
note, interdependent and interpenetrating."

[13] On the right to peace, see, for example, Philip Alston, *Peace as a Human Right,*
11 *Bulletin of Peace Proposals No. 4* 319 (1980). See also *U.N. General Assembly
Declaration on the Preparation of Societies for Life in Peace,* December 15, 1978,
General Assembly Resolutions 33/73, *U.N. General Assembly Official Records,* 33rd
Session, Supplement No. 45, p. 55, U.N. Doc. A/33/45 (1979), reprinted in 3 Weston
and Carlson III.S.1; *U.N. General Assembly Declaration on the Right of Peoples to
Peace,* November 12, 1984, General Assembly Resolutions 39/11 (Annex), *U.N.
General Assembly Official Records,* 39th Session, Supplement No. 51, 1t 22, U.N.
Doc. A/39/51 (1985), reprinted in 3 Weston and Carlson III.S.2.

[14] On the right to development, see, for example, Philip Alston, "The Right to
Development and the Need for an Integrated Human Rights Approach to Develop-
ment," in *Experts Discuss Some Critical Social Development Issues* (U.N. Division for
Social Policy and Development. U.N. Doc ESA/DSPD/BP.2, May 1999), pp. 71–88;
Stephen P. Marks, "The Human Right to Development: Between Rhetoric and
Reality," 17 *Harvard Human Rights Journal* 137 (2004); Arjun Sengupta, "On the
Theory and Practice of the Right to Development," 24 *Human Rights Quarterly* 837
(2002); N.J. Udombana, "The Third World and the Right to Development: Agenda
for the New Millennium," 22 *Human Rights Quarterly* 753 (2000). See also *U.N.
General Assembly Declaration on the Right to Development,* December 4, 1986,
General Assembly Resolutions 41/128 (Annex), *U.N. General Assembly Official
Records,* 41st Session, Supplement No. 53, p. 186, U.N. Doc. A/41/53 (1987),
reprinted in 3 Weston and Carlson III.R.2.

[15] On the right to a clean and healthy environment, see, for example, *Human
Rights Approaches to Environmental Protection* (A. Boyle and M. Anderson, eds.,
1998); Edith Brown Weiss, *In Fairness to Future Generations: International Law,
Common Patrimony, and Intergenerational Equity* (1989). See also Burns H. Weston,
"Climate Change and Intergenerational Justice: Foundational Reflections," 9 *Vermont
Journal of Environmental Law* 375 (2008).

[16] Thus: *life* (UDHR article 3 on the right to life, liberty, and security of the person); *bodily health* (UDHR articles 12 and 25 on the right to privacy, family, and
home and on the right to the highest attainable physical and mental health); *bodily
integrity* (UDHR articles 3–5 and 13 on the right to security of the person, to freedom from slavery or servitude, to freedom from cruel, inhuman, or degrading treatment, and to freedom of movement and residence); *senses, imagination, and thought*
(UDHR article 26 on the right to education and associated articles 18, 19, and 27 on
the right to thought, conscience, religion, opinion, and expression and to participate,
enjoy, and share in cultural life); *emotions* (UDHR article 12 on the right to privacy);
conscience (UDHR articles 18 and 19 on the right to thought, conscience, religion,
opinion, and expression); *affiliation qua friendship and respect* (UDHR articles 1, 20,
and 29 on the right to peaceful assembly and association and to community duties for
the free and full development of personality, all in a "spirit of brotherhood" *[sic]*);
play (UDHR article 24 on the right to rest and leisure); and *political and material*

control over one's environment (UDHR articles 12, 17, 19–21, and 23 on the right to privacy, property, speech, association, political participation, and to work and free choice of employment).

[17] See, for example, the country studies by Donald Mmari (Tanzania), Victoria Rialp (Philippines), and Benedito Rodrigues dos Santos (Brazil), in Weston 2005a, pp. 169–231.

[18] "[I]f a right is determined to be a human right, it is understood to be quintessentially general or universal in character, in some sense equally possessed by all human beings everywhere" (Weston, *Human Rights* [2005], *supra* note 6, p. 5). The universality of human rights has been much debated in recent years. For pertinent discussion, see Burns H. Weston, "The Universality of Human Rights in a Multicultured World: Toward Respectful Decision-Making," in Weston and Marks 1999, *supra* note 39, p. 65.

[19] Final Act of the Conference on Security and Co-operation in Europe: Declaration on Principles Guiding Relations between Participating States, Respect for Human Rights and Fundamental Freedoms, Including the Freedom of Thought, Conscience, Religion or Belief, ¶ 7 (August 1, 1975), reprinted in 14 *International Legal Materials* 1292 (1975) and 1 Weston and Carlson I.D.9.

[20] For much of what follows here, I am indebted to Slye 2001.

[21] See, for example, the website of the United States Institute of Peace (http://www.usip.org/library/truth.html).

[22] Replaced by the U.N. Human Rights Council on June 16, 2006. See General Assembly Resolutions 60/251, *U.N. General Assembly Official Records,* 16th Session, U.N. Doc. A/RES/60/251 (2006).

[23] See O'Neill 1992, p. 42. O'Neill asserts skepticism also because, she writes, "the ranks of childhood are continuously depleted by entry into adult life" (p. 39). Surely, however, this second argument is neutralized by the truism, curiously disregarded by O'Neill, that children, absent catastrophes such as AIDS and genocidal conflicts, continuously maintain the ranks of childhood by entering into life itself, replacing their seniors who mature into adulthood.

[24] See Final Declaration of the 2nd Meeting of the World Movement of Working Children and Adolescents, Berlin, Germany, April 19–May 2, 2004 (http://www.italianats.org/index.php?option=com_content&view=article&id=48:berlino&catid=40:dichiarazioniufficiali&Itemid=62&lang=en).

[25] At the Children's World Congress on Child Labor organized by Global March in Florence in mid-May 2004, for example, some 200 young persons from ages 10 to 17 shared their views and supported the creation of a "network for worldwide, youth-driven action to press international and national efforts towards integrating world resources and responses on poverty, child labour, and education, [including] the development of strategies to enhance national support for implementation of ILO conventions 138 and 182, as well as the 2015 commitment for education for all children" (quoted from the website of the Children's World Congress on Child Labour, http://www.globalmarch.org/events/worldcongress.php). A resulting Children's Declaration ("We Are the Present, Our Voice Is the Future") bears witness to these youth-defined intents. See http://www.globalmarch.org/events/dec.php.

[26] See, for example, Jennings and Entine 1998. For an exemplary illustration, see IKEA's website at http://www.ikea.com/ms/en_US/about_ ikea/social_environmental/ projects.html. On September 1, 2005, the IKEA Group, the Inter IKEA Group, and the IKANO Group together formed the "IKEA Social Initiative" to ensure a greater allocation of resources to global projects supporting children and their opportunities of learning and developing, including, for example, education, health issues, accessibility to clean water and solar energy.

[27] As Barnet and Müller pointed out in their germinal exposé of the power of multinational corporations three decades ago, "[a] global corporation is able to pay an annual retainer to a Wall Street law firm to represent its worldwide interests, which is perhaps five times the entire budget of the government agencies in poor countries that are supposed to regulate it" (Richard J. Barnet and Ronald E. Müller, 1974, *Global Reach: The Power of Multinational Corporations,* p. 138). See also Saman Zia-Zarifi, "Suing Multinational Corporations in the U.S. for Violating International Law," 4 *UCLA Journal of International Law and Foreign Affairs* 81 (1999) and documents cited therein, p. 84, note 6.

[28] According to this theory in its purest form, reflecting the dominance of the state as the primary organizational unit of human communities on the world stage since at least the Peace of Westphalia of 1648, states are the sole "subjects" of international law, the only actors with "standing" in the international legal order, the only beings competent to create and be bound by international legal obligations. See, for example, Malcolm N. Shaw, *International Law,* p. 126 (1997) and Mark W. Janis, *An Introduction to International Law,* p. 238 (4th ed., 2003).

[29] Regarding the global compact and its central purposes, see Global Compact, The Ten Principles, http://www.unglobalcompact.org/AboutTheGC/TheTen Principles/index.html. Regarding the former U.N. Commission on Human Rights, see U.N. Sub-Commission on Human Rights, Norms on the Responsibilities of Transnational Corporations and Other Business Enterprises with Regard to Human Rights, U.N. Doc. E/CN.4/Sub.2/2003/12/Rev.2 (2003), approved August 13, 2003, by Resolution 2003/16, U.N. Doc. E/CN.4/Sub.2/2003/L.11 p. 52 (2003), http://www.unhchr.ch/huridocda/huridoca.nsf/(Symbol)/E.CN.4.Sub.2.2003.12.Rev.2. En. And for scholarly commentary, see, for example, Monshipouri, Welch, and Kennedy 2003; Jordan J. Paust, "Human Rights Responsibilities of Private Corporations," 35 *Vanderbilt Journal of Transnational Law* 802 (2002); and Stephen R. Ratner, "Corporations and Human Rights: A Theory of Legal Responsibility," 111 *Yale Law Journal* 443 (2001).

[30] See also the following pertinent websites: Business for Social Responsibility (http://www.bsr.org), Business and Human Rights Resource Centre (http://www. business-humanrights.org), and Amnesty International (http://web.amnesty.org).

[31] See, for example, 1966 ICESCR, articles 7 (just and favorable conditions of work) and 8 (trade unions); American Convention on Human Rights, articles 6 (slavery and involuntary servitude) and 11 (privacy); and 1966 ICCPR, articles 8 (slavery, servitude, forced or compulsory labor) and 17 (privacy, family, home or correspondence).

[32] Examples include the U.S. Alien Tort Claims Act, 28 U.S.C. § 1350; also the German federal system's concept of *Völkerrechtfreundlichkeit,* or "friendliness" to human rights, whereby treaties are adopted by federal statute and treated as federal

law. See Stefan Oeter, "International Human Rights Law and National Sovereignty in Federal Systems: The German Experience," 47 *Wayne Law Review* 871 (2001).

[33] See, for example, Jennings and Entine 1998, pp. 10–16. See also David Gonzales, "Latin Sweatshops Pressed by U.S. Campus Power," *New York Times*, April 4, 2003, p. A3 (discussing the impact of American student actions on sweatshops); John Kelly, "For Some, an Uncomfortable Fit," *Washington Post*, May 14, 2002, p. C14 (discussing antisweatshop actions against various footwear companies); Jenne Mannion, "Lobby Groups Open Ethical Attacks," *Sunday Business*, December 9, 2001, p. 24 (discussing lobby groups' efforts to persuade pension funds to pull investments from companies accused of not being socially responsible).

[34] For a seemingly nihilistic critique and a convincing rebuttal to it, see Cassel 2001 and Slye 2001.

[35] Vienna Declaration and Programme of Action of the World Conference on Human Rights, U.N. Doc. A/Conf.157/24, pp. 20–46 (June 25, 1993; hereinafter "Vienna Declaration" or "1993 Vienna Declaration"), reprinted in 32 *International Legal Materials* 1661 (1993) and 3 Weston and Carlson III.U.2.

[36] Vienna Declaration, *supra* note 118, preamble ¶2. The declaration was adopted by acclamation by 171 states. "Because the [Declaration] was agreed to by virtually every nation on earth," opines Robert Drinan, "the document constitutes customary international law." See Drinan 2001.

[37] In her essay linking the capabilities approach with the UDHR, Nussbaum acknowledges that the language of rights retains an important place in public discourse, providing a normative basis for discussion, emphasizing the important and basic role of the entitlements in question and peoples' choice and autonomy, and establishing the parameters of basic agreement. See Nussbaum 1997.

[38] *Accord,* Freeman 2002, p. 67.

[39] In contrast to its almost complete lockout of even human rights talk in its prior leading reports on the subject in 2001 and 2002—see, for example, International Labour Organization 2001, *Every Child Counts: New Global Estimates of Child Labour;* and International Labour Organization 2002, *Report of the Director-General—A Future Without Child Labour: Global Report*—the ILO's apparent acceptance of child labor as a human rights problem in its *Global Report 2006* is noteworthy.

[40] Quoted from the Innocenti Research Centre website (http://www. unicef-icdc.org/aboutIRC). See also Santos Pais 1999.

[41] See UNICEF's edition of the Statement of Understanding in *The State of the World's Children 2004*, Annex B, pp. 91–3.

[42] Such is the approach of the United Nations Development Programme (UNDP) in the context of development and from which we draw inspiration. See *Integrating Human Rights with Sustainable Human Development: A UNDP Policy Document* (1998) and *Guidelines for Human Rights-Based Reviews of UNDP Programmes* (October 1, 2002). See also UNICEF, *Guidelines for Human Rights-based Programming Approach* (New York, F/EXD/1998–04, April 1998); Dorothy Rozga, *Applying a Human Rights Based Approach to Programming: Experiences of UNICEF* (UNICEF Presentation Paper prepared for the Workshop on Human Rights, Assets and Livelihood Security, and Sustainable Development, London, June 19–20, 2001;

http://www.crin.org/docs/resources/publications/hrbap/Applying_Human_Rights_App roach_to_Programming.pdf).

[43] In this connection, see the so-called "Paris Principles" relating to the status, competence, and responsibilities of national institutions for the promotion and protection of human rights, annexed to U.N. General Assembly Resolution 48/134 (on National Institutions for the Promotion and Protection of Human Rights), December 20, 1993, General Assembly Resolutions 49/134, *U.N. General Assembly Official Records*, 48th Session, Supplement No. 49, p. 9, U.N. Doc. A/RES/48/134 (1994).

[44] An independent entity appointed by the ILO governing body on the recommendation of the ILO director-general, the Committee of Experts is the ILO's primary body charged to interpret the ILO conventions.

[45] The Committee on the Rights of the Child is reported to be "keen to establish a permanent mechanism for interaction with state parties, in addition to the reporting system called for under the CRC" (*Report of the Expert Consultation on the Impact of the Implementation Process of the Convention on the Rights of the Child*, Florence: UNICEF Innocenti Research Centre, April 6–7, 2004).

[46] The Committee on the Elimination of Racial Discrimination was established under Article 8 of the International Convention on the Elimination of All Forms of Racial Discrimination, December 21, 1965, 660 *United Nations Treaty Series* 195, reprinted in 3 Weston and Carlson III.I.1. The Human Rights Committee was established under Article 28 of the 1966 ICCPR, *supra* note 37. The Committee against Torture was established under Article 17 of the Convention against Torture and Other Cruel, Inhuman or Degrading Treatment or Punishment, December 10, 1984, 1465 *United Nations Treaty Series* 85, reprinted in 3 Weston and Carlson III.K.2. The Committee on the Elimination of Discrimination against Women was established under Article 1 of the Optional Protocol to the Convention on the Elimination of All Forms of Discrimination against Women, October 15, 1999, General Assembly Resolutions 54/4 (Annex), *U.N. General Assembly Official Records*, 54th Session, Supplement No. 49, p. 4, U.N. Doc. A/54/4 (1999), reprinted in 39 *International Legal Materials* 281 (2000) and 3 Weston and Carlson III.C.16.

[47] 1989 CRC, article 45(b)–(c). A relatively recent example, highly pertinent to the issue of child labor, was the committee's request for an international study on the question of violence against children, honored in February 2003 by the U.N Secretary-General's appointment of an "independent expert" (Paulo Sergio Pinheiro) to lead a global study on the subject. For details, see the website of the Office of the U.N. High Commissioner for Human Rights, at http://www.unhchr.ch/html/menu2/6/crc/study.htm.

[48] "Representations" of treaty violations to the ILO's governing body by trade unions or employer organizations (not necessarily associated with the subject of the representation); "complaints" to the ILO governing body (and an assisting commission of inquiry) by governments, International Labor Conference delegates, or the governing body itself on its own motion; and "complaints" directly to the ILO governing body's Committee on Freedom of Association (CFA) and indirectly via the CFA to an assisting Fact-Finding and Conciliation Commission on Freedom of Association (FFCC) by governments or by employers' or workers' organizations alleging violations of the ILO's basic principles on freedom of association whether or not the state concerned is a party to any ILO convention on the subject. The first two mechanisms are prescribed by the ILO constitution. The FFCC may also examine complaints

referred to it by ECOSOC against states that are not members of the ILO. See Lee Swepston, "Human Rights Complaint Procedures of the International Labor Organization," in *Guide to International Human Rights Practice* 89, pp. 92–104 (Hurst Hannum ed., 4th ed., 2004).

[49] U.N. Economic and Social Council Resolution (No. 1503) Concerning Procedures for Dealing with Communications Relating to Violations of Human Rights and Fundamental Freedoms, 27 May 1970, E.S.C. Res. 1503, U.N. ESCOR, 48th Session, Supplement 1A, p. 8, U.N. Doc E/4832/Add.1 (1970), reprinted in 3 Weston and Carlson III.T.6 [hereinafter "ECOSOC Resolution 1503"].

[50] While its enabling resolution gave the quasi-judicial human rights complaint initiative for the first time to individuals and NGOs and initially in confidential format, and while it thus was seen by many around the time of its adoption as an important progressive step in human rights protection, the 1503 procedure was later widely criticized for being "painfully slow, complex, secret, and vulnerable to political influence at many junctures" (Frank C. Newman and David S. Weissbrodt, *International Human Rights: Law, Policy, and Process* 122 [1990]. See also Philip Alston, "The Commission on Human Rights," in *The United Nations and Human Rights: A Critical Appraisal* 151 [Philip Alston, ed., 1992]). Assuming radical reform, however, the procedure does hold out possibility. Unfortunately, procedural reforms adopted during the 56th session of the Commission on Human Rights in 2000 (see http://www.unhchr.ch/html/menu2/8/1503.htm) are not, in my judgment, sufficient.

[51] Norway established a commissioner, or ombudsman, with statutory rights to protect children and their rights in 1981 and was the first country in the world to do so. Since 1981, the Ombudsman for Children in Norway has worked continuously to improve national and international legislation affecting children's welfare. For details, see the Ombudsman for Children in Norway website at http://www.barneombudet.no/english.

[52] See Additional Protocol to the European Social Charter Providing for a System of Collective Complaints, November 9, 1995/July 1, 1998: ETS 158, reprinted in 34 *International Legal Materials* 1453 (1995) and 3 Weston and Carlson III.B.16c.

[53] See Protocol Amending the European Social Charter, October 21, 1991, *European Treaty Series* 142, reprinted in 31 *International Legal Materials* 155 (1992) and 3 Weston and Carlson III.B.15 (not in force pending acceptance by five states as of this writing—July 2008).

[54] See, for example, Pt. I (2)–(7), (17), (22), (24) and (26) of the 1996 European Social Charter (Revised), *supra* note 191, meant to safeguard rights to just conditions of work; safe and healthy working conditions; fair remuneration sufficient for a decent standard of living; freedom of association; collective bargaining; special protection for children against physical and moral hazards; appropriate social, legal, and economic protection for children; a role in determining and improving working conditions and environment; protection in cases of termination; and dignity at work.

[55] For eloquent expression and advocacy of this notion of human rights education, see the website of The People's Movement for Human Rights Education, formerly People's Decade for Human Rights Education (PDHRE) at http://www.pdhre.org/index.html. For scholarly treatment, see Richard Pierre Claude, "The Right to Education and Human Rights Education," *SUR: International Journal on Human Rights* No. 2 (2005), also http://www.surjournal.org/eng/?PHPSESSID=

59eb818edd9759689e0065a0c22d84b8, reprinted in abridged form in Claude and Weston 2006.

[56] From Seamus Heaney 1996, "Weighing In," in *The Spirit Level*, pp. 22–3.

References

Bachman, S.L. 2005. "Translating Standards into Practice: Confronting Transnational Barriers." In Burns H. Weston, ed., *Child Labor and Human Rights: Making Children Matter*. Boulder, CO: Lynne Rienner.

Beigbeder, Yves. 2001. *New Challenges for UNICEF: Children, Women and Human Rights*. New York: Palgrave Macmillan.

Black, Maggie. 2004. *Opening Minds, Opening Up Opportunities: Children's Participation in Action for Working Children*. London: Save the Children UK.

Cassel, Douglass. 2001. "International Human Rights in Practice: Does International Human Rights Law Make a Difference?" 2 *Chicago Journal of International Law* 121.

Charlesworth, Hilary, and Christine Chinkin. 2000. *The Boundaries of International Law: A Feminist Analysis*. Huntington, NY: Juris.

Claude, Richard Pierre, and Burns H. Weston, eds. 2006. *Human Rights in the World Community: Issues and Action* (3rd ed). Philadelphia: University of Pennsylvania Press.

Cullen, Holly. 2007. *The Role of International Law in the Elimination of Child Labor*. Leiden, The Netherlands: Martinus Nijhoff.

Cunningham, Hugh, and Shelton Stromquist. 2005. "Child Labor and the Rights of Children: Historical Patterns of Decline and Persistence." In Burns H. Weston, ed., *Child Labor and Human Rights: Making Children Matter*. Boulder, CO: Lynne Rienner, pp 55–83.

Donnelly, Jack. 1985. *The Concept of Human Rights*. Kent, UK : Croom Helm.

Donnelly, Jack. 1989. *Universal Human Rights in Theory and Practice*. Ithaca, NY: Cornell University Press.

Douzinas, Costas. 2000. *The End of Human Rights: Critical Legal Thought at the Turn of the Century*. Oxford: Hart.

Drinan, Robert F., S.J. 2001. *The Mobilization of Shame*. New Haven and London: Yale University Press.

Dugard, John. 1999. "Reconciliation and Justice: The South African Experience." In Burns H. Weston and Stephen P. Marks, eds., *The Future of International Human Rights*. Ardsley, NY: Transnational.

Dworkin, Ronald. 1977. *Taking Rights Seriously*. Cambridge, MA: Harvard University Press.

Freeman, Michael D.A. 2002. *Human Rights: An Interdisciplinary Approach*. Cambridge: Polity.

Garcia, Frank J., and Soohyun Jun. 2005. "Trade-Based Strategies for Combating Child Labor." In Burns H. Weston, ed., *Child Labor and Human Rights: Making Children Matter*. Boulder, CO: Lynne Rienner, pp. 401–24.

Gewirth, Alan. 1996. *The Community of Rights*. Chicago: University of Chicago Press.

Grimsrud, Björne. 2002. "Too Much Work at Too Early an Age." In Björne Grimsrud, ed., *The Next Steps: Experiences and Analysis of How to Eradicate Child Labour*. Oslo: Fafo, pp. 9–24.

Gross, James A. 2003. "A Long Overdue Beginning: The Promotion and Protection of Workers' Rights as Human Rights." In James A. Gross, ed., *Workers' Rights as Human Rights*. Ithaca, NY: Cornell University Press, pp. 1–22.

Howard-Hassmann, Rhoda. 2005. "The Second Great Transformation: Human Rights Leapfrogging in the Era of Globalization." 27 *Human Rights Quarterly* 1 (February).

International Labour Organization. 2004. *Helping Hands or Shackled Lives? Understanding Child Domestic Labor and Responses to It.* Geneva: International Labour Office.

International Labour Organization. 2006. *The End of Child Labor: Within Reach.* Geneva: International Labour Office.

International Labour Organization. 2008. *IPEC Action Against Child Labour 006–2007: Progress and Priorities.* Geneva: International Labour Office.

Jennings, Marianne M., and Jon Entine. 1998. "Business with a Soul: A Reexamination of What Counts in Business Ethics." 20 *Hamline Journal of Public Law and Policy*, 1, 72.

Kennedy, David. 2002. "The International Human Rights Movement: Part of the Problem?" 15 *Harvard Human Rights Journal* 102.

Kennedy, David. 2004. *The Dark Sides of Virtue: Reassessing International Humanitarianism.* Princeton, NJ: Princeton University Press.

Kielburger, Craig. 1998. *Free the Children.* New York: Harper Perennial.

Leary, Virginia A. 1994. "The Right to Health in International Human Rights Law." 24 *Health and Human Rights* 28.

Leary, Virginia A. 1996. "The Paradox of Workers' Rights as Human Rights." In Lance A. Compa and Stephen F. Diamond, eds., *Human Rights, Labor Rights, and International Trade.* Philadelphia: University of Pennsylvania Press.

Lippman, Matthew. 1985. "Multinational Corporations and Human Rights." In George W. Shepherd, Jr., and Ved P. Nanda, eds., *Human Rights and Third World Development.* Westport, CT: Greenwood Press, pp. 249–72.

Marks, Stephen P. 1999. "The United Nations and Human Rights: The Promise of Multilateral Diplomacy and Action." In Burns H. Weston and Stephen P. Marks, eds., *The Future of International Human Rights.* Ardsley, NY: Transnational, pp. 291–350.

McDougal, Myres S. 1960. "Perspectives for an International Law of Human Dignity." In *Studies in World Public Order* 987. New Haven, CT: Myres S. McDougal & Associates.

McDougal, Myres S., Harold D. Lasswell, and Lung-chu Chen. 1980. *Human Rights and World Public Order: The Basic Policies of an International Law of Human Dignity.* New Haven, CT: Yale University Press.

Miljeteig, Per. 2000. *Creating Partnerships with Working Children and Youth.* Washington, DC: World Bank.

Minow, Martha. 1999. *Between Vengeance and Forgiveness: Facing History after Genocide and Mass Violence.* Boston: Beacon Press.

Mock, William B.T. 2000. "Human Rights, Corporate Responsibility, and Economic Sanctions: Corporate Transparency and Human Rights." 8 *Tulsa Journal of Comparative and International Law* 15.

Monshipouri, Mahmood, Claude E. Welch Jr., and Evan T. Kennedy. 2003. "Multinational Corporations and the Ethics of Global Responsibility: Problems and Possibilities." 24 *Human Rights Quarterly* 965.

Nasaw, David. 1986. *Children of the City at Work and at Play*. Oxford: Oxford University Press.

Nussbaum, Martha C. 1997. "Capabilities and Human Rights." 66 *Fordham Law Review* 273.

Nussbaum, Martha C. 1999. "Capabilities, Human Rights, and the Universal Declaration." In Burns H. Weston and Stephen P. Marks, eds., *The Future of International Human Rights*. Ardsley, NY: Transnational, pp. 25–64.

O'Neill, Onora. 1992. "Children's Rights and Children's Lives." In Philip Alston, Stephen Parker, and John Seymour, eds., *Children, Rights, and the Law*. Oxford: Clarendon Press, pp. 24–42.

Rawls, John. 1971. *A Theory of Justice*. Cambridge, MA: Belknap Press of Harvard University Press.

Robinson, Mary. 1999. "Foreword." In Marta Santos Pais, ed., *A Human Rights Conceptual Framework for UNICEF*. Innocenti Essay No. 9. May. Florence: UNICEF International Child Development Centre.

Rodley, Nigel S., and David Weissbrodt. 2004. "United Nations Non-Treaty Procedures for Dealing with Human Rights Violations." In Hurst Hannum, ed., *Guide to International Human Rights Practice*. Ardsley, NY: Transnational.

Rorty, Richard. 1993. "Human Rights, Rationality, and Sentimentality." In Stephen Shute and Susan Hurley, eds., *On Human Rights*. New York: Basic Books, pp. 112–34.

Röselaers, Frans. 2002. "Foreword." In *Unbearable to the Human Heart: Child Trafficking and Action to Eliminate It*. Geneva: International Labour Office, International Programme for the Elimination of Child Labour.

Rotberg, Robert I., and Dennis Thompson, eds. 2000. *Truth v. Justice: The Morality of Truth Commissions*. Princeton, NJ: Princeton University Press.

Santos Pais, Marta. 1999. *A Human Rights Conceptual Framework for UNICEF*. Innocenti Essay No. 9. May. Florence: UNICEF International Child Development Centre.

Schrage, Elliot J. 2004. *Promoting International Worker Rights Through Private Voluntary Initiatives: Public Relations or Public Policy?* Iowa City: University of Iowa Center for Human Rights.

Sen, Amartya K. 1985. *Commodities and Capabilities*. Amsterdam and New York: Elsevier Science.

Sen, Amartya K. 1997. "Equality of What?" In Amartya K. Sen, ed., *Choice, Welfare and Measurement*. Cambridge, MA: Harvard University Press, pp. 353–69.

Sen, Amartya. 2000. *Development as Freedom*. New York: Anchor Books.

Shelton, Dinah. 1999. "The Promise of Regional Human Rights Systems." In Burns H. Weston and Stephen P. Marks, eds., *The Future of International Human Rights*. Ardsley, NY: Transnational, pp. 351–98.

Shelton, Dinah. 2002. "Protecting Human Rights in a Globalized World," 25 *Boston College International and Comparative Law Review* 273.

Slye, Ronald C. 2001. "International Human Rights Law in Practice: International Law, Human Rights Beneficiaries, and South Africa: Some Thoughts on the Utility of International Human Rights Law." 2 *Chicago Journal of International Law* 59.

Swift, Anthony. 1999. *Working Children Get Organized*. London: Save the Children UK.

Tolfree, David. 1998. *Old Enough to Work, Old Enough to Have A Say: Different Approaches to Supporting Working Children*. Stockholm: Save the Children–Sweden.

UNICEF. 1997. *State of the World's Children 1997*. New York: UNICEF.

UNICEF. 1999a. *State of the World's Children 1999*. New York: UNICEF.

UNICEF. 1999b. *Human Rights for Children and Women: How UNICEF Helps Make Them a Reality*. New York: UNICEF.

UNICEF. 2001. *Beyond Child Labour: Affirming Rights*. New York: UNICEF.

UN High Commissioner for Human Rights. 2000. *Business and Human Rights: A Progress Report*. January.

Van Boven, Theo C. 1982. "Survey of the Positive Law of Human Rights." In Karel Vasak, ed., Philip Alston, trans., *The International Dimensions of Human Rights*. Westport, CT: Greenwood Press, Vol. 1, p. 87.

Weston, Burns H., ed. 2005a. *Child Labor and Human Rights: Making Children Matter*. Boulder, CO: Lynne Rienner.

Weston, Burns H. 2005. "Human Rights." In 20 *Encyclopaedia Britannica* 656 (15th ed). <http://www.britannica.com/eb/article?tocID=219350>. [June 28, 2009].

Weston, Burns H. and Jonathan C. Carlson, eds. 1994. *International Law and World Order: Basic Documents*. Ardsley, NY: Transnational.

Weston, Burns H., and Stephen P. Marks, eds. 1999. *The Future of International Human Rights*. Ardsley, NY: Transnational.

Weston, Burns H., and Mark B. Teerink. 2006. *Child Labor through a Human Rights Glass Brightly*. Human Rights and Welfare Working Paper No. 35. October. http://www.du.edu/gsis/hrhw/working/2006/35-weston_terrink-2006.pdf [June 28, 2009].

Williams, Bernard. 1987. "The Standard of Living: Interests and Capabilities." In G. Hawthorn, ed., *The Standard of Living*. New York: Cambridge University Press, pp. 94–102.

Wiseberg, Laurie S. 2005. "Nongovernmental Organizations in the Struggle against Child Labor." In Burns Weston, ed., *Child Labor and Human Rights: Making Children Matter*. Boulder, CO: Lynne Rienner , pp. 343–76.

CHAPTER 5

Workers' Freedom of Association

TONIA NOVITZ

University of Bristol

Freedom of association, including the right to join a trade union, is recognized under international human rights instruments as well as domestic constitutions and labor legislation. To the extent that there are these legal sources, workers' entitlement to associate freely is uncontroversial. Insofar as countries, including the United States (U.S.), Canada, and the United Kingdom (U.K.), are in breach of their international legal obligations regarding freedom of association, the case can be made for legal and institutional reform, as well as litigation for the realization of workers' human rights (Adams 2002; Compa 2002; Ewing and Hendy 2002; Swidorski 2003).

There is, however, significant controversy over the nature and scope of an entitlement to freedom of association. There is, for example, the preliminary issue as to what forms of "association" are protected under this freedom. Notably, in the workplace, there is scope to argue that an employer should not be able to discriminate against workers on grounds of their religious affiliations or their intimate association in personal relationships. These can be seen as a reflection of an individual's desire to worship or enjoy a private life. Freedom of association can also be connected to freedom of speech, since collective protest is an effective means of voicing opinions and is arguably vital to the democratic process. More often, the term has come to be associated with trade unions and their activities, and here arise the debates that are the chief focus of this chapter.

The idea of "freedom of association" fuses the entitlement to form and belong to a collective association, such as a trade union, with the notion of individual freedom. If the trade union cannot lawfully pursue the interests of its members, their entitlement to associate would seem to be meaningless. Nevertheless, there are instances where conflict arises between collective action and individual choice. In particular, at least two issues have emerged, both of significant concern to workers and their organizations.

The first issue is whether freedom of association encompasses not only *the positive entitlement* to associate with others, but also *the negative entitlement* to refuse to do so. Where emphasis has been placed on the negative aspect of freedom of association (or the right to disassociate), priority has been given to an employer's freedom not to negotiate with a trade union. Moreover, in some legal contexts, permission has been given to "free riders" to take the benefit of collectively negotiated terms and conditions where they have not been members of a trade union or have not participated in strike action. Intertwined with this issue are the questions of whether and to what extent workers should have the freedom to choose which union should represent them. There would seem to be a case for achieving a balance between effectiveness of trade union representation and individual freedom, but there is little consensus as to where that balance should lie.

The second issue is whether freedom of association extends, beyond the formal ability of an individual to form and join an organization without state interference, to *the ability to act collectively* as an organization by engaging in consultative processes, bargaining, and potentially industrial action. Recognition of the ability to act collectively (as a facet of freedom of association) would require recognition of trade unions as entities capable of enforcing their members' legal entitlements or even of going against the views of a minority of their members. Also arguably connected with this issue are the questions of whether and to what extent the state should act to facilitate collective action by trade unions and the extent to which they can be compelled to do so by judicial institutions.

I begin the chapter by discussing the appeal of individual choice and the desirability of collective action, then review the treatment of these issues under international labor law and specifically in the legal systems of Canada, the U.K., and the U.S. There is scope here to consider the role of constitutional protection, human rights, and labor legislation as well as the role that can be played by the courts within each jurisdiction. With respect to the U.K., the European Union and the Council of Europe also wield significant influence over the development of domestic labor law.

It emerges that instruments adopted under the auspices of the International Labour Organization (ILO), as well as the supervisory bodies responsible for authoritative interpretation of those instruments, advocate a particular balance between collective association and individual freedom whereby the effectiveness of trade unions will not altogether be sacrificed to the preservation of individual personal freedom. Nevertheless, Canadian, U.K., and U.S. legal systems demonstrate variance in application of these international labor standards. As a regulatory strategy, reliance on freedom of association as a human right within Canada, the U.K., and the U.S. may not therefore be very helpful to workers seeking to protect trade union activity. It may, however, serve an important ideological function, which is not to be underestimated.

The Appeal of Individual Choice and Arguments for Collective Action

The appeal of individual choice lies in the priority placed in a liberal tradition on the autonomy of individuals, as opposed to coercion by the state (Berlin 1969:171; Dworkin 1996). Rights necessary for individual freedom have been designated "civil liberties" (see, for example, Marshall 1950). Where freedom of association is viewed solely as a civil liberty, a decision to join an organization, whether an employer's association or a trade union, is regarded as personal and individual. At least two consequences might seem to follow. First, the same status is given to the negative entitlement to disassociate as to positive manifestations of association. Second, the state would seem to have performed its duty to protect freedom of association merely when there are laws that prohibit interference with the formal rights to join and form trade unions. There is little basis for an obligation to be placed on the state to promote and facilitate collective bargaining.

There is no doubt that the idea of freedom of association originated in assertions of individual freedom of conscience in the context of organizations established for charitable, religious, and scientific purposes. It was only gradually that this freedom was extended to the industrial sphere (Alkema 1994; Jenks 1957). However, workers' purpose in forming these organizations was notably different from those claiming the freedom to associate for other purposes. In joining trade unions, workers sought to address long-standing inequalities of bargaining power between employer and worker. Through trade unions, workers could appoint representatives to give their opinions voice, argue for improved terms and conditions in collective bargaining, and, if necessary, organize industrial action. This fundamental difference in aim did not go unnoticed, such that for a considerable period of time, additional restrictions were placed on workers' collective organizing not experienced by other charitable, religious, and scientific associations (Pelling 1963). The fear was that workers' organizations in particular would upset the power relations between management and labor and thereby the fabric of society. Nevertheless, by 1927, the conclusion of an ILO survey was that governments "which recognised the right of association and of assembly in general, could not indefinitely maintain the paradox of forbidding a certain category of citizens from combining and meeting."[1]

It is commonly conceded, even by neoliberal scholars, that every person has a right to form and join a trade union. What commentators like Frederich Hayek have objected to, specifically, is legislation that is designed to promote collective bargaining or protect collective action, on the basis that such laws constitute distortions of the market in a way that impinge unacceptably on individual freedom (Hayek 1980). On such reasoning, the private legal order—the common law of contract, tort, restitution, and property—is the precondition for human freedom and is to be preferred to state interference and coercion through legislation. Legislation that provides immunity from liability for striking workers and their organizations is therefore unpalatable. For example, Hayek's view was that each worker individually has a right to strike, in the sense of an entitlement to withdraw his or her labor from the service of an employer, but that each worker should bear the consequences under private law of withdrawing labor, namely, breach of contract and liability in tort (Hayek 1984). Further, as Lord Bill Wedderburn has commented on the consequences of the neoliberal perspective on freedom of association, "those propounding individualist philosophies interpret this freedom with emphasis, like Hayek, upon the right to *disassociate*" (Wedderburn 1989:17).

It is, however, important to be reminded that there are alternative ways to approach the liberal discourse. For example, Sheldon Leader has argued that freedom of association entails not so much that individual choice be protected, but rather the freedom "to do collectively what they are allowed to do individually" (Leader 1992:23). His view is that persons should not have less freedom as a group than they have as individuals. He phrases this claim in "the language of equal protection" (Leader 1992:189). Were Leader's arguments to be regarded generally as compelling, there may be considerable scope for arguing that wide-ranging permission should be given by the state to the pursuit of trade union activities.

One difficulty with Leader's argument, however, is his attempt to treat with formal parity individual and collective action. Coordinated collective action, by virtue of its scale, has much greater effect than action taken solo, as Hayek and others have observed. One might therefore usefully supplement Leader's arguments with an appeal to what collective action, specifically in a work context, can achieve by redressing the imbalance of power between worker and employer.

The very point of joining a trade union is to have more impact in bargaining, with its clearly detrimental effect on the interests of the employer. It seems sensible to make these claims, rather than asserting that they are irrelevant. I suggest that this is an instance where it may make sense to make the claim for a right to join a trade union on the basis of freedom of speech, for association allows workers to gain an effective voice in challenging terms and conditions that affect their working lives. One can also explain the role of trade unions in terms of the scope for democratic representation that they offer to workers in formulating the positions presented to employers. Moreover, we may want to appeal to the actual material benefits that action taken through a trade union offers to workers, arguing that this constitutes a socioeconomic right.

Leader's work is of interest, however, because it offers, from a liberal perspective, reasons for giving priority to a trade union's entitlement to compel association (such as through a "closed shop") over and above the right to disassociate. For some theorists, this has proved an intractable problem (see von Prondzynski 1987). Leader attempts to achieve this by virtue of a "free rider" argument, namely that no one should be able to benefit from collective action without providing one's own contribution. On this basis, he considers that not only should one pay union dues when benefiting from collective bargaining, but that workers have an obligation to join a strike called by their union where this is likely to be beneficial to them (Leader 1992). Notably, this argument is said not to apply in the absence of such benefits, namely where a union does not represent one's interests (Leader 1992).

Clyde Summers takes a skeptical view of this supplement to Leader's main argument, because Leader does not explain why it is not applicable to "a wide range of private associations," such as the community association that performs a good deed. Summers therefore presents the alternative explanation "that the appeal to the free rider argument on behalf of unions has more to do with the special role unions play in our society than with conceptions of freedom of association" (Summers 1995:268). He is also concerned by Leader's insistence that one should have entirely free choice as to which union one joins, without any appreciation of the ways in which this may in practice undermine collective bargaining (Summers 1995).

In my view, there are many reasons specific to the context of work, which are political and socioeconomic in nature, for protecting freedom of association. If we acknowledge these, in addition to the exercise of individual liberty, then it becomes possible to also have regard for the practical reasons not to equate positive and negative dimensions of freedom of association. For example, if (as is generally the situation in the U.K.) "union-negotiated terms and conditions are available to everyone (or extended to everyone by the employer), paying and non-paying employees alike, it generally makes no sense for a self-interested, utility-maximising person to join a union and pay dues. . . . If free riding becomes pervasive, union dues could rise, in principle, to an excessive level and effectively discourage anyone from joining" (Harcourt and Lam 2006:255–6).

Harcourt and Lam point, moreover, to the resource problems posed for trade unions that continually have to mount organizing drives to reach non-unionized workplaces and to the limited bargaining power that most workers have in the absence of trade union representation. They note that workers' freedom of contract will not lead to genuine contractual diversity, since it will be the employer who, in the absence of the correction in collective bargaining power offered by trade unions, will generally set terms and conditions of employment. Furthermore, collective bargaining can set minimum terms and conditions above which differentiation can occur (Harcourt and Lam 2006).

International Legal Sources

The entitlement to freedom of association is to be found in international human rights instruments as well as domestic constitutions and legislation. This section reviews the legal sources of this entitlement under international law and the extent to which they reflect the conflict between the individual and collective dimensions of freedom of association already identified.

International Labour Organization

The preamble to the first constitution of the International Labour Organization (ILO) in 1919 stated that freedom of association was a principle of "special and urgent importance" applied, for "all lawful purposes," to both "the employed" and "employers." In this sense, it was expected to have parity of application. The particular significance to workers of freedom of association was stressed by the international community in the Declaration of Philadelphia of 1944, subsequently appended to the ILO constitution. Article I asserted, inter alia, that "freedom of expression and of association are essential to sustained progress." Article III went further in that ILO objectives were to include "the effective recognition of the right of collective bargaining." There is no doubting the centrality of freedom of association to the tripartite makeup of the ILO and its practical significance in domestic legal systems of ILO member states at that time. These constitutional statements have since been elaborated upon, in particular through the medium of ILO Conventions No. 87 on Freedom of Association and Protection of the Right to Organise, 1948, and No. 98 on the Right to Organise and Collective Bargaining, 1949.

Convention No. 87 establishes, in Article 2, the freedom of workers and employers to organize and, subject only to the rules of the organizations concerned, join organizations of their own choosing. This freedom includes, by virtue of Article 3, "the right to draw up their constitutions and rules, to elect their representatives in full freedom, to organise their administration and activities and to formulate their programmes." This entitlement is extended, through Articles 5 and 6, to trade union and employer federations and confederations. Convention No. 87 is thereby concerned with the exercise of freedom to associate by workers and employers alike, without undue interference from the state. In this sense, it maps on to the liberal view of freedom of association outlined above. The only positive onus placed on ratifying ILO member states, under Article 11, is to take "measures appropriate to national conditions . . . where necessary, to encourage and promote the full development and utilisation of machinery for voluntary negotiation between employers or employers' organizations and workers' organizations, with a view to the regulation of terms and conditions of employment by means of collective agreements."

Convention No. 98 again, under Article 4, obliges the state to take such "measures." This convention also goes further in that Article 3 places an onus on the state to establish machinery to protect workers from anti-union discrimination and to protect both workers' and employers' associations from undue interference with one another or with each other's agents or members.

It should be noted that the freedom to association, the right to organize, and the right to engage in collective bargaining do not remain unqualified. ILO Convention Nos. 87 and 98 both exclude the armed forces and the police, who are to be covered by national law and regulation. Convention No. 98, by virtue of Article 6, "does not deal with the position of public servants engaged in the administration of the State, nor shall it be construed as prejudicing their rights or status in any way." Rights to protection from anti-union discrimination and protection of public employees' organizations from "acts of interference by a public authority" are extended to public employees by virtue of ILO Convention No. 151 concerning Protection of the Right to Organise and Procedures for Determining Conditions of Employment in the Public Service, 1978. Article 8 makes specific provision for the settlement of disputes in this sector, "through negotiation between the parties or through independent and impartial machinery, such as mediation, conciliation and arbitration, established in such a manner as to ensure the confidence of the parties involved."

More recently, "freedom of association and the effective recognition of the right to collective bargaining" have been recognized as "fundamental rights" under Article 2 of the ILO Declaration on Fundamental Principles and Rights at Work, 1998. This declaratory instrument has a peculiar follow-up mechanism, which is intended to encourage best practice rather than identify breach of international legal obligations (Bellace 2001) but has since been used as a basis for trade conditionality, such as under the generalized system of preferences operated by the European Union (Novitz 2008; Orbie, forthcoming).[2]

The bare text of these ILO instruments does not assist in appropriately interpreting the guarantees of freedom of association contained therein. This apparent lacuna has been remedied by the ILO Governing Body Committee on Freedom of Association (CFA), founded in 1951, which has developed a substantial jurisprudence relating to freedom of association. The CFA views freedom of association as a constitutional principle, protectable regardless of ratification of ILO Convention Nos. 87 and 98.[3] In this way, its jurisprudence provides an important supplement to the views expressed by the ILO Committee of Experts on the Application of Conventions and Recommendations (CEACR), which monitors state reports regarding ratified conventions.

The ILO has not made any pronouncement on the right not to be a member of a trade union, but it has adopted what has been described as a "liberal interpretation of freedom of association" (Caraway 2006:219), which emphasizes the free choice to join a trade union, including determination of trade union constitutions, and criticizes preconditions for establishment or registration of a trade union (International Labour Organization 2006). Caraway has observed that, when applied to a country like Argentina, "the ILO's understanding of freedom of association, if implemented would result in greater fragmentation of the labour movement and the emergence of more decentralized bargaining" (2006:225).

Nevertheless, it is important to stress that the ILO CFA does not prevent the most representative trade unions' being given certain privileges in terms of negotiating rights and the collective agreements that they conclude being extended to other workers (International Labour Organization 2006). Moreover, the CEACR has criticized U.K. legislation that does not permit trade unions to discipline nonstriking workers.[4] There is, apparently, limited toleration of "free riding" by ILO supervisory bodies and a concern with the effectiveness of collective bargaining. Indeed, the CFA has expressed concern "that the emphasis on individual responsibility for bargaining . . . can be detrimental to collective bargaining."[5] The committee considered it important for not only employers but also workers to have freedom of choice. It acknowledged that, unless the state intervened and introduced suitable mechanisms for the promotion of collective bargaining, workers would be unable to choose collective bargaining, given the superior bargaining power of an employer.[6]

The CFA has accepted that certain restrictions may be placed by governments on trade union organization and collective action in the army and police force and among other public servants. For example, "recognition of the principle of freedom of association in the case of public servants does not necessarily imply the right to strike" (International Labour Organization 2006:paragraph 572). However, it has been adamant that any restrictions placed on such a right must be proportionate to the harm potentially caused and must be accompanied by "compensatory guarantees" such as the provision of "adequate, impartial and speedy conciliation and arbitration proceedings in which the parties concerned can take part at every stage and in which the awards, once made, are fully and promptly implemented" (International Labour Organization 2006:paragraphs 595–6).

Universal Declaration of Human Rights, 1948

The notion of negative freedom of association is not so much a feature of ILO jurisprudence, but it was recognized in the foundational human rights instrument, the Universal Declaration of Human Rights (UDHR), adopted under the auspices of the United Nations in 1948. Article 20 stated that "(1) [e]veryone has the right to freedom of peaceful assembly and association; and (2) No one may be compelled to belong to an association."

In this context, the right to associate and the right to disassociate were placed side by side, as if two sides of the same coin. Notably, there was no mention in this instrument of trade unions as a manifestation of freedom of association. Instead, Article 23(4) provided independently that "[e]veryone has the right to form and to join trade unions for the protection of his interests."

European Convention on Human Rights, 1950

When deliberating whether the wording of the UDHR should be applied in a European context, the drafters of the European Convention on Human Rights (ECHR), 1950, deliberately selected a different formulation, whereby freedom of association was explicitly linked to the right to form and join trade unions, and no mention was made of the negative freedom to disassociate (Novitz 2003). They did, however, envisage that restrictions could be placed on such an entitlement, especially in relation to members of the armed forces, police, or administration of the state. This entitlement and restrictions thereto were also subsequently elaborated upon in Articles 6 and 31 of the European Social Charter, 1961. Article 31 stated that restrictions or limitations could be permissible insofar as they were "prescribed by law and are necessary in a democratic society for the protection of the rights and freedoms of others or for the protection of public interest, national security, public health, or morals." Notably, the European Court of Human Rights (ECtHR) has subsequently found (and recently reiterated) that negative freedom of association is implicit in Article 11 of the ECHR,[7] such that the efforts of the drafters in this regard were in vain. This is despite a trend toward citation of ILO Conventions and jurisprudence in the court's judgments (see Mantouvalou 2006).

UN Covenants, 1966

It was the formulation of freedom of association set out in the ECHR that was reflected in the wording of Article 22 of the 1966 International Covenant on Civil and Political Rights (ICCPR) adopted by the UN General Assembly: "Everyone shall have the right to freedom of association with others, including the right to form and join trade unions for the protection of his interests." Article 8 of its twin instrument, the 1966 International Covenant on Economic, Social and Cultural Rights (ICESCR), contained more far-reaching provisions relating to trade unions, rather than freedom of association per se, including qualified recognition of the right to strike. Both instruments, however, indicate the extent of the "freedom," which is not to be restricted or limited other than as "prescribed by law" and "necessary in a democratic society in the interests of national security or public order or for the protection of the rights and freedoms of others" and does not extend to members of the armed forces or police.

In both UN human rights instruments, provisions relating to the right to form and join trade unions were also made expressly subject to the proviso that "[n]othing in this article shall authorize States Parties to the International Labour Organisation Convention of 1948 concerning Freedom of Association and Protection of the Right to Organise to take legislative measures which would prejudice, or to apply the law in such a manner as to prejudice, the guarantees provided for in that Convention." This suggests that ILO jurisprudence, which states that a right to strike is a vital aspect of freedom of association (International Labour Organization 2006), might have influenced the views of the UN Human Rights Committee responsible for supervising implementation of the ICCPR. However, the committee has been hesitant to adopt ILO jurisprudence uncritically. In 1982, a complaint was considered inadmissible by the majority of that supervisory body, on the basis that Article 22 of the ICCPR did not encompass a right to strike, given that specific provision had been made for such a right under the ICESCR.[8] However, several concluding observations of the Human Rights Committee on compatibility with Article 22 indicate that restriction of a right to strike under national laws may amount to a violation of that provision (Joseph, forthcoming).[9] The artificial divide between civil and political rights on the one hand and socioeconomic rights on the other, reflected in the division between the ICCPR and the ICESCR, may well be responsible for the uncertainty that continues to prevail as to the link between freedom of association and collective action.

While it might seem that the ILO should be regarded as the primary source of norms in relation to freedom of association, this has not altogether been the case. ILO supervisory bodies have stressed the significance of choice as an aspect of freedom of association and the importance of freedom from government intervention in the formation and activities of employer and worker organizations, but they have sought to do so in a manner that also protects effective collective bargaining. Despite reference to ILO standards in the two UN Covenants of 1966 and even in the recent judgments of the European Court of Human Rights, there is more emphasis in these institutional settings on negative freedom of association and less on promotion of collective bargaining through the effective legal protection of a right to strike (Novitz 2003). Given the unresolved tensions between the individual and collective aspects of freedom of association at the international level, can they be resolved at a domestic level?

Constitutional, Legislative, and Judicial Protection of Freedom of Association

In countries such as Canada, the U.K. and the U.S., indications are that trade union membership has declined over the past 50 years. For example, in the U.S., union density reached its peak in the 1950s, when over 30% of all U.S. workers belonged to unions, and nearly 40% of those in the private sector did. By 1999, only 13.9% of workers and 9.4% of private sector workers belonged to trade unions (Swidorski 2003). In 2007, these figures were 12.1% of workers and 7.5% of private sector workers.[10]

This decline might not be seen as problematic if it actually reflected a preference of workers not to be represented by trade unions, but social research points to a significant "representation gap," "in which the proportion of workers indicating a clear preference for union representation has exceeded, often considerably, the proportion actually represented by a union with the same preference" (Harcourt and Lam 2006:254). In the U.S., that gap is 42%, in Canada it is 44%, and in the U.K., where trade union membership is higher, it is 36% (Bryson et al. 2005). "It essentially means that many workers are unable to exercise their freedom to associate with a union" (Harcourt and Lam 2006:255).

The question, then, is what has happened in these countries that has allowed such a situation to occur. Much may be attributed to changes in the labor market (Kochan 2003), but at least part of the answer may be attributed to the content and implementation of domestic labor law and human rights law. As we shall see, Canadian, U.K., and U.S. domestic labor law do not wholly comply with ILO standards or the "balance" between individual and collective dimensions of freedom of association advocated by ILO supervisory bodies. Indeed, in Canada and the U.S., noncompliance has prevented ratification of key international instruments relating to freedom of association.

Moreover, when we examine the application of human rights standards by courts, we find that the judiciary places considerable reliance on the rhetoric of "choice" and treats freedom of association primarily as an individual entitlement. This is evident particularly when engaged in an exercise of "balancing" rights of the employer and employee. Here, collective action, especially when it has a coercive element aimed at achieving conclusion of a collective agreement, does not tend to win sympathy. Where there has been judicial reference to ILO standards, it has been accompanied by recognition that freedom of association may have a significant collective dimension. However, the overriding climate for promotion of collective bargaining via litigation asserting entitlement to freedom of association seems far from favorable.

Canada

Canada has ratified both the ICCPR and the ICESCR. However, while there has been ratification also of ILO Convention No. 87, Convention No. 98 has not been ratified.[11] The reason would seem to be the narrow range of exceptions envisaged in Convention No. 98 to the entitlements set out therein. As we shall see, various Canadian provinces exclude from union representation not only agricultural and professional workers, but also workers in the public sector, such as teachers. Canadian trade unions have brought a significant number of complaints to the ILO Committee on Freedom of Association, with Canadian provincial legislation being found in violation of ILO principles.

Two such complaints were brought against the Canadian government by virtue of legislation adopted by the Province of Quebec. The first complaint, on which the CFA issued recommendations in 2006, concerned legislation that canceled the trade union registrations of certain workers in social, health, and childcare services, depriving them of employee status under the Labour Code and making them independent contractors. In response, the committee called upon the government "to amend the Act in order for the workers concerned to be able to benefit from the general collective labour rights system."[12]

The second complaint, on which the CFA commented in 2007, concerned Quebec legislation that imposed conditions of employment in the public sector (allegedly without prior bargaining or consultation) and took away the right to strike without granting an alternative procedure for the settlement of disputes, such as mediation, conciliation, or arbitration. The complaint was exceptionally complex, and it is difficult to do it justice in its entirety here. Nevertheless, the recommendations are notable for various reasons, among them being the committee's reiteration of "the fundamental importance that it attaches to the right of workers to have recourse to strike action and that it has always maintained that the right to strike is one of the essential means through which workers and their organizations may promote and defend their economic and social interests."[13] The CFA went on to set out the limitations that may legitimately be placed on that right in respect of public servants exercising authority in the name of the state and essential services "in the strict sense of the term, that is, services the interruption of which would endanger the life, personal safety or health of the whole or part of the population."[14] In the absence of a right to strike for such workers, the Government of Quebec was requested to make the necessary "compensatory guarantees," namely, to "establish a bargaining procedure that has the confidence of the parties concerned and allows them to settle their differences especially by having recourse to conciliation or mediation and by voluntarily calling on an independent arbitrator to resolve their differences, on the understanding that the arbitration decisions are binding on both parties and are fully and swiftly executed."[15]

There have sometimes been positive outcomes following the outcome of complaints to the ILO CFA. For example, the Government of Ontario, through the Colleges Collective Bargaining Act, sought to exclude various part-time workers from collective bargaining. The CFA responded that it failed to see why the principles "on the basic rights of association and collective bargaining afforded to all workers should not also apply to part-time employees" and requested that legislative measures be taken accordingly.[16] This recommendation was issued in 2006, and in June 2008, the Colleges Collective Bargaining Act 2008, which will remove the part-time exclusion clause, was introduced in a statement to the Ontario Legislative Assembly.[17]

However, some complaints have not led to any greater willingness to comply with ILO standards. Indications of frustration on the part of the ILO CFA can be found in complaints brought regarding the enactment of labor legislation in British Columbia. The committee had previously criticized legislation that granted an arbitrator jurisdiction to eliminate hundreds of provisions contained in a collective agreement covering 42,000 teachers and associated professional workers in the public education sector.[18] The British Columbia Supreme Court also ruled that the legislation was fundamentally flawed. The legislature retaliated by seeking to adopt retroactive legislation that achieved the same goal. Unsurprisingly, the committee was "particularly concerned at this new unilateral intervention, within a very short lapse of time, in view of its previous conclusions."[19] "Emphasizing the utmost importance attached to the voluntary nature of collective bargaining and to the autonomy of the bargaining partners, as fundamental aspects of freedom of association principles, the Committee once again firmly requests the Government to refrain in future from having recourse to such legislative intervention in the collective bargaining process."[20] However, within a few months there came another case relating to further legislation adopted in British Columbia seeking unilaterally to extend the term of the teachers' collective agreement so that they could not bargain a wage increase or other working conditions or engage in industrial action.[21] There would seem to be an ongoing struggle between trade unions and the Campbell administration in British Columbia from 2001 onward that has yet to be resolved,[22] although one may expect a more immediate response to 2007 judgment of the Supreme Court of Canada in the case of *Health Services and Support—Facilities Subsector Bargaining Association* v. *British Columbia.*[23]

Indeed, what may yet operate as a more effective constraint on provincial legislation, following recent decisions of the Canadian Supreme Court, is the Canadian Charter of Rights and Freedoms, 1989, which is Part I of the Canadian Constitution Act, 1982. Section 2 of the Charter states the following:

Everyone has the following fundamental freedoms:

(a) freedom of conscience and religion;

(b) freedom of thought, belief, opinion and expression, including freedom of the press and other media of communication;

(c) freedom of peaceful assembly; and

(d) freedom of association.

This statement remains subject to the proviso in section 1 that these freedoms may be "subject only to such reasonable limits prescribed by law as can be demonstrably justified in a free and democratic society." There are echoes here of corresponding statements in international human rights instruments. In the *Health Services* case, the Canadian Supreme Court concluded that "the section 2(d) guarantee of freedom of association protects the capacity of labour unions to engage in collective bargaining on workplace issues."[24] This conclusion constituted a substantial departure from "20 years of jurisprudence that interpreted the freedom of association as excluding collective bargaining" (Fudge 2008:25).

To understand this development, one has to trace this jurisprudence back to what has come to be known as the "Labour Trilogy" of cases, in which the majority of the Canadian Supreme Court reached the conclusion that statutes that restricted strikes did not violate the provision made for freedom of association in section 2(d) of the charter.[25] Indeed, the assertion was made that freedom of association did not require any judicial intervention for the protection of collective bargaining. Justice Le Dain, who delivered the majority judgment in the *Alberta Reference* case, asserted that the freedom of association guaranteed under the charter extended only to association for the purpose of exercising other fundamental rights and that collective bargaining and industrial action could not constitute such rights, being legislative creations whose exercise involved the balancing of competing interests. The latter was a task for the legislature, not the courts.[26] Justice MacIntyre went further and sought to limit freedom of association to the protection of activities that a person could lawfully pursue as an individual, but he rejected the view that because an individual employee could withdraw his or her labor, the action of union members engaging a strike should be regarded as constitutionally protected.[27] In this respect, he took the directly opposing view to Sheldon Leader (detailed in an earlier section). Notable, however, was Chief Justice Dickson's dissent, which relied explicitly on the "clear consensus amongst the ILO adjudicative bodies that Convention No. 87 goes beyond merely protecting the formation of labor unions and provides protection of their essential activities—that is of collective bargaining and the freedom to strike"[28] (see Norman 2004 and Fudge 2004). Judy Fudge's view was that "the Supreme Court of Canada's emphasis on individualism and negative freedoms in the context of repeated attempts by unions to obtain constitutional protection for workers' rights reinforced the tendency in neo-liberal politics to treat unions as coercive monopolies rather than as democratic organizations and to treat workers'

rights as special interests rather than as fundamental human rights"
(Fudge 2004:427). It was a position that accorded most closely with that
of Hayek (described earlier).

The Supreme Court's position was reconsidered in 2001 in *Dunmore* v.
Ontario (Attorney General),[29] a case that challenged the exclusion of
agricultural workers from the Ontario Labour Relations Act on the basis
of a violation of freedom of association. Given the Supreme Court's insistence in the "Labour Trilogy" that it would leave such matters to the
appropriate provincial legislature, one might have expected that this
would not be considered a legitimate complaint. Nevertheless, a seven-
judge majority of the court found that the exclusion of agricultural workers constituted an unjustifiable infringement of freedom of association
under section 2(d) of the charter. The majority judgment delivered by
Justice Bastarache relied on ILO sources, including a recent complaint
before the ILO CFA.[30] Also notable was the statement that freedom of
association could constitute not only an individual, but also a collective
right. The court ordered Ontario to enact positive freedom of association
protection for agricultural workers.

What may prove even more interesting are the reasons that Justice
Bastarache gave for his conclusions, which indicate the basis for protection of freedom of association, which goes beyond the instantiation of
personal liberty. These related to the ways in which trade unions facilitate democratic collaboration: "In addition to permitting the collective
expression of employee interests, trade unions contribute to political
debate. At the level of national policy, trade unions advocate on behalf of
disadvantaged groups and present views on fair industrial policy. These
functions, when viewed globally, affect all levels of society and constitute
'an important subsystem in a democratic market-economy.'"[31]

The *Healthcare Services* litigation was a response to the swift adoption of legislation in British Columbia, without consultation with unions
representing the affected workers, that sought to facilitate restructuring
in the health service by altering terms relating to employment security
previously established by collective agreement. In *Healthcare Services*,
Chief Justice McLachlin and Justice LeBel, the authors of the judgment
with which five other members of the court concurred, revisited "the
grounds advanced in the earlier decisions for the exclusion of collective
bargaining from the *Charter's* protection of freedom of association,"
which they found did not withstand principled scrutiny and should be
rejected.[32] In so doing, they systematically rejected the reasoning in the
Labour Trilogy cases. In particular, they recognized, following *Dunmore*,
"that certain collective activities have no individual analogue and yet are
deserving of protection" (Fudge 2008:32). Moreover, they sought to take

a purposive approach to the protection of freedom of association in a trade union context, for ignoring the differences between organizations would have "the unfortunate effect . . . of overlooking the importance of collective bargaining."[33] Their judgment also explicitly drew on international legal sources, such as the 1966 Covenants and ILO Convention No. 87.[34]

Yet, as the judgment stated and Fudge has observed, the right to collective bargaining that follows from freedom of association is a "limited right" (Fudge 2008): "First, as the right is to a process, it does not guarantee any substantive outcome. Moreover, the right is to a general process of collective bargaining, not to a particular model of labor relations, nor to a specific bargaining method."[35] It is also notable that the charter only applies to state action and not private action. Moreover, in order to seek positive intervention by the government (for example, to extend the range of persons covered by legislation protecting those engaging in a collective bargaining regime), "there must be evidence that the freedom would be next to impossible to exercise without positively recognizing a right to access a statutory regime."[36] Most commonly, it will be a right exercised to restrain the interference by government with collective bargaining, but only in respect of an interference "so substantial that it interferes not only with the attainment of the union members' objectives (which is not protected), but with the very process that enables them to pursue these objectives by engaging in meaningful negotiations with the employer."[37] The legislature of British Columbia has been given a year's grace to consider how to address the findings of the court; Fudge and others, however, do not hold out much hope of an enthusiastic response, but expect one that is grudging and minimalist, as was the response of the Ontario government to the finding in *Dunmore* (Fudge 2008). But Fudge does consider that, regardless of the lack of compensation for affected workers and the unions (which also lost thousands of members), the court's decision "is an important symbolic and moral victory" (Fudge 2008:48).

United Kingdom

The U.K. was the first member of the ILO to ratify either ILO Convention No. 87 or 98, but its enthusiasm for compliance with ILO standards relating to freedom of association has waned considerably in recent years. Since 1984, the U.K. has remained stubbornly intransigent, such that concerns expressed both by the ILO CEACR and CFA have not been heeded. These supervisory bodies have indicated that various aspects of U.K. law are in breach of ILO Convention Nos. 87 and 98, which relate to the right to organize and to engage in collective bargaining.

For example, the CEACR has found repeatedly that lack of any legal protection for sympathy action in the U.K. is highly problematic,[38] but no legislative reform is contemplated by the current U.K. Labour government in this regard. Also, the CEACR has expressed concern regarding various aspects of the U.K. statutory recognition procedure introduced in 1999, revised in 2004. These include the absence of protection from anti-union discrimination and acts of interference with trade union affairs outside a very limited "balloting period"; the exclusion of small workplaces (fewer than 21 employees) that are exempt from the statutory recognition provisions; the inability to be represented by a trade union in a collective bargaining period if the majority of a designated "bargaining unit" (and at least 40% of those voting) do not agree; and the capacity for an employer to voluntarily recognize a non-independent union for collective bargaining purposes so as to thwart an application by an independent trade union under the statutory procedure.[39]

In 2005, the CFA determined that protection of freedom of association is unduly hindered by restrictions placed on the right to strike in the prisons service insofar as these have not been accompanied by adequate, impartial, and speedy conciliation and arbitration proceedings the outcomes of which are fully and properly implemented. This was because the U.K. government was not prepared to articulate the scope of exceptional circumstances in which it would not comply with the findings of the arbitrator.[40] It is notable that this last finding of the ILO CFA has been cited in a judgment of the English High Court delivered by Mr. Justice Wyn Williams. In this case, the Ministry of Justice sought the issue of an injunction by the court to prevent any future industrial action by prison officers, on the basis that the strike was in breach of a "joint industrial relations procedural agreement," under which prison officers forego industrial action and agree instead that their pay be determined in response to recommendations made by an independent pay review body. The union alleged that since the government had not fully implemented the findings of the pay review body, the injunction should not be issued, and it relied on the findings of the CFA. However, the recommendations of the CFA were not considered to be determinative, because the U.K. government continued to assert its entitlement to depart from the findings of the pay review body on the basis of "affordability" and, in the absence of a monist legal system, the policy taken by the government must prevail. The government certainly did not heed the view of the CFA, but proceeded instead to introduce legislation so as to ensure that prison officers would be, in the future, under an unconditional statutory obligation not to strike.[41] ILO sources, one might therefore conclude, have relatively little weight in U.K. courts or with the U.K. legislature.

The lack of commitment to collective bargaining of the U.K. government may also be gathered from the conduct of its embassy in the U.S., where it refused to recognize and negotiate with the trade union chosen by locally engaged staff to represent them and sought instead to set up an internal management-led "staff representative council" whereby staff would be "invited" to act as representatives.[42] In this context, the U.K. sought to rely on diplomatic immunity, a contention that was rejected by the CFA, which recommended that the government "take all necessary measures with a view to encouraging and promoting negotiations . . . with a view to reaching agreement on the nature of their relationship and on the terms and conditions of locally engaged staff."[43]

There is no straightforward constitutional protection of freedom of association in the U.K., since there is no single written source of a constitution. The requirement of the state to protect freedom of association arises by virtue of the Human Rights Act 1998, which domesticates "convention rights" set out in the ECHR. In this manner, Article 11 of the ECHR, which makes provision for protection of human rights, operates as a constraint on the content and application of the key piece of U.K. legislation governing collective bargaining, the Trade Union and Labour Relations (Consolidation) Act 1992 (TULRCA). The findings of the ECtHR are considered binding, and the U.K. legislature is obliged to implement its rulings. The ECHR has proved significant insofar as it has resulted in the dismantling of the "closed shop," or compulsory trade unionism in the U.K., following the 1979 judgment of ECtHR in *Young, James and Webster*.[44] This was the seminal case that determined that Article 11 includes the individual entitlement to refuse to be a member of a trade union, or "negative" freedom of association.

What is perhaps more curious is that the influence that the principle of negative freedom of association has had on the recent case of *ASLEF* v. *UK*,[45] in which a U.K. union sought to exclude a Mr. Lee, a member of the British National Party, which advocates racist policies contrary to the constitutional objectives of the union, despite the findings of two U.K. employment tribunals to the effect that they had to admit him to membership by virtue of TULRCA, section 174. In finding that the union, ASLEF, was entitled to expel Lee, the ECtHR took the significant step of finding that a trade union as an organization could claim a human right, such as the negative right not to associate. This was also a freedom that could be exercised by a collective entity. However, otherwise, the court's reasoning betrayed a curiously neutral view of the entitlement to freedom of association, which reveals the liberal underpinnings of their jurisprudence. The court has attempted to give parity of treatment to the right of individuals not to join associations and the rights of associations not to have them join. The court also failed to distinguish between trade unions and other sorts of associations.[46] The judgment suggested how such a formalistic application of the rule of law may sometimes assist workers' organizations (Thomas 1976). However, despite its importance as a means of protecting trade union interests (Ewing 2007), the court's reasoning remains troubling. The conclusions of the court were at least stated to be subject to the proviso in Article 11(2) of the convention that trade union autonomy can be restricted to the extent that this is prescribed by law and "necessary in a democratic society" for one of a number of aims. The court was also prepared to recognize that "a balance must be achieved which ensures the fair and proper treatment of minorities and avoids any abuse of a dominant position."[47]

In addition, the more market-focused law of the European Union (EU) takes precedence over domestic law by virtue of the European Communities Act 1972. This means that, while the EU has no specific competence to make legislation applicable to member states relating to freedom of association, where U.K. labor law or that of another member state impinges on a vital aspect of EU law, such as freedom of movement of goods, services, persons, and establishment between member states, that legislation may be subject to challenge before national courts and, ultimately, the European Court of Justice (ECJ). The ECJ has also, in its interpretation of EU law, sought to be guided in its general principles of jurisprudence by the rights guaranteed under the ECHR, as well as the constitutional traditions of member states. The court now also refers explicitly to the provisions set out in the EU Charter of Fundamental Rights, 2000, an instrument that also makes self-conscious reference to the ECHR.[48] There have been three very recent and significant decisions before the ECJ that will have an impact on U.K. domestic law relating to collective bargaining.

First was the case of *Werhof*,[49] which concerned the extent to which a new employer should be considered to be bound by a collective agreement after a transfer of an undertaking. Under EU law, it is standard for all of a worker's terms and conditions that apply before the sale of a business (a transfer of an undertaking) to apply afterward. However, while the ECJ determined that terms set out in a collective agreement at the time of transfer could be incorporated into each individual worker's contract of employment, the court stated that the employer could not be considered bound by provisions contained in a subsequent collective agreement without the employer's consent, nor was the employer obliged to try to maintain relations with the relevant trade union. The justification given was the principle of negative "freedom of association," namely, the right of an employer not to have to associate or enter into an agreement with a union.[50] This is an approach that prioritizes individual freedom of contract as opposed to collective bargaining within the EU labor market. It also circumscribes the obligation of states to promote collective bargaining under Article 4 of ILO Convention No. 98.

The second case, which arose from an application for an injunction before U.K. courts, was *Viking*.[51] This litigation concerned an attempt by an employer to prevent industrial action in Finland (and support for such action by the International Transport Workers' Fereration in the U.K.), which had sought to prevent the reflagging of a ship in Estonia. The employer brought the action on the basis that the industrial action breached its right to freedom of establishment under EU law. The judgment delivered by the ECJ in this case was remarkably similar to its judgment in another case, *Laval*,[52] referred from the Swedish courts. In both, the court cited ILO Convention No. 87 in support of the existence of a right to strike, which had to be respected under EU law,[53] and then went on to consider whether the industrial action in question could constitute a legitimate exception to the application of EU law. Ultimately, in both *Viking* and *Laval*, the ECJ concluded that, on the facts of the two cases, the industrial action could not be legitimate. In so doing, the court imposed strict requirements both as to the objectives of legitimate action (which involved a very narrow interpretation of what was in workers' interests),[54] and whether such action could be regarded as necessary and proportionate[55] (see Davies 2008; Syrpis and Novitz 2008). This was the first explicit recognition of a right to strike by the ECJ, but it was at best a pyrrhic victory.

The United States

The U.S. has not ratified either ILO Convention Nos. 87 or 98, nor has it ratified the ICESCR. The U.S. ratified the ICCPR only in 1992, while declaring that this would not have any ramifications regarding ratification of other key instruments concerning freedom of association (Compa 2004). The Clinton administration did support the adoption of the ILO Declaration of Fundamental Principles and Rights at Work, but this was viewed skeptically by Philip Alston in light of U.S. lack of enthusiasm for the ratification of ILO Conventions relating to freedom of association. The suspicion remains that the aim of the U.S. was to dilute the content of core labor standards, such as freedom of association, while using these as a basis for trade conditionality (Alston 2004).[56]

There is no explicit constitutional protection of freedom of association in the U.S. Instead, the U.S. Supreme Court has regarded a right to associate with others as implicit in the First Amendment. Two dimensions of this entitlement have emerged: first, a right to associate for the purpose of speech or assembly; and second, a right to intimate association, such as expression of a sexual preference (Long 2007; Magrid and Prenkert 2004–5).[57] Alternative sources of protection for workers' rights could have been "the Thirteenth Amendment's affirmation of free labor, and the Fourteenth Amendment's guarantee of equal protection." Instead, the decision was taken to adopt the National Labor Relations Act (NLRA) "under the commerce clause of the constitution empowering Congress to regulate interstate business" (Compa 2004:214; see also Compa, forthcoming).

Section 7 of the NLRA makes provision for workers to "self-organize" and to "form, join, or assist labor organizations." The legislation also goes further, stating that they may "engage in concerted activities" for their "mutual aid and protection." This is the legacy of the Wagner Act of 1935, which sought to give effect to the principle of association. The constitutionality of this piece of legislation was upheld on the basis that Congress had power to grant rights to organize, bargain, and engage in collective activity to promote the free flow of commerce—not on the grounds that these rights were fundamental.[58] Section 7 rights are protected under Section 8 by giving workers and employers the ability to complain and prevent "unfair labor practices," an innovative legal device that could be used to prevent the kinds of practices later proscribed by Article 3 of ILO Convention No. 98. However, the Labor Management Relations (or Taft-Hartley) Act of 1947 amended and restricted the effect of the NLRA in significant ways, such that U.S. law departs from ILO standards in various respects. Examples include the ban that the NLRA now places on sympathy strikes and the exclusion of agricultural workers and other categories of workers from the act's protection.[59]

More recently, a complaint determined by the ILO Committee on Freedom of Association in 2008 concerned three decisions made by the National Labor Relations Board (NLRB), "the federal agency which has primary responsibility for interpreting and enforcing the NLRA, although the United States Supreme Court has final authority to decide over the meaning of statutory terms."[60] The way in which political appointments are made to the NLRB means that, during a Republican presidency, workers cannot expect decisions in their favor (Gross 1995, as cited in Swidorski 2003). For example, in 2004 the NLRB excluded new categories of workers from collective bargaining, such as graduate student employees.[61]

The NLRB also, in a trio of cases that has come to be known as the Oakwood Trilogy,[62] sought to further extend the definition of a "supervisor" under Section 2(3) of the NLRA. As the complainant union before the CFA, the American Federation of Labor and Congress of Industrial Organizations (AFL-CIO) observed that "the original NLRA, commonly known as the Wagner Act granted organizing and bargaining rights to supervisors in bargaining units separate from those of supervised employees. . . . But in 1947 a reactionary Congress stripped supervisors of these rights." The complaint did not, however, focus on the existence of the supervisor exclusion, which the complainant viewed as violating workers' freedom of association, but its extension by the NLRB to employees who possess only minor or sporadic oversight over coworkers, as little as 10% to 15% of the employee's work time. The decision of the NLRB had followed a decision of the U.S. Supreme Court that had set out a test determining when "supervisor status" should be applied to charge nurses (in which ILO standards were not mentioned at all),[63] while the lead case in the Oakwood Trilogy likewise concerned registered nurses, some of whom were charge nurses and others of whom took on charge roles on a rotational basis. Notably, the U.S. government defended the status quo by adopting a narrow interpretation of what would constitute freedom of association. The U.S. government noted that supervisors had a right to associate and could seek collective bargaining under the U.S. Constitution and the NLRA,[64] even if they were barred from protection from anti-union activity and employers could dismiss them and refuse to bargain with them with impunity. The CFA regarded the U.S. government's response as inadequate and considered that "the NLRB interpretation in the Oakwood trilogy" appeared to "give rise to an overly wide definition of supervisory staff that would go beyond freedom of association principles."[65] Further, the CFA noted that the lack of clarity in the definition of a supervisor "might lead to the exclusion of wide categories of workers from protection of their freedom of association rights, and to a clogging of the representation and collective bargaining process through an increase in appeals filed by employers with a view to challenging the status of employees in bargaining units."[66] The government was therefore requested "to take all necessary steps, in consultation with the social partners, to ensure that the exclusion that may be made of supervisory staff under the NLRA is limited to those workers genuinely representing the interests of employers."[67]

In a case concerning the exclusion of public sector workers from collective bargaining rights, the ILO CFA also had cause to express concern. A North Carolina general statute had declared any agreement or contract between the government of any city, town, county, other municipality, or the State of North Carolina and "any labor union, trade union or labor organization, as bargaining agent for any public employees" to be illegal and null and void.[68] Notably, this aspect of the statute was held by a three-judge panel of the federal district court to be constitutional, since there was nothing in the U.S. Constitution, including the First Amendment's right to associate freely, that compelled a party to enter into a contract with any other party, and the State of North Carolina was free to decide through the people's democratic representatives that they would not enter into such an agreement. Moreover, freedom of association for public sector employees was still protected in that they could still address, through the legislative process, issues that collective bargaining standardly addressed.[69]

In response to this assertion in the judgment given in *Atkins*, the CFA sought to emphasize "that the voluntary negotiation of collective agreement, and therefore the autonomy of the bargaining partners, is a fundamental aspect of the principles of freedom of association," but "while a legislative provision that would oblige a party to conclude a contract with another party would be contrary to the principle of free and voluntary negotiations, a legislative provision, such as [the relevant provisions of the North Carolina general statutes], which prohibits authorities and public employees, even those not engaged in the administration of the State, from concluding an agreement, even if they are willing to do so, is equally contrary to this principle."[70] Moreover, the CFA stressed the link between the right to form and join trade unions and actual access to collective bargaining: "[P]rovisions which ban trade unions from engaging in collective bargaining unavoidably frustrate the main objective and activity for which such unions are set up."[71]

Notably, in submissions made in both the 2007 and 2008 cases determined by the ILO CFA, the U.S. government sought to assert that the CFA lacked jurisdiction under the principles of international law to apply the elements of Convention Nos. 87 and 98 to the U.S., because the U.S. had not ratified either convention.[72] The U.S. has also stressed that it "has no formal obligations under the ILO Declaration on Fundamental Principles and Rights at Work and its Follow-up," as the latter "is a non-binding statement of principles."[73] In response to these submissions, the CFA has continued to assert "that, since its creation in 1951, it has been given the task to examine complaints alleging violations of freedom of association whether or not the country concerned has ratified the relevant ILO Conventions. Its mandate is not linked to the 1998 ILO Declaration—which has its own built-in follow-up mechanisms, but rather stems directly from the fundamental aims and purposes set out in the ILO Constitution."[74] In light of this continued assertion of ILO jurisdiction, it will also be interesting to see how the CFA responds to a further "mega-complaint" brought by the AFL-CIO concerning "the cumulative effect of NLRB decisions under the Bush administration," to be determined in the near future (Compa 2008:7). The state of U.S. law does not therefore seem to reflect either legislative or judicial respect for ILO standards regarding freedom of association. Nevertheless, there remains a glimmer of hope. For example, at a preliminary stage in the case of *Rodriguez et al. v. Drummond Co.*, relating to the applicability of the Alien Torts Claims Act, the judge denied the U.S.-based coal company's motion to dismiss the case:

> Although this court recognizes that the United States has not ratified ILO Conventions 87 and 98, the ratification of these conventions is not necessary to make the rights to associate and organize norms of customary international law. As stated above, norms of international law are established by general state practice and the understanding that the practice is required by law. . . . This court is cognizant that no federal court has specifically found that the rights to associate and organize are norms of international law for purposes of formulating a cause of action under the ATCA. However, this court must evaluate the status of international law at the time this lawsuit was brought under the ATCA. After analyzing "international conventions, international customs, treatises, and judicial decisions rendered in this and other countries" to ascertain whether the rights to associate and organize are part of customary international law, this court finds, at this preliminary stage in the proceedings, that the rights to associate and organize are generally recognized as principles of international law sufficient to defeat defendants' motion to dismiss.[75]

The key question is whether other U.S. judges will come to a similar realization and follow the example set by Canadian courts or will follow those in the U.K. It may be that, as Carl Swidorski has observed, the appealing aspect of a strategy aimed at realizing workers' human rights, including freedom of association, is not so much that there will be immediate judicial recognition of their importance and force, but rather that "it urges an ideological struggle to get workers to once again think of their labor, and the expression which accompanies organizing and defending it, as their rights as citizens in a democracy" (Swidorski 2003:79).

Conclusion

I have argued in this chapter that tensions between the individual and collective dimensions of freedom of association may be explained in terms of whether this entitlement can be categorized as a civil liberty, as a political right, or as socioeconomic in nature. Stark differences emerge depending on whether one views this freedom as a negative entitlement to be protected from intervention by the state or other social actors; as a democratic political right, which can be linked to meaningful participation in governance in the workplace or society at large; or as a means by which workers can make socioeconomic claims to a standard of living or a meaningful share in societal wealth.

If one views freedom of association as a civil liberty involving primarily individual choice to exercise contractual freedoms and autonomy from the state, protection of the right to disassociate would seem appropriate. Nevertheless, this does not mean that negative freedom of association must always be given the same weight as positive freedom of association. The argument presented here has been that the simple equation of a right *to* join a trade union and the right *not to* join a trade union is problematic because the effect of the two choices on other people may be quite different. Indeed, if freedom of association is viewed as a democratic and socioeconomic entitlement, it becomes possible to present arguments as to why a positive approach could prevail, at least in certain circumstances.

Further, freedom of association may best be understood as multifaceted, since a case can be made for workers that freedom of association can be claimed as a civil, political, *and* socioeconomic right. Indeed, so much follows from the notion that the state must respect, protect, and fulfill human rights. The obligation to "respect" human rights expresses the state's negative duty not to interfere with a person's legitimate exercise of their freedoms. The obligation of "protection" is linked to the state's duty to prevent human rights violations, including those committed by nonstate actors. These obligations are in turn fulfilled through the enactment and enforcement of legislation and other appropriate policy-based measures, including resource (re)allocation where appropriate. Just as freedom from torture cannot be guaranteed without state respect for the dignity of the individual; protection of that individual from the actions of the state's officials or other private persons; and fulfillment of these obligations by the provision of systems of training, deterrence, inspection, and enforcement, so too does this threefold understanding of states' obligations come into play with respect to the entitlement to freedom of association that workers claim. There is therefore no necessary barrier to the three species of claim being made in conjunction with one another.

The ILO provides an example of such an approach in practice. The outstanding question remains whether, given the limited influence of the ILO on domestic labor law and protection of human rights, legislatures and courts are interested in (and capable of) responding to such arguments. The survey provided here of Canadian, U.K., and U.S. domestic legal regimes suggests that a litigious human rights strategy for workers may not be the most successful in terms of gaining additional protection for participation by workers' organizations in collective bargaining. It is no doubt worth trying, but it may be that appreciation of the multifaceted arguments for workers' freedom of association is what is significant, and when fully understood, may provide a vital rallying cry for workers, such that they can address the representation gap that exists in all three countries, and elsewhere.

Acknowledgment

I am very grateful to Lance Compa and James Gross for their comments on a draft of this chapter.

The legal materials discussed are accurate as of 1 November 2008, the date the chapter was submitted for publication. Since then, there have been significant decisions by the European Court of Human Rights (ECtHR), especially in May 2009, which significantly change the ECHR jurisprudence on freedom of association.

Endnotes

[1] International Labour Organization (ILO), *Freedom of Association: Report and Draft Questionnaire* (1927) ILC, 10th Session, International Labour Office, Geneva, 12.

[2] Council Regulation (EC) No. 980/2005 of 27 June 2005 applying a scheme of generalized tariff preferences.

[3] *Case No. 102 (South Africa)*, 15th Report of the CFA (1955), paragraph 128; see also International Labour Organization 2006, paragraph 2. It should be noted, however, that under paragraph 8, "[t]he Committee's mandate is not linked to the 1998 ILO Declaration on Fundamental Principles and Rights at Work—which has its own built-in follow-up mechanisms—but rather stems directly from the fundamental aims and purposes set out in the ILO Constitution."

[4] See CEACR: Individual Observation concerning Convention No. 87, Freedom of Association and Protection of the Right to Organise, 1948 United Kingdom (ratification 1949), 2005, paragraph 1; and CEACR: Individual Observation concerning Convention No. 87, Freedom of Association and Protection of the Right to Organise, 1948 United Kingdom (ratification 1949), 2003, paragraph 1: "It recalls that unions should have the right to draw up their rules without interference from public authorities and so to determine whether or not it should be possible to discipline members who refuse to comply with democratic decisions to take lawful industrial action."

[5] Case No. 1698 (New Zealand), 292nd Report (1994), paragraph 726.

[6] Case No. 1698 (New Zealand), 295th Report (1994), paragraphs 253–8.

[7] *Young, James and Webster* v. *UK* (1982) 4 EHRR 38; most recently confirmed in *Application Nos. 52562/99 and 52620/99 Sørensen* v. *Denmark* and *Rasmussen* v. *Denmark*, judgment of the European Court of Human Rights, January 11, 2006.

[8] *J.B. et al* v. *Canada*, CCPR/C/28/D/118/1982.

[9] See, for example, *Concluding Observations on Lithuania*, 2004, UN document CCPR/CO/80/LTU, paragraph 17. See also *Concluding Observations on Chile*, 1999, UN document CCPR/C/79/Add. 104, paragraph 25.

[10] See U.S. Department of Labor, Bureau of Labor Statistics, *Union Membership in 2007*, at http://www.bls.gov/news.release/union2.toc.htm [September 1, 2008].

[11] It should be noted that this has not prevented criticism under ILO Convention No. 87. For example, see CEACR: Individual Direct Request concerning Freedom of Association and Protection of the Right to Organise Convention, 1948 (No. 87) Canada (ratification 1972) submitted 2006.

[12] Case No. 2314 (Canada–Quebec), 340th Report (2006), paragraph 432.

[13] Case No. 2467 (Canada–Quebec), 344th Report (2007), paragraph 577.

[14] Case No. 2467 (Canada–Quebec), 344th Report (2007), paragraph 577.

[15] Case No. 2467 (Canada–Quebec), 344th Report (2007), paragraph 587.

[16] Case No. 2430 (Canada–Ontario), 343rd Report (2006), paragraph 362.

[17] John Milloy, Minister of Training, Colleges and Universities: Statement to the Legislative Assembly, available at http://www.edu.gov.on.ca/eng/document/nr/08.06/hs0610b.html.

[18] Case Nos. 2166, 2173, 2180 and 2196 (Canada–British Columbia), 330th Report (2005), paragraphs 295–300.

[19] Case No. 2405 (Canada–British Columbia), 340th Report (2006), paragraph 452.

[20] Case No. 2405 (Canada–British Columbia), 340th Report (2006), paragraph 455.

[21] Case No. 2405 (Canada–British Columbia), 343rd Report (2006).

[22] See the chronology of events from 2001 available at http://bctf.ca/Advocacy/Campaigns/ChronologyOfLegislation.aspx.

[23] 2007 SCC 27 (the *Health Services* case).

[24] 2007 SCC 27, paragraph 35.

[25] *Reference re Public Service Employee Relations Act (Alta.)*, [1987] 1 S.C.R. 313 ("*Alberta Reference*"), *PSAC* v. *Canada*, [1987] 1 S.C.R. 424, and *RWDSU* v. *Saskatchewan*, [1987] 1 S.C.R. 460.

[26] "*Alberta Reference*" (see note 25), at 390–1.

[27] "*Alberta Reference*" (see note 25), at 411–2.

[28] "*Alberta Reference*" (see note 25), at 359.

[29] *Dunmore* v. *Ontario (AG)*, [2001] 3 S.C.R 1016.

[30] *Dunmore* v. *Ontario (AG)*, [2001] 3 S.C.R 1016, paragraphs 145–6, citing Complaint Against Ontario Report No. 308, Case No. 1900, vol. LXXX, 1997, Series B. No. 3.

[31] *Dunmore* v. *Ontario (AG)*, [2001] 3 S.C.R 1016, at paragraph 38. (Cited by Norman 2004.)

[32] *Health Services* case (see note 23), paragraph 22.

[33] *Health Services* case (see note 23), paragraph 30.

[34] *Health Services* case (see note 23), paragraph 77.

[35] *Health Services* case (see note 23), paragraphs 2 and 91.

[36] *Health Services* case (see note 23), paragraph 34.

[37] *Health Services* case (see note 23), paragraphs 2 and 91.

[38] ILO CEACR: Individual Observation concerning Convention No. 87 (UK), 2007. See also 2004.

[39] ILO CEACR: Individual Observation concerning Convention No. 98 (UK), 2007.

[40] Case No. 2383 (UK), 336th Report (2005), paragraphs 773 and 777, cited in *The Ministry of Justice* v. *POA* [2008] EWHC 239 (QBD) at paragraph 42.

[41] Criminal Justice and Public Order Act 1994, since amended by Criminal Justice and Immigration Act 2008.

[42] See Case No. 2437 (UK), 344th Report (2007).

[43] See Case No. 2437 (UK), 344th Report (2007), paragraph 1321.

[44] *Young, James and Webster* v. *UK* (1982) 4 EHRR 38; most recently confirmed in *Application Nos. 52562/99 and 52620/99 Sørensen* v. *Denmark* and *Rasmussen* v. *Denmark*, judgment of the European Court of Human Rights, January 11, 2006.

[45] Application No. 11002/05 (2007) IRLR 361.

[46] Application No. 11002/05 (2007) IRLR 361, paragraph 39.

[47] Application No. 11002/05 (2007) IRLR 361, paragraph 43.

[48] Case C–303/05 *European Parliament* v. *Council* (2006) E.C.R. I-5769, paragraph 38.

[49] Case C-499/04 *Werhof* v. *Freeway Traffic Systems GmbH & Co. KG* (2006) IRLR 400.

[50] Case C-499/04 *Werhof* v. *Freeway Traffic Systems GmbH & Co. KG* (2006) IRLR 400, at paragraph 33.

[51] Case C-438/05 *International Transport Workers' Federation (ITF) and Finnish Seamen's Union (FSU)* v. *Viking Line*, judgment of 11 December 2007 [2008] All E.R. (EC) 127; [2008] 1 C.M.L.R. 51; [2008] I.R.L.R. 143; Times, December 14, 2007 (hereafter *Viking*).

[52] Case C-341/05 *Laval un Partneri* v. *Svenska Byggnadsarbetareförbundet*, judgment of 18 December 2007 [2008] All E.R. (EC) 166; [2008] I.R.L.R. 160 (hereafter *Laval*).

[53] *Viking*, at paragraphs 42–4; *Laval*, at paragraphs 89–91.

[54] *Viking*, paragraphs 81–9; *Laval*, at paragraphs 103–11.

[55] *Viking*, paragraph 87.

[56] See, for example, the labor rights amendment in the U.S. Generalized System of Preferences (GSP), 19 U.S.C.A. § 2461 *et. seq*. Also U.S. trade agreements, available at http://www.ustr.gov. Cited by Compa, forthcoming.

[57] See also *Roberts* v. *US Jaycees*, 468 US 609 (1984).

[58] *NLRB* v. *Jones and Laughlin Steel Company*, 301 U.S.1 (1937).

[59] Case No. 1543 (U.S.), 278th Report (1991), paragraph 92.

[60] Case No. 2524 (U.S.), 349th Report (2008), paragraph 805.

[61] *Brown University*, 342 NLRB No. 42 (2004).

[62] *Oakwood Healthcare, Inc.*, 348 NLRB No. 37; *Croft Metal, Inc.*, 348 NLRB No. 38; and *Golden Crest Healthcare Center*, 348 NLRB No. 39 (October 2, 2006) are the cases referred to as the Oakwood Trilogy.

[63] *NLRB* v. *Kentucky River Community Care Inc.* 532 US 706.

[64] Case No. 2524 (U.S.), 349th Report (2008), paragraph 842.

[65] Case No. 2524 (U.S.), 349th Report (2008), paragraph 854.

[66] Case No. 2524 (U.S.), 349th Report (2008), paragraph 855.

[67] Case No. 2524 (U.S.), 349th Report (2008), paragraphs 856 and 858.

[68] Case No. 2460 (U.S.), 344th Report (2007), paragraph 946.

[69] *Atkins* v. *City of Charlotte*, 296 F.Supp 1068 (WDNC 1969). Discussed in Case No. 2460 (U.S.), 344th Report (2007), at paragraphs 954–63.

[70] Case No. 2460 (U.S.), 344th Report (2007), at paragraph 990.

[71] Case No. 2460 (U.S.), 344th Report (2007), at paragraph 991.

[72] Case No. 2460 (U.S.), 344th Report (2007), at paragraph 958; Case No. 2524 (U.S.), 349th Report (2008), paragraph 845.

[73] Case No. 2460 (U.S.), 344th Report (2007), at paragraph 958; and see in respect of U.S. government representations to similar effect in a case concerning freedom of association rights of migrant workers *(Hoffman)*, Case No. 2227 (U.S.), 332nd Report (2003), paragraph 578.

[74] Case No. 2524 (U.S.), 349th Report (2008), paragraph 846; Case No. 2460 (U.S.), 344th Report (2007), at paragraph 985; Case No. 2227 (U.S.), 332nd Report (2003), paragraph 600.

[75] *Rodriguez et al.* v. *Drummond Co.* (2003) 256 F.Supp. 1250. Cited in Compa, forthcoming.

References

Adams, Roy J. 2002. "Implications of the International Human Rights Consensus for Canadian Labour and Management." *Canadian Labour and Employment Policy Journal*, Vol. 9, no. 1, pp. 119–40.

Alkema, E. 1994. "Freedom of Associations and Civil Society." In Council of Europe, *Freedom of Association Proceedings*. Strasbourg: Council of Europe Press.

Alston, Philip. 2004. "'Core Labour Standards' and the Transformation of the International Labour Rights Regime." *European Journal of International Law*, Vol. 15, no. 3, pp. 457–521.

Bellace, Janice. 2001. "The ILO Declaration of Fundamental Principles and Rights at Work." *International Journal of Comparative Labour Law and Industrial Relations*, Vol. 17, no. 3, pp. 269–87.

Berlin, I. 1969. "Two Concepts of Liberty." In I. Berlin, ed., *Four Essays on Liberty*. Oxford: Oxford University Press.

Bryson, A., R. Gomez, M. Gunderson, and N. Meltz. 2005. "Youth–Adult Differences in the Demand for Union Organization: Are American, British and Canadian Workers All That Different?" *Journal of Labor Research*, Vol. 26, no. 1, pp. 155–67.

Caraway, Teri L. 2006. "Freedom of Association: Battering Ram or Trojan Horse?" *Review of International Political Economy*, Vol. 13, no. 2, pp. 210–32.

Compa, Lance. 2002. "Pursuing International Labour Rights in U.S. Courts: New Uses for Old Tools." *Industrial Relations*, Vol. 57, no. 1, pp. 48–76.

Compa, Lance. 2004. *Unfair Advantage: Workers' Freedom of Association in the United States under International Human Rights Standards* Ithaca, NY, and London: ILR Press, Cornell University Press.

Compa, Lance. 2008. "Coming Together for 'Human Rights.' " *International Union Rights*, Vol. 15, no. 2, pp. 6–7.

Compa, Lance. Forthcoming. "Legal Protection of Workers' Human Rights: Regulatory Changes and Challenges: The United States." In Colin Fenwick and Tonia Novitz, eds., *Human Rights at Work: Perspectives on Law and Regulation*. Oxford: Hart Publishing.

Davies, Anne. 2008. "One Step Forward, Two Steps Back? The *Viking* and *Laval* Cases in the ECJ." *Industrial Law Journal*, Vol. 37, no. 2, pp. 126–48.

Dworkin, Ronald. 1996. *Freedom's Law: The Moral Reading of the American Constitution*. Cambridge, MA: Harvard University Press.

Ewing, Keith. 2007. "The Implications of the *ASLEF* Case." *Industrial Law Journal*, Vol. 36, no. 4, pp. 425–45.

Ewing, Keith, and John Hendy. 2002. *A Charter of Workers' Rights*. London: Institute of Employment Rights.

Fudge, Judy. 2004. "'Labour Is Not a Commodity': The Supreme Court of Canada and the Freedom of Association." *Saskatchewan Law Review*, Vol. 67, no. 2, pp. 25–52.

Fudge, Judy. 2008. "The Supreme Court of Canada and the Right to Bargain Collectively: The Implications of the *Health Services and Support* Case in Canada and Beyond." *Industrial Law Journal*, Vol. 25, no. 1, pp. 25–48.

Gross, James A. 1995. *Broken Promise: The Subversion of US Labor Relations Policy, 1974–1994*. Philadelphia: Temple University Press.

Harcourt, Mark, and Helen Lam. 2006. "Freedom of Association, Freedom of Contract and the Right-to-Work Debate." *Employee Responsibilities and Rights Journal*, Vol. 18, no. 4, pp. 249–66.

Hayek, F. 1980. *Law, Legislation and Liberty: A New Statement of the Liberal Principles of Justice and Political Economy*. London: Routledge.

Hayek, F.A. 1984. *1980s Unemployment and the Unions: Essays on the Impotent Price Structure of Britain and Monopoly in the Labour Market* (2nd ed), London: Institute of Economic Affairs.

International Labour Organization. 2006. *Freedom of Association: Digest of Decisions of the Freedom of Association Committee of the Governing Body of the ILO* (5th rev. ed). Geneva: International Labour Organization.

Jenks, C. Wilfred. 1957. *The International Protection of Trade Union Freedoms*. London: Stevens.

Joseph, Sarah. Forthcoming. "UN Covenants and Labour Rights." In Colin Fenwick and Tonia Novitz, eds., *Human Rights at Work: Perspectives on Law and Regulation*. Oxford: Hart Publishing.

Kochan, Thomas A. 2003. "A US Perspective on the Future of Trade Unions in Britain." In Howard Gospel and Stephen Wood, eds., *Representing Workers: Union Recognition and Membership in Britain*. London: Routledge, pp. 166–77.

Leader, Sheldon. 1992. *Freedom of Association: A Study in Labor Law and Political Theory*. New Haven, CT/London: Yale University Press.

Long, Alex. 2007. "The Troublemaker's Friend: Retaliation against Third Parties and the Right of Association in the Workplace." *Florida Law Review*, Vol. 59, pp. 931–90.

Magrid, Julia Manning, and Jamie Darin Prenkert. 2004–5. "The Religious and Associational Freedoms of Business Owners." *University of Pennsylvania Journal of Labor and Employment Law*, Vol. 7, no. 2, pp. 191–224.

Mantouvalou, Virginia. 2006. "Servitude and Forced Labour in the 21st Century: The Human Rights of Domestic Workers." *Industrial Law Journal*, Vol. 35, no. 4, 395–414.

Marshall, T.H. 1950. *Citizenship and Social Class*. Cambridge: Cambridge University Press.

Norman, Ken. 2004. "ILO Freedom of Association Principles as Basic Canadian Human Rights: Promises to Keep." *Saskatchewan Law Review*, Vol. 67, no. 2, pp. 591–608.

Novitz, Tonia. 2003. *International and European Protection of a Right to Strike*. Oxford: Oxford University Press.

Novitz, Tonia. 2008. "Social Policy: Normative Power Europe at Work?" In J. Orbie, ed., *Europe's Global Role: External Policies of the European Union*. Aldershot: Ashgate, pp. 139–56.

Orbie, Jan. Forthcoming. "Core Labour Standards in Trade Policy: The GSP Regime of the European Union." In Colin Fenwick and Tonia Novitz, eds., *Human Rights at Work: Perspectives on Law and Regulation*. Oxford: Hart Publishing.

Pelling, Henry. 1936. *A History of British Trade Unionism*. Harmondsworth: Penguin.

Summers, Clyde. 1995. "Book Review: *Sheldon Leader, Freedom of Association: A Study in Labor Law and Political Theory*." *Comparative Labor Law and Policy Journal*, Vol. 16, no. 2, pp. 262–72.

Swidorski, Carl. 2003. "From the Wagner Act to the Human Rights Watch Report: Labor and Freedom of Expression and Association, 1935–2000." *New Political Science*, Vol. 25, no. 1, pp. 55–80.

Syrpis, Phil, and Tonia Novitz. 2008. "Economic and Social Rights in Conflict: Political and Judicial Approaches to Their Reconciliation." *European Law Review*, Vol. 33, no. 3, pp. 411–27.

Thomas, E.P. 1976. *Whigs and Hunters: The Origins of the Black Act*. London: Pantheon.

von Prondzynski, Ferdinand. 1987. *Freedom of Association and Industrial Relations: A Comparative Survey*. London: Mansell.

Wedderburn, Lord. 1989. "Freedom of Association and Philosophies of Labour Law." *Industrial Law Journal*, Vol. 18, no. 1, pp. 1–38.

CHAPTER 6

Prosecute, Prevent, Protect: Migrant Labor, Forced Labor, and Human Rights

REBECCA SMITH
National Employment Law Project

In the Dominican Republic, Haitian sugar-cane cutters are housed in deplorable living conditions, their labor rights ignored (Kennedy and Tilly 2001). In the United States, Indian "guest workers" live in sweltering labor camps, crowded 24 workers to a room, under curfew (Preston 2008).

In Ireland, a work permit regime for migrant workers that ties immigrant workers to one employer is criticized for leading to abuse of migrant workers (*Irish Independent* 2001). The same system exists in the United States and around the world.

In South Korea, despite a court ruling to the contrary, the government refuses to recognize a union because its members include unauthorized workers. In the United States, despite an international court ruling to the contrary, unauthorized workers illegally fired for union activities are not entitled to compensation.

One out of every 35 persons living on Earth is an international migrant (Global Commission on International Migration 2005). Nearly 200 million people (including migrant workers and their families, refugees, and permanent migrants) are now living permanently or temporarily outside of their country of origin, and at least 50% of these are economically active. The United States is home to some 20% of the world's migrants. Six to seven million of these are unauthorized immigrant workers. Another 155,000 are temporary guest workers in seasonal industries (U.S. Department of Homeland Security 2007).

A number of trends have meant both that companies can make huge profits by moving money and people around the globe and that, for increasing numbers of people, migration has become the only option for a better future. These include the traditional "push" and "pull" factors of poverty and war and the more recent militarization of borders. They also include newer economic and political developments that come under the heading of "globalization"—internationalization of financial markets, the increasing role of the International Monetary Fund and the World Trade Organization on governance policies, new technologies in communication and transportation, deregulation and privatization, and the surge in multinational corporations. At the same time that the pressure to migrate intensifies, governments have enacted restrictive immigration policies and harsher practices and penalties for violations of these laws. It has become at once more difficult, costly, and dangerous to migrate and impossible to stay home.

In the United States, as in many countries, would-be immigrants must choose between migrating illegally and taking their chances at living in the shadows engaging in low-paid, high-risk jobs, or entering the country as legal, temporary guest workers, often after paying huge "recruitment fees" to labor contractors that must be worked off in this country. While migration patterns, economic opportunities, and national laws vary greatly from country to country, migrants worldwide face eerily similar treatment: legal schemes that exclude them, whether they are lawfully or unlawfully present in a country, from labor protections; unregulated recruitment practices that force them into debt bondage; and temporary worker programs that deny workers the ability to change jobs or work toward permanent settlement in the host country. At the same time, tepid protection schemes and practices mean that abuses go unremedied and that victims of trafficking are left without recourse.

This paper represents a modest effort to gather the law and practices that would represent a more comprehensive protection scheme. I argue that migrant workers will continue to fall into situations of forced labor without, first, correcting imbalances in labor rights between migrants (both documented and undocumented), on the one hand, and nationals of a country on the other; second, without confronting three aspects of the guest worker program (unregulated labor brokers, the "single employer" rule, and the lack of a pathway to permanent residence in a country); and, third, without aggressive efforts to identify and protect victims of trafficking. The United States, which sees itself as a champion in the fight against slavery worldwide, must confront these causes of slavery at home in order to live up to its obligations under international law and to lead by example. Fortunately, models exist—in treaties, judicial pronouncements, and the approaches of some governments and migrant communities themselves—that policy makers within the United States and worldwide can consult, study, and adapt.

Current U.S. Policies and Practices

Treatment of Unauthorized Workers under the Law

The United States' highest court and various state courts have excluded unauthorized workers from employment rights and remedies available to their documented and U.S. citizen counterparts.[1] Discrimination against unauthorized workers has always been with us in practice, but discrimination in law was further fueled by a United States Supreme Court decision, *Hoffman Plastic Compounds, Inc.* v. *National Labor Relations Board,* in which the country's highest court limited unauthorized workers' right to an effective remedy for violation of their freedom of association.[2]

In *Hoffman*, the United States Supreme Court held that an unauthorized worker, fired in retaliation for participating in a union organizing campaign, was not entitled to the remedy of back pay (compensation for wages lost because of unlawful firing) under the National Labor Relations Act (NLRA) due to his immigration status. Although unauthorized workers are considered "employees" under the NLRA, after *Hoffman,* they are no longer entitled to back pay when illegally fired in retaliation for having exercised their right to freedom of association (unless they can show that they currently have lawful employment status; National Labor Relations Board General Counsel 2002). After *Hoffman,* the only remedies available when unauthorized workers are wrongfully terminated are the following: the employer who illegally fires an unauthorized worker may be ordered to post a notice at the workplace and may be told to "cease and desist" violating the law. There are no monetary remedies available to the unauthorized individual who suffers the retaliatory termination.

Though unauthorized workers have always been subject to arguments that they are without labor rights and to retaliation for claiming those rights, the impact of *Hoffman* has extended far beyond its narrow holding and created an explosion in litigation over migrant workers' rights. As a consequence, some states have relied on the *Hoffman* decision to sanction unequal treatment under other core labor and employment laws, by either eliminating or severely restricting state-law-based workplace protections for unauthorized workers. These include access to state workers' compensation for workplace injuries, protection from workplace discrimination, and entitlement to lost wages for injuries causing loss of work.[3] Under the current legal scheme, whether an unauthorized worker is entitled to the protection of a variety of labor rights depends largely on the law of the state in which he or she is employed.

Lack of formal remedies, coupled with the "enforcement only" approach to migration that is exemplified in the tenfold increase in workplace immigration raids, with many of them carried out in military-like fashion, and with subsequent criminal prosecutions of migrants, have pushed increasing numbers of unauthorized workers underground. Policies and practices that focus on immigrants as criminals rather than victims of crime are sure to miss exploitative situations. Perhaps the clearest recent example of this dynamic is the May 2008 immigration raid at Agriprocessors, at the time the largest raid in the history of the United States. Of the some 600 workers arrested in Postville, Iowa, 306 were turned over to the U.S. Attorney's office to face criminal charges for working with false papers, including Social Security fraud and identity theft (Leopold 2008). At the time, Agriprocessors was under investigation by at least three state and federal labor agencies, and the Immigration and Customs Enforcement agency (ICE) knew this. In fact, in a section of the warrant application used to gain entry into the plant, an ICE agent cites repeated serious health and safety and wage and hour violations as evidence, not that workers may have been victims of labor trafficking, but that the company may be guilty of harboring unauthorized workers (Hoagland 2008). Rather than interview the workers as potential victims of trafficking, ICE chose to prosecute them.

Treatment of Guest Workers under the Law

There are currently two guest worker programs for temporary work lasting less than a year in the U.S.: the H-2A program, for temporary agricultural work, and the H-2B program, for temporary nonagricultural work. In 2007, the United States issued about 155,000 H-2B visas and about 87,000 H-2A visas, primarily to Mexicans, though the number of guest workers from other, non-Spanish-speaking countries is on the rise.

Many of these workers face abuse before they ever leave home. Labor contractors and recruiters may impose significant fees, ranging from $500 to well over $10,000, on workers as a condition of gaining access to the job-applicant pool in the foreign country (Southern Poverty Law Center 2007). They may charge high interest rates for lending the money to pay those fees. They may threaten that family members in the home country will be harmed if the participating worker does not comply with the recruiters' demands. They may also threaten the worker inside the U.S. with dire consequences if the worker challenges unfair or illegal conduct during the employment.

Workers have little recourse to recover these fees. While courts have ruled that H-2A and H-2B workers are entitled to the protection of the Fair Labor Standards Act (covering minimum wage and overtime pay) and that certain recruitment fees and travel costs must be repaid by employers at the beginning of employment to the extent that they reduce wages below the minimum wage, the U.S. Department of Labor (DOL) has refused to enforce the rulings, leaving vulnerable workers to attempt to recover these costs on a case-by-case, court-by-court basis.[4]

Once workers arrive in the United States, promises of steady work at lucrative wages frequently go unmet, with many workers kept idle, particularly at the beginning or end of the season. Nor are guest workers entitled to safety-net benefits such as unemployment compensation or Social Security benefits. For employees injured at work, workers' compensation benefits are often cut off when they return to their home countries. Even worse, in the case of death of an employee, many individual state statutes provide for payment of lower amounts of survivors' benefits to family members living outside the United States.

These violations of the guest worker contract often go unremedied, for a number of reasons. Like guest workers in other countries, H-2A and H-2B workers are allowed to work only for the employer that sponsors their visa. If a job is lost, so too is the right to remain in the United States. The common practice of withholding passports, though illegal, serves to ensure that workers stay put. Many workers find the potential consequences of a complaint, which include not only job loss and loss of a visa, but potentially loss of the deed to a home, too high a price to pay.

Further, there is frequently no one to complain to: U.S. DOL takes the position that it cannot legally enforce the contractual rights of guest workers. Efforts of nonprofit organizations that operate transnationally cannot meet the enforcement need.[5] Rather than making efforts either legislatively or administratively to strengthen its administrative powers, DOL has recently proposed rules that would exacerbate its weaknesses, by reducing its level of oversight and continuing a disavowal of an enforcement role for itself (U.S. Department of Labor, Employment and Training Administration 2008a, 2008b). Nor are most guest workers entitled to the assistance of legal aid lawyers: except in the context of H-2B reforestation workers, H-2B workers are explicitly denied the right to representation by no-cost lawyers under the Legal Services Corporation Act.

Trafficking in Forced Labor and the U.S. Response

Migrants can be taken advantage of or be subjected to exploitation by those who facilitate their journey. Many migrants or their families who cannot repay their debts are forced into slave-like working conditions and life-long debt or bondage. Others may become targets of human traffickers who force them to toil in sweatshops, fields, brothels or construction sites and to live under inhumane conditions (International Red Cross 2007).

In the United States and around the world, the situation of migrant workers, both lawfully and unlawfully present in the country of employment, is almost by definition one of forced labor, marked by coercion, deception, confinement, exploitation, and, frequently, violence. Cases of forced labor and debt bondage have been chronicled by many sources, ranging from the Central Intelligence Agency to the Southern Poverty Law Center (Knudsen 2005; McKee 2005; Nam 2007; Richard 2000; Southern Poverty Law Center 2007). The unauthorized construction worker or domestic worker, often dependent on the employer for both housing and employment, isolated by language and geography, and kept working by the implicit or explicit threat of deportation, is easy prey for an employer who is disinclined to comply with labor laws. In many guest worker programs, the lack of visa portability, putting control of workers' immigration status in the hands of the employer, combined with exploitation in recruitment and subcontracting, leaves workers extremely vulnerable.

The U.S. Department of State estimates that 800,000 people are trafficked across international borders annually (U.S. Department of State 2008). The International Labour Organization (ILO) estimates that, at any given time, there are 12.3 million people in forms of involuntary servitude worldwide (International Labour Office 2005a). Of these, estimates of numbers of workers trafficked into the United States vary from a low of 14,500 to a high of 50,000 per year (U.S. Department of State 2008).

In various statutes, the United States has long pledged not only to end slavery but to eradicate its "badges and incidents" (McKee 2005). Toward that end, in 2000, Congress passed key legislation—the Trafficking Victims Protection Act of 2000 (TVPA)—that provides for prosecution, prevention, and protection of victims of trafficking within the United States. The TVPA included broad definitions of trafficking, including debt bondage and involuntary servitude. It also created new trafficking-related crimes based in part on these expanded definitions (18 U.S.C. §§ 1589–1594). It provided that a victim of trafficking would be eligible to remain in the United States, under a newly created T visa, if he or she (1) were a victim of a severe form of trafficking, (2) had complied with any reasonable request for assistance in investigation or prosecution (or was under 18); and (3) would suffer extreme hardship if removed from the country. Social benefits are available to provide a safety net while victims recover. The TVPA also provides a U visa for survivors of crime who have suffered substantial physical or mental abuse and have been helpful or are likely to be helpful in prosecuting the crime. In 2003, the statute was amended to include a private right of action for victims of trafficking, after advocates noted than only a few hundred victims per year were being offered T visas.

After nearly a decade, the numbers of victims who receive T and U visas has remained low, with fewer than 300 T visas issued in 2007 (U.S. Department of State 2008). To date, no U visas have been issued.

Critics point out a number of shortcomings in the law. Foremost is that law enforcement tends to view trafficking victims only in the context of the stereotypical—a female worker, literally sold into work for the purposes of prostitution (as one commentator put it, "chained to a bed in a brothel"; Haynes 2007). The broad, nuanced, continuum represented by what is regarded only as "smuggling" on the one hand (in its simplest case, where a worker pays to be guided across international boundaries and does not remain in the control of the smuggler) and "trafficking" on the other (the stereotypical case of sexual slavery) often escapes law enforcement's understanding. In a number of cases, law enforcement has declined to prosecute cases unless there was an actual physical barrier preventing the workers' escape (Kim 2007).

Second, within these stereotypical cases, the linkage to prosecution means that law enforcement tends to see as victims only those whom law enforcement itself has rescued. The U.S. Department of Justice has also taken the position that victims of trafficking must be processed as deportable aliens by ICE before any interview to determine whether they are victims of trafficking. This relatively new requirement, which is very intimidating and has potentially serious ramifications for the victim, has undoubtedly prevented some trafficked people from reporting their cases to the Department of Justice.

The reluctance of victims to come forward may also be related to the juxtaposition of large-scale immigration raids against a protectionist scheme. As exemplified in the Agriprocessors raid, ICE does not screen potential victims of trafficking who are picked up in immigration raids, even when it knows that labor abuse is being investigated at a workplace. Victims arrested in a raid may face detention and deportation, rather than help with visa applications, should they come forward. Victims who have not been "rescued" by law enforcement but instead identified by nongovernmental organizations must engage in a complicated dance with the Department of Homeland Security to ensure that they can make their applications without being exposed to detention.

Third, prosecutions under the TVPA have been overwhelmingly against sex traffickers as opposed to labor traffickers. The focus of labor trafficking prosecutions has not been on large corporations who, directly or through labor recruiters, subject workers to debt bondage and forced labor; instead they have targeted individual homeowners or small businesses.

As a recent example of this narrow view of the law, Indian welders employed as guest workers for Signal International, based in Pascagoula, Mississippi, left their jobs and filed litigation in March 2008. The workers claimed that they had been forced to work through force, fraud, and coercion. The guest workers were charged recruitment fees of up to $20,000 and were housed in closely guarded, overcrowded labor camps. They faced aggressive retaliation when they organized to defend themselves against what they viewed as illegal activity (Preston 2008; Rosenbaum 2008). Despite pleas by members of Congress and the amassing of reams of evidence in their case, nearly a year after reporting the trafficking crimes, the Department of Justice has continued to refuse to grant them "continued presence," or the temporary right to remain in the United States as victims of trafficking.

Finally, particularly in a post-9/11 world, there are political pressures to treat smuggling and trafficking as distinct phenomena, with the vast majority of immigrants treated as lawbreakers rather than victims (Anderson and O'Connell Davidson 2003). The Signal workers were subject to surveillance by ICE officials as they engaged in a "truth tour" in support of their cause, traveling from Louisiana to Washington, DC (Bureau of National Affairs 2008).

As part of the TVPA, the United States took on a role of monitoring anti-trafficking efforts worldwide. In a yearly report, the U.S. State Department reviews the indicia of trafficking, conducts case studies worldwide, makes recommendations for "best practices," and grades countries on their performance. The report is an invaluable tool and contribution to anti-trafficking efforts.

However, there is a disconnect between the State Department's recommendations and the practices of law enforcement, including those of ICE, within the U.S. For example:

- The State Department criticizes countries that focus on the voluntary nature of transnational movement and that do not see undocumented workers as potential victims of transnational organized crime.
- The State Department recommends that destination countries have systems in place to screen workers, in order to identify victims of

trafficking before they are deported for immigration violations. However, the United States has no such screening system.

- While the State Department identifies debt bondage for foreign temporary workers as a form of trafficking, the Department of Labor refuses to follow court rulings that would serve to cancel these debts.

- The State Department identifies confiscation of documents as a trafficking tool, but the U.S. has never prosecuted a major employer for document confiscation.

Law and Practice: What Can the U.S. Learn from the International Community?

Prevention of slavery and forced labor are the first principles of international human rights law. The 1815 Declaration Relative to the Universal Abolition of the Slave Trade was the first international human rights instrument, issued in condemnation of the trans-Atlantic slave trade. It was further refined in two League of Nations Conventions in 1926 and 1930, the latter of which added a prohibition on forced labor, and in a series of ILO Conventions; it made the Universal Declaration of Human Rights a feature of the ICCPR; and is recognized in a number of regional instruments, such as the American Declaration of Human Rights, the American Convention, and the European Convention. More recently, the modern versions of slavery were addressed in the UN Transnational Organized Crime Convention and its protocols on smuggling and trafficking (Weissbrodt and Anti-Slavery International 2002).

The United States has recognized the primacy of anti-slavery efforts in international law in the preamble to the TVPA (18 U.S.C. 7101(b)(23)). If the U.S. and other countries are committed to eradicating slavery, all emblems of slavery, and all of its forms in the world, they must adopt the best practices that exist worldwide in anti-trafficking conventions and policies. But countries must also go further, as I hope this modest review of experiences has shown. If, as the State Department has said in its annual report on trafficking, there is a strong correlation between forced labor and policies that exclude groups of workers from the protection of labor laws, then the U.S. and other countries must have a more comprehensive response. States must take more seriously other human rights principles, including those that outlaw discrimination and that provide for labor rights such as free access to employment, and apply these principles against their policies toward unauthorized workers and in guest worker programs. With respect to exclusions of both unauthorized workers and guest workers from core labor protections, states are bound by ratification of particular treaties, as elaborated in judicial pronouncements, to remove such exclusions. Finally, states, including the United States, must look seriously not only at substantive law but at the best practices that have emerged as part of the worldwide debate on migration.

The Principle of Nondiscrimination and Its Implications for Labor-Migration Policies

Principles of international law, including several instruments signed and ratified by the United States, offer protection for migrant workers with respect to a destination country's labor laws. Most instruments, either explicitly or through interpretation, make no distinction between the rights of migrants in either regular or irregular situations on the one hand and nationals of a country on the other. For example, the International Covenant on Civil and Political Rights (ICCPR), is open-ended; it prohibits discrimination based on race, color, sex, language, religion, political or other opinion, national or social origin, property, birth, or other status. The United States is directly bound by the ICCPR, having ratified the treaty in 1992. Of specific relevance to migrant workers, the ICCPR protects equality before the law in Articles 2 and 26, protects freedom of association and trade union rights in Article 22, and prohibits slavery and forced labor in Article 8.

Similarly, the International Covenant to End Racial Discrimination (ICERD) guarantees a range of civil, political, economic, social, and cultural rights to all persons without discrimination. In its General Recommendation No. 30 on Discrimination Against Non-Citizens (2004), the Committee on the Elimination of Racial Discrimination (CERD) observed that states are obligated under the ICERD to guarantee equal treatment between citizens and noncitizens, with limited exceptions allowed for some political rights, such as the right to vote and stand for election. Differential treatment based on citizenship or immigration status is allowed under the ICERD only if it pursues a legitimate aim and is proportional to achievement of that aim.

Recent court pronouncements in both U.S. and international forums have interpreted principles of nondiscrimination in a way that makes it clear that labor rights of migrant workers must be equivalent to those of a country's nationals. In September 2003, the Inter-American Court of Human Rights issued a landmark advisory opinion on the juridical condition and rights of unauthorized immigrants. The court held that "the migratory status of persons can never constitute a justification in depriving them of the enjoyment and exercise of their human rights, including those related to work." The court found that international principles of equal protection and nondiscrimination, including those contained in the American Declaration, the American Convention, the Organization of American States Charter, and the ICCPR prohibit discrimination, in that case against unauthorized immigrants, with respect to their labor rights (Inter-American Court of Human Rights 2003).

The court's advisory opinion followed an ILO Committee on Freedom of Association case, in which the committee concluded that a Spanish law that provided that foreigners could exercise trade union rights only "when they obtain authorization of their stay or residence in the country" violated the fundamental right to freedom of association (International Labour Office 2001). The committee confirmed in the Spain case that Article 2 of Convention No. 87 "recognize[s] the rights of all workers, without distinction whatsoever, to establish and join organizations of their own choosing," with the only permissible exception relating to the armed forces and police (International Labour Office 2001).

Subsequent to the ILO and Inter-American Court decisions, South Korean courts have also dealt with this issue.[6] A High Court decision handed down on February 1, 2007, called for government recognition of the Migrant Workers' Trade Union. The case arose when the South Korean government rejected calls for the formation of a migrant workers' trade union. The Ministry of Labor rejected the migrant workers' application for union status and demanded the list of members (including unauthorized workers from Bangladesh, Nepal, Vietnam, the Philippines, Sri Lanka, and Indonesia), arguing that irregular migrant workers did not qualify as workers under South Korean law. A lower court upheld the ministry's rejection of the permit, but on appeal the High Court overturned the decision, recognizing the right of unauthorized immigrants to form a union. The ministry appealed to the Supreme Court and a decision is expected sometime in 2009. On March 25, 2009, the governing body of the ILO adopted a report made by the Committee on Freedom of Association supporting the rights of the workers to form and join labor unions and asking the government to end arrests and deportations that interfere with labor rights (Amnesty International 2007; Goss 2008; *Illegal Aliens Can Form Unions, High Court in Seoul, Korea, Has Ruled* 2007; International Labour Office 2009).

In its earlier advisory opinion, the Inter-American Court reiterated the principle that discrimination is allowable only if it is both legitimate and narrowly tailored, but the court did not elaborate on the kinds of discrimination that it would consider legitimate and proportional. However, a 2004 English House of Lords judgment relied on the nondiscrimination principles of the ICERD and ICCPR in finding unlawful discrimination in the U.K.'s racial profiling of Roma immigrants at

Prague Airport, after a high number of Czech nationals sought asylum at the airport and were subjected to longer and more intrusive questioning than others there.[7] That opinion confirms that the standard for justifying unequal treatment under the ICERD and the ICCPR is higher than the "rational basis" standard that American lawyers are familiar with: the House of Lords indicated that governmental recitation of even the fight against terrorism as a basis for unequal treatment would not justify discrimination (*Regina* v. *Immigration Officer at Prague Airport* 2004).

The developing international law around discrimination has obvious implications for the unwillingness of the U.S. and other countries to grant full labor rights to unauthorized workers and guest workers, at least in the context of freedom of association, wage and hour laws, and compensation for injuries and for discrimination. Further, the definition of "discrimination" as articulated broadly in treaty and judicial decisions might be extended to require countries to allow guest workers to change jobs freely or to work toward residency status, especially given the potential for labor trafficking inherent in the systems. It remains to be seen whether a state's objective to protect its national workforces and labor markets would justify treating guest workers with less than adequate protections.

The Siliadin Case, Forced Labor, and the Right to Seek Employment Freely

In 2005, the European Court of Human Rights issued a landmark decision finding that a Togolese domestic worker in Paris had been subjected to both forced labor and involuntary servitude at the hands of her employers (*Siliadin* v. *France* 2005). Brought to France by her father to perform domestic labor, then transferred to a second employer, Ms. Siliadin worked as many as 15 hours per day for the family. Her work went essentially unpaid. Her papers were confiscated by her employer, who had promised that her immigration status would be regularized. The Paris Court of Appeal, an intermediate court, had acquitted the defendants of the criminal offense of not paying Siliadin on the grounds that she had some "autonomy" in her situation (Mantouvalou 2006).

The court found that Ms. Siliadin had been subjected both to forced labor and to involuntary servitude. The European and ILO Forced Labour Conventions provide that forced or compulsory labor is work "exacted . . . under the menace of any penalty" and also performed against the will of the person concerned, that is work for which the person "has not offered himself voluntarily." The court found sufficient "menace of penalty" in that Siliadin "was an adolescent girl in a foreign land, unlawfully present on French territory and in fear of arrest by the police. Indeed, Mr and Mrs B. [Siliadin's employers] nurtured that fear and led her to believe that her status would be regularized" (*Siliadin* v. *France* 2005:paragraph 118).[8]

The *Siliadin* case has some potential to broaden the international community's understanding of forced labor and its broad application to many common immigrant worker situations. While the court did not explicitly say so, it indicated that the fact that Ms. Siliadin was undocumented and fearful of arrest, coupled with her employer's assurances of regularization of status, perhaps even apart from her age and absent severe violations of labor standards, may be sufficient to show that a worker has been subjected to forced labor; that is, even subtle exploitations of a worker's vulnerabilities may constitute sufficient coercion to amount to forced labor. If the understanding of forced labor is, as the *Siliadin* ruling suggests, broad enough to include false immigration status–related promises or threats made to a worker who is by definition vulnerable because of his or her precarious immigration position, the case has potential to significantly broaden the protections of anti-slavery laws. Although the TVPA is arguably open to the same interpretation, thus far U.S. courts have not been willing to extend the definition of "involuntary servitude" that far.[9]

Further, like the discrimination decisions noted above, *Siliadin* may also have some implications for further articulating the CERD's Article 5 right to "free choice of employment," in the context of guest worker programs. While such programs may not lead inevitably to forced labor, the fact that workers in the program have no option to leave their employment might violate human rights principles of forced labor or free choice of employment. *Siliadin* represents some forward movement in understanding the complexity of migration pressures and in overcoming the tendency to treat all unauthorized workers as "consenting" to their situation.[10]

Migration and Labor in the International Community: The Context for Debate

In recent years, many international bodies have turned their attention to the potential and the challenges of migration. A Global Commission on International Migration (GCIM) set up by the governments of Sweden and Switzerland to place migration on the global agenda presented recommendations to then–UN Secretary General Kofi Annan in 2005. The following year, Secretary Annan issued his own report and recommendations on migration, appointed a Special Representative on International

Migration, and convened a High Level Dialogue on Migration and Development in September 2006 in New York. The dialogue was followed by the first meeting of the Global Forum on Migration in Brussels, Belgium, in 2007, with a second meeting in Manila in 2008 and a third meeting in Greece in 2009.

While the records of these meetings, reports, and recommendations frequently include practices that would end labor discrimination against migrant workers and promote protection against forced labor, they focus on migration from a trade-based standpoint, often centering on agreements between governments for the temporary movement of workers and on the potential for migration to contribute to development of both sending and receiving countries, rather than placing the human rights of migrants at center stage. The UN's Special Representative has said he believes that the international discussion on migration is more usefully approached from an "economic, rather than rights-based" criteria (Sutherland 2006:3). Given the chronic unwillingness of migrant-receiving countries to enter into binding multilateral obligations such as the Migrant Workers Convention, this approach may have merit. Yet the frame leaves little room for discussion of the treatment of migrant workers in a way that addresses their developing rights under international law and the steps that governments can take to guarantee their rights. Groups operating on the ground, working with migrants in both sending and receiving countries, who are in a position to see the dire needs and daily human rights abuses, have not been fully incorporated into this process.[11]

The efforts that offer up the most useful practices emerge from the work of the ILO, because of its traditional focus on human rights as a central focus of migration discussions. The Conference of the ILO has adopted a plan focused on the 86 million migrant workers in the global economy (International Labour Office 2004). It has developed a non-binding multilateral framework on labor migration, which along with promoting decent work at home, so that the pressure to migrate is reduced, emphasizes equality of treatment for migrants and nationals (Article V, Section 8); promotes effective labor inspection schemes, including sanctions for violations of workers rights and legal services to assist in proceedings (Article V, Section 10; Article VI, Section 11); and calls for licensing, supervision, and regulation of private employment agencies (Article VI, Section 13; International Labour Office 2006). It has developed manuals to guide a country's decision making on combating forced labor and on establishing effective labor migration policies, directed toward protection of human rights (International Labour Office 2005b; International Labour Office et al. 2006). The ILO has repeatedly called on the international community to incorporate migrant organizations themselves into its policy development (International Labour Office 2007).

Model Practices: Trafficking and the Council of Europe Response

As the international community became more aware of the modern form of the slave trade and especially of the involvement of organized crime in exploitation of women and children, it developed new instruments to combat it. In 2000, 148 countries gathered in Palermo, Italy, to open the UN Convention against Transnational Organized Crime. Eighty countries drafted two new protocols for dealing with trafficking and smuggling. The Trafficking Protocol, which came into force on December 23, 2003, offers an internationally agreed-upon definition of trafficking (Article 3, Section a)—"recruitment, transportation, transfer, harbouring or receipt of persons, by means of the threat or use of force or other forms of coercion, of abduction, of fraud, of deception, of the abuse of power or of a position of vulnerability or of the giving or receiving of payments or benefits to achieve the consent of a person having control over another person, for the purpose of exploitation" (United Nations 2000). It further defines exploitation as the "exploitation of the prostitution of others or other forms of sexual exploitation, forced labour or services, slavery or practices similar to slavery, servitude or the removal of organs" (United Nations 2000) While its wording differs slightly from the United States' TVPA, it generally covers the same ground and raises some of the same questions.

The UN protocol is an advance over the TVPA in that it expressly provides that consent of a victim of trafficking to exploitation is irrelevant, when any of enumerated means (coercion, abduction, fraud, deception, abuse of power, etc.) were used. While the U.S. State Department has said that consent is irrelevant under the TVPA, in practice cases involving the individual's initial consent have not generally been viewed as "trafficking" cases. Perhaps because of its origins as an amendment to the transnational crime protocol, like the TVPA, the Trafficking Protocol is written from a perspective of *prosecution* of crime, rather than *protection* of human rights or labor rights (Zalewski 2005). As a consequence of this perspective, the protocol recommends, but does not require, that states provide care, support, and relief from deportation to victims (Kapur 2005).

These flaws were corrected in the Council of Europe's Convention on Action against Trafficking in Human Beings, which entered into force on February 1, 2008. The convention breaks new ground in emphasizing protection of victims of trafficking. In particular, it delinks protective visas for victims of trafficking from criminal prosecution of traffickers.

The 14 states that have thus far ratified the convention agree to criminalize trafficking, but they also commit to ensuring that a mechanism is in place for the accurate identification of trafficked persons. Under the convention, trafficking victims are granted time to recover and are offered medical care, counseling, education for their children, housing, and a suitable standard of living, regardless of whether they agree to participate in any proceedings the authorities may decide to pursue against those responsible for their ordeal. The states offer victims access to redress, including provisions for corporate liability for trafficking.

Most importantly, Article 14 provides that each party shall issue a renewable residence permit to victims, in one or other of the two following situations or in both: the competent authority considers that their stay is necessary owing to their personal situation; or the competent authority considers that their stay is necessary for the purpose of their cooperation with the competent authorities in investigation or criminal proceedings.

Two of the biggest flaws in the UN Protocol and in the TVPA are thus corrected in the Council of Europe's Convention: access to a visa is made nearly mandatory, and the high burden of cooperation in prosecution—a burden that many victims are not able to meet since cooperation could jeopardize the lives of themselves or their family members—is lifted.

Model Practices

Labor inspection. As noted, under international law, workers' immigration status should be irrelevant to their protection under core labor standards (UN Secretary-General 2006; UN Committee on the Protection of the Rights of All Migrant Workers and Members of Their Families 2006; Global Forum on Migration and Development 2007b). Ensuring, through labor inspection and appropriate screening of migrant workers as victims of labor abuse or trafficking, that such standards are met is a complementary, necessary, and no-less-crucial undertaking.

Experience on enforcement of labor standards in the United States has shown that workers are best able to enforce their rights when they have two complementary means of enforcement: access to an active enforcement agency and to the right to sue privately in their own name. This is true because when budgetary shortfalls or lack of will prevent agencies from protecting workers, a private right of action means that individuals may continue to assert their claims. But if private litigation is the only route, lack of access to lawyers prevents many low-wage workers from enforcing their own rights.

Access to agency enforcement is limited in the United States as it is elsewhere in the world. In its simplest terms, adequate labor inspection is a question of staffing. The ILO recommends a ratio of one inspector per 10,000 workers in industrial market economies (International Labour Office et al. 2006). At present, the U.S. Department of Labor's Wage and Hour Division has one inspector per 110,000 workers in the country (Smith and Ruckelshaus 2007). A recent Government Accountability Office (GAO) review of the division concludes that the DOL is not effective and calls for strong measures to reverse this trend (U.S. Government Accountability Office 2008). A series of case studies by the GAO paint a chilling picture of the Wage and Hour Division's response to worker complaints, including instances where the division inappropriately rejects complaints, fails to adequately investigate complaints, and neglects investigations until it is too late. The general GAO report finds that overall Wage and Hour Division enforcement dropped by more than one third in the period 1997 to 2007, and it admonishes the DOL for not keeping adequate and very basic data on incoming complaints, not using its commissioned study to target and enhance its effectiveness, and failing to confer with external groups, such as worker advocates and the states. The ILO's recommendations for adequate labor inspection systems include a recommendation for consultation with both employer and worker groups (International Labour Office et al. 2006).

In terms of private enforcement, international law, including the ICCPR, the Universal Declaration of Human Rights, and a number of regional instruments to which the United States is a party, require that workers have unimpeded access to the courts and legal assistance. The Organization of American States' OC-18 advisory opinion emphasized that American states are obliged to ensure effective protection of the law, including access to the services of lawyers. To meet this obligation, the United States must ensure that unauthorized workers and all H-2B guest workers are eligible for legal aid.

Regulation of labor intermediaries. Costs imposed on laborers for the "privilege" of working abroad can place laborers in a situation highly vulnerable to debt bondage. When combined with exploitation by unscrupulous labor agents or employers in the destination country, these costs or debts, when excessive, can become a form of debt bondage (U.S. Department of State 2008).

As more migrants are hired through profit-making recruitment agencies worldwide and as complaints of debt bondage have proliferated, a number of UN and other agencies have struggled with the role of private recruitment agencies. Both the GCIM report and the UN's Committee on Migrant Workers have cited lack of regulation of these agencies as a hurdle to protection of migrant workers, and the ILO calls dependence of migrants on private intermediaries a major factor behind forced labor.

It recommends regulation of labor intermediaries as a primary means of combating labor trafficking (Global Commission on International Migration 2005; UN Committee on the Protection of the Rights of All Migrant Workers and Members of Their Families 2006; International Labour Office 2005b). The U.S. Department of State advocates that they be criminally punished (U.S. Department of State 2008).

These recruiters must be regulated, but experience has shown that they cannot be adequately regulated without placing responsibility on the employers who use them. As noted earlier, in the U.S. advocates have sought to make employers liable for the excessive recruitment fees charged to workers, with limited success. There exists no system of oversight of foreign recruiters, and, as noted, the DOL takes the position that it cannot enforce H-2B workers' contracts.[12]

In the Philippines, recruiters are jointly liable with employers for protection of migrants' rights and working conditions (Global Forum on Migration and Development 2007b). In that country, recruitment agencies must be licensed, bonded, and subject to direct enforcement of contracts by workers, and they must disclose the identity and biography of each of their recruiters (International Labour Office 2005b; International Labour Office et al. 2006). Up to 90% of all overseas Filipino workers are deployed by licensed recruiters and staffing agencies, of which there are some 1,400 operating in the Philippines (Global Forum on Migration and Development 2007b).

To ensure compliance, the ILO recommends a system of monitoring labor recruiters that includes records inspection and physical inspection, publicizing lists of recruiters who have been sanctioned or blacklisted, and a thorough review of workers' contracts both prior to signature and during employment (International Labour Office et al. 2006). Licensing systems also exist in Pakistan, Israel, and Russia.

Countries vary in their approaches to recruitment fees. In the Philippines, these are allowed up to the sum of one month's pay. In India, low-skilled workers may be charged up to $45 US. In Canada, intermediaries such as labor recruiters are excluded from the overseas recruitment process: there are no recruitment fees, workers are selected directly from the field, and they are processed by the Canadian Embassy. Employers are obligated to cover the up-front travel costs (Global Forum on Migration and Development 2007b).

Each of these approaches presents its own challenges in terms of governance and monitoring, adequate funding for monitoring, and choices to be made between government-operated recruitment systems and privately operated, licensed systems. Advocates in the Philippines have criticized their system for its lack of adequate oversight and funding (Center for Migrant Advocacy 2008). But each presents a model worth further study in order to ban the debt-bondage-inducing system that now pervades guest worker programs.

The role of NGOs. Just as they do in establishing migration labor policies, nongovernmental organizations, such as trade unions and worker centers, have a pivotal but underappreciated role in monitoring labor abuse, guarding against forced labor and slavery. Diaspora organizations, made up of migrant workers themselves, exist in many countries. They have first-hand experience of the major labor and immigration abuses that workers face on a daily basis. These groups are in the best position to supplement government-provided orientations and to know what policies will provide the best protection for migrant workers before, during, and after their journeys. As organizations that workers trust, they are in the best position to provide orientation to workers both before their departure and in their destination countries, to negotiate and monitor fair contracts, and to identify abusive employment agencies and those involved in trafficking.

Migrant information or resource centers are a useful conduit for migrants and others to better inform themselves prior to going abroad, lack of information also having been identified as a contributor to forced labor (International Labour Office et al. 2006). In a number of countries, including the Philippines and Guatemala, worker centers overseas dispense information, advice, counseling, skills upgrading, and help to stranded migrants, particularly women (Global Forum on Migration and Development 2007b).

The Migrant Forum in Asia is one example of a cross-border network devoted to advancing the human rights of migrant workers in both sending and receiving countries. The forum, with members in Bangladesh, Hong Kong, India, Indonesia, Korea, Malaysia, and the Philippines, works on many levels to protect workers' rights. Many of its member groups operate as migrant centers, much like worker centers in the United States, and they are connected to workers in both sending and receiving countries. The forum operates an active e-mail listserv where members can share issues, actions, and strategies. Working from a base in migrant communities, it is able to develop, across borders, best human rights policies and practices.

Here in the United States, both major agricultural unions, the United Farm Workers (UFW) and the Farm Labor Organizing Committee, have organized agricultural guest workers. The UFW recently signed an agreement with the Mexican State of Michoacan, which has a long history of migration to states in the western United States (United Farm Workers' Union 2008). Under the agreement, UFW and the State of Michoacan will exercise joint oversight of the H-2A recruitment process to ensure that workers are not charged recruitment fees, and workers will be connected to the UFW to present grievances for their treatment within the U.S. (Ferris 2008).

For its part, the Farm Labor Organizing Committee has had an agreement since 2004, with the North Carolina Growers Association, covering some 7,000 H-2A guest workers and 800 growers in the southern part of the United States. A recent renewal of the contract eliminates recruitment fees and incorporates a seniority provision, as well as continuing the existing grievance procedure that guarantees workers' voice at the work site.

Recently, Mexican guest workers present in Canada under the Seasonal Agricultural Workers Program won a union contract that guarantees them a grievance procedure and a right to be recalled each season based on seniority. The contract also contains language to protect workers from being evicted from their employer-owned lodgings or expelled from Canada until their case is heard by an independent arbitrator, one year after the Manitoba Labor Board certified the union election (UFCW Canada 2008). In South Korea and in Germany, respectively, trade unions have incorporated migrant workers into their ranks and conducted know-your-rights campaigns directed toward unauthorized workers.

Conclusion

As it is currently practiced, globalization has meant displacement of millions of families worldwide. In this context—with so many human beings working outside their countries of origin and so many of them delivered into situations of wage exploitation, discrimination, and retaliation should they speak up about it—the need to protect the human rights of migrant workers in countries of destination is as urgent and compelling as it is daunting. Systems that create unequal labor rights for unauthorized workers and guest workers are ready-made for modern-day slavery. Most well-intentioned governmental efforts to combat involuntary servitude and debt bondage have not addressed either the causes or the effects of forced labor in a comprehensive way that incorporates labor protections, adequate screening and labor inspection systems, and adequate protection of victims. Nevertheless, in just a few years, judicial decisions, models of worker organizing, and covenants have developed that can, with more study and development, create a level playing field for migrant workers. The task for U.S. policy makers and advocates alike is to look both within and beyond our borders for the practices that move toward migration as a choice freely engaged in and undertaken by workers who have a full voice at work in the global economy.

Endnotes

[1] I use the term "unauthorized" worker to describe immigrant workers who do not possess authorization to be employed pursuant to U.S. law. This group includes workers who are in the United States legally for various reasons (holders of student visas, asylum applicants, etc.) but who nevertheless lack authorization to work. The term "undocumented" immigrant, a more common but less precise term, is often used to describe immigrants whose presence in the U.S. is illegal. These workers form a subset of the immigrant population that is unauthorized to work. Most relevant court decisions are based on the presence or absence of work authorization.

[2] 535 U.S. 137 (2002). See also National Labor Relations Act, 29 U.S.C. § 157 (2006).

[3] *Crespo* v. *Evergo Corp.*, 366 N.J. Super. 391 (App. Div. 2004), cert. denied, *Crespo* v. *Evergo Corp.*, 180 N.J. 151 (2004), holding that an unauthorized worker suing for discriminatory termination could not recover either economic or non-economic damages absent egregious circumstances during the period of employment such as extreme sexual harassment. See *Sanchez* v. *Eagle Alloy, Inc.*, 254 Mich. App. 651 (Mich. Ct. App. 2003), cert. denied, *Sanchez* v. *Eagle Alloy, Inc.*, 471 Mich. 851 (Mich. 2004), finding that unauthorized workers are covered by Michigan's workers compensation law and are entitled to full medical benefits if injured on the job but that their right to wage-loss benefits ends at the time that the employer "discovers" they are unauthorized to work; *Reinforced Earth Co.* v. *Workers' Compensation Appeal Board (Astudillo)*, 570 Pa. 464 (2002), holding that although an unauthorized worker is entitled to medical benefits after experiencing a workplace injury, illegal immigration status might justify terminating workers compensation benefits for temporary total disability; *Rosa* v. *Partners in Progress, Inc.*, 152 N.H. 6 (2005), holding that an unauthorized worker asserting a tort claim for workplace injury could recover lost wages only at the wage level of his country of origin unless he could prove his employer knew about his irregular immigration status at the time of hiring; *Balbuena* v. *IDR Realty LLC*, 6 N.Y. 3d 338 (N.Y. 2006), holding that immigration status can be a factor to reduce benefits received by an unauthorized worker's family in a wrongful workplace death claim; *Ramroop* v. *Flexo-Craft Printing*, 896 N.E. 2d 69 (N.Y.Ct. Apps. June 26, 2008).

[4] Compare *Arriaga* v. *Fla. Pac. Farms*, 305 F.3d 1228, 1231 (11th Cir. 2002); *Avila-Gonzalez* v. *Barajas*, 2006 U.S. Dist. LEXIS 9727 (M.D. Fla. Mar. 2, 2006); *Rivera* v. *Brickman Group, Ltd.*, 2008 U.S. Dist. LEXIS 1167 (E.D. Pa. Jan. 7, 2008) with *Close to Slavery*, at 30 (Southern Poverty Law Center 2007). In the waning days of the Bush administration, the Department of Labor issued rules that would have overruled these decisions, but that interpretation of the law is currently under review by the Obama administration. See U.S. Department of Labor, Employment and Training Administration, Wage and Hour Division, "Withdrawal of Interpretation of the Fair Labor Standards Act Concerning Relocation Expenses Incurred by H-2A and H-2B Workers," *Federal Register*, Vol. 74, no. 57, p. 13261 (March 26, 2009).

[5] In a Freedom of Information Act response, Connie Klipsch, regional administrator, Employment Standards Administration, Atlanta Regional Office, U.S. DOL, to Ivy Hernandez (January 9, 2008) stated, "I regret to inform you that in fact this agency does not have jurisdiction over the H2B visa program under the Immigration Reform and Control Act of 1986. Your request should have been directed to Department of Homeland Security." At least two nonprofit organizations, the Global Workers

Justice Alliance and the Centro de los Derechos del Migrante, coordinate U.S. lawyers' attempts to represent clients who have already returned home, but the need for legal services is much greater than their present capacity.

[6] A court judgment in South Korea in 2007 held that unauthorized workers who are already on the job must be considered "laborers" under that country's trade union and labor relations adjustment act and held that the union involved, Migrant's Trade Unions of Seoul, Gyeonggi and Incheon Region, could not condition the establishment of the union on MTU's submission of a list of the names of its members. Appeal is pending to the Supreme Court (Goss 2008; *Illegal Aliens Can Form Unions, High Court in Seoul, Korea, Has Ruled* 2007).

[7] *Regina* v. *Immigration Officer at Prague Airport,* ex parte European Roma Rights Center (cited in Cholewinski 2008).

[8] With respect to "servitude," the court said that case law had established that this means an obligation to provide one's services that is imposed by the use of coercion. The court said that her work was not voluntary because she had not chosen it in the first instance. It relied on the facts that Ms. Siliadin was a minor without resources, she had no other accommodation, her papers had been confiscated and she had been promised regularization of her status, and she was rarely permitted to leave the house.

[9] In a pre-TVPA case, the Ninth Circuit Court of Appeals said, for example, "We recognize that economic necessity may force persons to accept jobs that they would prefer not to perform or to work for wages they would prefer not to work for. Such persons may feel coerced into laboring at those jobs. That coercion, however, results from societal conditions and not from the employer's conduct. Only improper or wrongful conduct on the part of an employer subjects him to prosecution. To illustrate this point further, an employer who truthfully informs an individual that there are no other available jobs in the market, merely provides an opportunity for a person to work for low wages, or simply takes advantage of circumstances created by others is not guilty of an offense" *U.S.* v. *Mussry,* 726 F.2d 1448 (9th Cir. 1984).

[10] One writer has also analyzed guest worker programs in the context of the Thirteenth Amendment's prohibition of slavery, saying, in much the same way as the European Court did, "a highly textured understanding of the realities faced by deported immigrants reveals that quitting is an unacceptable option" (Ontiveros 2007:927–8) and that the visa programs, from an economic standpoint, exert the same downward pressure on "free" wages that were present in slavery systems.

[11] The approach has left some international migrant rights organizations and some countries wondering how this new frame will advance the human rights of migrants. They view with dismay the Secretary-General's failure to include in his report a recommendation that governments ratify the Migrant Workers Convention (United Nations Non-Governmental Liaison Service 2006). Advocates view critically as well the GFMD relative noninclusiveness, in which civil society is relegated to a separate event preceding the meetings of the Global Forum, with a separate report (UN Non-Governmental Liaison Service 2006; Global Forum on Migration and Development 2007a).

[12] The department does not claim that it lacks authority to enforce H-2A contracts, but advocates have found its oversight of that program lacking as well. In regulations that took effect on January 18, 2009, the department states that it now believes it does

have the authority to protect workers in the H-2B program under their contracts. See U.S. Department of Labor, Employment and Training Administration, "Labor Certification Process and Enforcement for Temporary Employment in Occupations Other Than Agriculture or Registered Nursing (H-2B Workers)," *Federal Register*, Vol. 73, no. 245, 78020 at 78047, and 20 C.F.R. §655.60.

References

Amnesty International. 2007. *South Korea: Crackdown Against Migrants' Trade Union,* December 3. <http://www.amnesty.org/en/library/asset/ASA25/007/2007/en/dom-ASA250072007en.html>. [April 20, 2009].

Anderson, Bridget, and Julia O'Connell Davidson. 2003. *Is Trafficking in Human Beings Demand Driven? A Multi-Country Pilot Study.* IOM Migration Research Series No. 15. <http://www.compas.ox.ac.uk/about/publications/Bridget/Anderson04.pdf?event=detail&id=2932>. [September 5, 2008].

Bureau of National Affairs. 2008. "Immigration: Guestworkers Seek 'Continued Presence' to Participate in DOJ Trafficking Investigation." *Daily Labor Report,* June 12, p. 5. <http://subscript.bna.com/SAMPLES/wil.nsf/85256269004a991e8525611300214487/20aef77070ab80b7852574670080f1b4?OpenDocument>. [September 5, 2008].

Center for Migrant Advocacy. 2008. *The Philippines: A Global Model on Labor Migration?* Third Dr. Alfredo J. Ganapin Advocacy Forum Series, September 19.

Cholewinski, Ryszard. 2008. "The Human and Labor Rights of Migrants: Visions of Equality." *Georgetown Immigration Law Journal,* Vol. 22, no. 2 (winter), 177–219.

Ferris, Susan. 2008. "UFW Signs Pact with Mexican State for Guest Workers on U.S. Farms." *Sacramento Bee,* April 18, p. A4. <http://www.sacbee.com/101/story/871903.html>. [September 5, 2008].

Global Commission on International Migration. 2005. *Migration in an Interconnected World: New Directions for Action* (October). <http://www.gcim.org/en/finalreport.html>. [September 5, 2008].

Global Forum on Migration and Development. 2007a. *Final Report on the First Session of the Global Forum on Migration and Development* (Brussels, July 9–11, 2007). <http://www.gfmd-fmmd.org/en/press-release/publication-final-report-first-session-global-forum-migration-and-development>. [September 17, 2008].

Global Forum on Migration and Development. 2007b. *Report of the Civil Society Day of the Global Forum on Migration and Development.* (Brussels, July 9–11, 2007). <www.gfmd2007.org/downloads/EN_MigraDev.pdf>. [April 20, 2009].

Goss, William. 2008. Migrant Forum in Asia, Manila, Philippines. E-mail exchange with the author. July 17, 2008.

Haynes, Dina Francesca. 2007. "(Not) Found Chained to a Bed in a Brothel: Conceptual, Legal and Procedural Failures to Fulfill the Promise of the Trafficking Victims Protection Act." *Georgetown Immigration Law Journal* Vol. 21, no. 3 (spring), 337–81.

Hoagland, David M. 2008. *Enforcement Affidavit and Application for a Search Warrant in the Matter of Agriprocessors, Inc., and/or Neval Properties.* Case No. 08-MJ-110 (N.D. Iowa, May 8, 2008).

Hoffman Plastic Compounds, Inc. v. *National Labor Relations Board,* 535 U.S. 137 (2002).

Illegal Aliens Can Form Unions, High Court in Seoul, Korea, Has Ruled. 2007. February 2. <http://www.digitaljournal.com/article/105113>. [September 17, 2008].

Inter-American Court of Human Rights. 2003. "Juridical Condition and Rights of the Undocumented Migrants." Commission on Human Rights Advisory Opinion, Report No. 18/03, OEA/Ser. A., doc. 18. <http://www.corteidh.or.cr/docs/opiniones/seriea_18_ing.pdf>. [September 5, 2008].

International Labour Office. 2001. Committee of Freedom of Association, Report No. 326 (Vol. LXXXV, 2002, Series B, No. 1), Spain, ¶561 (Case No. 2121 of March 23).

International Labour Office. 2004. *Towards a Fair Deal for Migrants in the Global Economy, International Labor Conference,* 92nd Session. <www.ilo.org/public/english/standards/relm/ilc/ilc92/pdf/rep-vi.pdf>. [April 20, 2009].

International Labour Office. 2005a. *A Global Alliance against Forced Labour.* Geneva: International Labour Organization. <http://www.yaleglobal.yale.edu/pdfs/globalalliance.pdf>. [April 20, 2009].

International Labour Office. 2005b. *Trafficking for Forced Labour: How to Monitor the Recruitment of Migrant Workers* (training manual). <http://www.ilo.org/sapfl/Informationresources/ILOPublications/lang—en/docName—WCMS_081894/index.htm>. [September 5, 2008].

International Labour Office. 2006. *Multilateral Framework on Labour Migration: Non-binding Principles and Guidelines for a Rights-Based Approach to Labour Migration.* TMMFLM/2005/1/(Rev.). Geneva: International Labour Office.

International Labour Office, International Organization for Migration, and Organization for Security and Co-operation in Europe. 2006. *Handbook on Establishing Effective Labour Migration Policies in Countries of Origin and Destination.* <http://www.osce.org/item/19187.html>. [September 5, 2008].

International Labour Organization. 2007. *The Quest for a Fair Globalization Three Years On: Assessing the Impact of the World Commission on the Social Dimension of Globalization.* Geneva: International Institute for Labour Studies.

International Labour Office, Governing Body. 2009. *Sixth Item on the Agenda, 353rd Report of the Committee on Freedom of Association.* <http://www.ilo.org/wcmsp5/groups/public/——ed_norm/——relconf/documents/meetingdocument/wcms_104130.pdf>. [April 20, 2009].

International Red Cross. 2007. 30th International Conference of the Red Cross and Red Crescent (Geneva, November 26–30, 2007). p. 17. <http://www.icrc.org/web/eng/siteeng0.nsf/htmlall/30-international-conference-working-documents-121007/$File/30IC_5-1_Obj1_ChallengesBackground_ENG_FINAL.pdf>. [September 18, 2008].

Irish Independent. 2001. "Immigrant Workers Being Exploited, Warn Unions." April 2. <http://www.unison.ie/irish_independent/stories.php3?ti=41&ca=9&si=394880&issue_id=4221>. [September 17, 2008].

Kapur, Ratna. 2005. "Travel Plans: Border Crossings and the Rights of Transnational Migrant." *Harvard Human Rights Journal,* Vol. 18, pp. 107–38 (Spring).

Kennedy, Marie, and Chris Tilly. 2001. "Haiti in 2001: Political Deadlock, Economic Crisis." *Dollars and Sense,* November 1. <http://www.thirdworldtraveler.com/Haiti/Haiti_2001.html>. [September 17, 2008].

Kim, Kathleen. 2007. "Psychological Coercion in the Context of Modern-Day Involuntary Labor: Revisiting *United States* v. *Kozminski* and Understanding Human Trafficking." *University of Toledo Law Review,* Vol. 38, no. 3 (spring), pp. 941–72.

Knudsen, Tom. 2005. "The Pineros: Men of the Pines." *Sacramento Bee,* November 13–15. <http://www.sacbee.com/static/content/news/projects/pineros/c1/>. [September 17, 2008].

Leopold, David Wolfe. 2008. *On Behalf of the American Immigration Lawyers Association Before the Subcommittee on Immigration, Citizenship, Refugees, Border Security, and International Law Committee on the Judiciary United States House of Representatives Hearing on the Arrest, Prosecution, and Conviction of Undocumented Workers in Postville, Iowa from May 12 to 22*. July 24.

Mantouvalou, Virginia. 2006. "Servitude and Forced Labour in the 21st Century: The Human Rights of Domestic Workers." *Industrial Law Journal*, Vol. 35, no. 4 (December), pp. 395–414.

McKee, Kathleen. 2005. "Modern-Day Slavery: Framing Effective Solutions for an Age-Old Problem." *Catholic University Law Review*, Vol. 55, no. 1 (fall), pp. 141–91.

Nam, Jennifer. 2007. "The Case of the Missing Case: Examining the Civil Right of Action for Human Trafficking Victims." *Columbia Law Review*, Vol. 107, no. 7 (November), pp. 1655–701.

National Labor Relations Board General Counsel. 2002. "Procedures and Remedies for Discriminatees Who May Be Unauthorized Aliens after *Hoffman Plastic Compounds, Inc.*" July 19. <http://www.lawmemo.com/nlrb/gc02-06.htm>. [September 17, 2008].

Ontiveros, Maria L. 2007. "Noncitizen Immigrant Labor and the Thirteenth Amendment: Challenging Guest Worker Programs." *University of Toledo Law Review*, Vol. 38, no. 3 (spring), pp. 923–39.

Preston, Julia. 2008. "Workers on Hunger Strike Say They Were Misled on Visas." *New York Times*, June 7. <http://www.nytimes.com/2008/06/07/washington/07immig.html>. [September 4, 2008].

Regina v. Immigration Officer at Prague Airport. 2004. Opinions of the Lords of Appeal for Judgment in the Cause. UKHL 55. <http://www.publications.parliament.uk/pa/ld200405/ldjudgmt/jd041209/roma-1.htm>. [April 20, 2009].

Richard, Amy O'Neill. 2000. *International Trafficking in Women to the United States: A Contemporary Manifestation of Slavery and Organized Crime*. U.S. Central Intelligence Agency, Center for the Study of Intelligence. <https://www.cia.gov/library/center-for-the-study-of-intelligence/csi-publications/books-and-monographs/trafficking.pdf>. [September 17, 2008].

Rosenbaum, Jennifer. 2008. New Orleans Worker Center for Racial Justice, New Orleans, Louisiana. E-mail exchange with the author, September 16.

Siliadin v. France. App No 73316/01, Judgment of 26 July 2005 ([2005] ECHR 545).

Smith, Rebecca, and Catherine Ruckelshaus. 2007. "Solutions, Not Scapegoats: Abating Sweatshop Conditions for All Low-Wage Workers as a Centerpiece of Immigration Reform." *New York University Journal of Legislation and Public Policy*, Vol. 10, no. 3 (October), pp. 555–602.

Southern Poverty Law Center. 2007. *Close to Slavery: Guestworker Programs in the United States*. <http://www.splcenter.org/pdf/static/SPLCguestworker.pdf>. [September 17, 2008].

Sutherland, Peter. 2006. *Global Challenges, Global Responses? Migration and Development*. Brussels: European Policy Center. October 12.

UFCW Canada. 2008. *Ratification of UFCW Canada First-Contract at Manitoba Farm Historic Breakthrough for Migrant Workers*. June 23. <http://www.ufcw.ca/Default.aspx?SectionId=af80f8cf-ddd2-4b12-9f41-641ea94d4fa4&LanguageId=1&ItemId=7a46affd-9f50-40a4-9ccf-d3b917af6fa0>. [September 17, 2008].

United Farm Workers' Union. 2008. *Agreement with the State of Michoacan*. <http://www.ufw.org/_board.php?mode=view&b_code=org_key_back&b_no=4640>. [September 17, 2008].

United Nations. 2000. *Protocol to Prevent, Suppress and Punish Trafficking in Persons, Especially Women and Children, Supplementing the United Nations Convention against Transnational Organized Crime.* <untreaty.un.org/english/notpubl/18-12-a.E.doc>. [April 20, 2009].

United Nations Committee on the Protection of the Rights of All Migrant Workers and Members of Their Families. 2006. *Contribution by the High-level Dialogue on Migration and Development of the General Assembly.* Item 54(b), delivered to the General Assembly, U.N. Doc. A/61/120 (July 3). <http://www2.ohchr.org/english/bodies/cmw/docs/CMW.C.4.CRP.2.pdf>. [September 17, 2008].

United Nations Office of the High Commissioner for Human Rights. 2004. *General Recommendation No.30: Discrimination Against Non-Citizens.* <http://www.unhchr.ch/tbs/doc.nsf/(Symbol)/e3980a673769e229c1256f8d0057cd3d?Opendocument>. [April 20, 2009].

United Nations Non-Governmental Liaison Service. 2006. *Non-Governmental Organizations Response to the Secretary-General's Report, Migration and Development.* A/60/871. Geneva: United Nations.

United Nations Secretary-General. 2006. *Report of the Secretary-General on International Migration and Development.* Item 54(c), delivered to the General Assembly, U.N. Doc. A/60/871. <http://www.un.org/Docs/journal/asp/ws.asp?m=A/60/871>. [September 17, 2008].

U.S. Department of Homeland Security. 2007. *Yearbook of Immigration Statistics.* Table 25. <http://www.dhs.gov/ximgtn/statistics/publications/YrBk07NI.shtm>. [April 20, 2009].

U.S. Department of Labor, Employment and Training Administration. 2008a. "Proposed Rule, Labor Certification Process and Enforcement for Temporary Employment in Occupations Other Than Agriculture or Registered Nursing in the United States (H–2B Workers), and Other Technical Changes." *Federal Register,* Vol. 73, no. 100 (May 22), pp. 22941–75.

U.S. Department of Labor, Employment and Training Administration. 2008b. "Proposed Rule, Temporary Agricultural Employment of H-2A Aliens in the United States; Modernizing the Labor Certification Process and Enforcement." *Federal Register,* Vol. 73, no. 30 (February 13), pp. 8537–85.

U.S. Department of State. 2008. *Trafficking in Persons Report.* <http://www.state.gov/documents/organization/105501.pdf>. [September 2, 2008].

U.S. Government Accountability Office. 2008. *Department of Labor: Case Studies from Ongoing Work Show Examples in Which Wage and Hour Division Did Not Adequately Pursue Labor Violations.* GAO-08-973T (July 15). <http://www.gao.gov/new.items/d08973t.pdf>. [September 17, 2008].

Weissbrodt, David, and Anti-Slavery International. 2002. *Abolishing Slavery and Its Contemporary Forms.* New York and Geneva: United Nations. <http://www.antislavery.org/homepage/resources/Weissbrodt%20report%20final%20edition% 202003.pdf>. [September 18, 2008].

Zalewski, Anna. 2005. "Migrants for Sale: The International Failure to Address Contemporary Human Trafficking." *Suffolk Transnational Law Review,* Vol. 9, no. 1 (winter), pp. 113–38.

CHAPTER 7

Human Rights and Sustainability: A Corporate Perspective

EDWARD E. POTTER
MARIKA MCCAULEY SINE
The Coca-Cola Company

One of the most important social phenomena resulting from the spread of capitalism, democracy, and market economics has been the recognition of global, immutable human rights, driven principally through treaties and declarations of the International Labour Organization and the United Nations. A principal catalyst has been the dominant economic and political position played by the United States in the post–World War II world community.

However, the mindset of American business on human rights since the 1950s has been complex. Business leaders have been proponents of free markets, the rule of law, adherence to the laws of the countries in which they operate, and the application of their workplace best practices globally. But they also have consistently taken the position that their internal workplace practices should reflect the normal legislative and regulatory process of the country in which they operate and should not be imposed by treaty. In particular, upholding internationally recognized human rights based on declarations and treaties has not been viewed as part of business activity. In our view, this is not a position on which global U.S. business can hope to survive and thrive in today's globalized economy.

Notwithstanding the substantial overall economic gains in the last century, we live in a world of vast economic inequality and social diversity. The difference in income per head between the richest industrial and the poorest non-industrial nation today is about 400 to 1 (Landes 1998). Two hundred fifty years ago, the gap between the richest and poorest countries was around 5 to 1, and the difference between Europe and South Asia was about 2 to 1 (Bairoch 1979). At the extremes, the gap is still growing, and some countries continue to grow poorer in absolute terms (De Long 2004).

181

Meanwhile, today's world is increasingly interconnected and increasingly more complex. Falling trade barriers, instant communications, relatively fast and inexpensive transportation, and rapidly changing technologies are shaping the world economy. More recently, rising energy, food, and commodity costs; higher levels of consumer consumption; and increased urbanization have built further stresses into the global economy.

As a consequence of these global dynamics, it has become clear that many pressing social problems, ranging from lack of respect for human rights to adequate food supply and high food prices to climate change, are beyond the capacity of any sector or nation to solve in isolation. The emerging consensus is that cross-sector international collaboration, creativity, and courage will be required to address these major global problems.

In this context, the 21st century brings a new set of expectations to international business. It is no longer sufficient to provide a quality product or service. Today, expectations of business are broader, and social dynamics are inextricably linked to business success. For a business to maintain quality and its license to operate, make a profit, minimize burdensome regulation, serve consumers, and obey the law, it must address the following social expectations.

First, business should help enhance the sustainability of the communities it serves. Leading companies understand that if the communities they serve are not sustainable, the business itself will not be sustainable. Companies must devise sustainability strategies linked to their core business and capabilities in order to enhance their license to operate in communities and to garner the trust and goodwill of business partners and consumers both locally and worldwide. Their sustainability strategies must meet the needs and objectives of the business and its shareholders while simultaneously enhancing the factors driving community-level business success.

Second, any successful sustainability strategy must build on the aligned efforts of the business as well as relevant government and civil society actors as the key to accelerating sustainable development. It is in businesses' interest to harness the collective resources and skills of other sectors in order to address the social issues that are barriers to continued business success. To effectively address the world's most pressing problems, these efforts need to capitalize on the comparative advantages that civil society, government, and business can each bring to the table.

And third, a successful business must be—in both perception and reality—a functioning part of every community in which it operates. In the 21st century, successful companies are genuinely and routinely engaged in the public debate in the communities where they do business. Particularly for global companies, this engagement helps preserve their vital license to operate, building trust and goodwill, and helps ensure that businesses address risks and opportunities at the community level in a timely manner.

Business and Human Rights

Human rights are universal and indivisible—their realization enables a wide range of social goods, including freedom, wealth, opportunity, and equality. Governments have a duty to uphold their citizens' rights as reflected in national laws and regulations. And yet many countries are failing to uphold this responsibility, largely as a result of inadequate labor inspection, judicial systems, or budgetary resources.

Beginning in the early 1990s, media, civil society, and social investors began pressing companies to step into this void by providing social compliance systems for their global supply chains. Ever since, companies have faced practical and institutional barriers in substituting themselves for the labor inspection and enforcement role of governments. Nevertheless, the primary accountability remains with government to protect its citizens and enforce the law.

The debate about the role of business in addressing human rights is following the same pattern as the environmental debate, which began in earnest 20 years ago. Companies are moving from denial of responsibility for human rights to signing the United Nations Global Compact commitment to human rights principles and adopting codes of conduct, supplier standards, and social compliance activities. Moreover, companies are increasingly realizing that good human rights practice can be a source of competitive advantage, and they are reaching across industries to build cross-sector solutions to human rights issues. Businesses increasingly understand that positively impacting human rights is in the interest of their employees, the communities in which they operate, and their own bottom line.

Historical Perspective

The foundation of today's human rights doctrine and international law is the Universal Declaration of Human Rights (UDHR), unanimously adopted by the members of the United Nations on December 10, 1948. At a fundamental level, it clarified for the first time the internationally accepted rights that all people could consider indivisible and interdependent.

To further codify the declaration, the United Nations in 1966 adopted two covenants that now enjoy almost universal ratification worldwide—the International Covenant on Civil and Political Rights (http://www2.ohchr.org/english/law/ccpr.htm) and the International Covenant on Economic, Social and Cultural Rights (http://www.unhchr.ch/html/menu3/b/a_cescr.htm). Together, these three landmark documents make up what is considered the International Bill of Human Rights. They encompass traditional labor and employment rights, along with a wide range of other rights.

These human rights documents were targeted toward states—and, indeed, states remain the organs of society responsible for ratifying the covenants and for reflecting their standards in national law. Although the UDHR calls on "every organ of society" to strive to respect rights and to contribute to ensuring their universal recognition and enjoyment, until the 1980s there was very little focus on the role of business in respecting human rights.

In 1984, one of the world's worst industrial disasters took place in Bhopal, India, raising a wide range of new questions about businesses' obligations to the health and safety of workers and the remuneration of victims of industrial accidents. Civil society and student campaigns on divestment from South Africa on the issue of apartheid also began gaining traction in the mid-1980s. Civil society took its arguments against apartheid straight to American companies' shareholder meetings, forcing discussions about complicity and the responsibilities of foreign business operations in states violating human rights. By 1988, more than 170 American companies had sold their holdings in South Africa (Paul 1988).

The 1990s saw a growing intensity of the debate among the media, companies, and civil society on human rights issues. In many cases, companies were perceived as more powerful than states, and society began to ascribe to companies the responsibilities that had in the past been limited to states. Most often, working conditions in the developing-country supply chains of major multinationals came into question in circumstances where governments were unable or unwilling to enforce their own labor laws.

In the absence of government action to uphold human rights, businesses began to self-regulate to act in their own defense. Nike, Reebok, Levi Strauss, and Gap, Inc. were among the retailers first pushed by media and civil society campaigns to address the complex issue of low labor standards in the developing world. When these multinational companies began to look into labor conditions in their supply chains, they found that many of their suppliers' workplaces had standards far below their own and far below what most Western consumers would consider acceptable.

Particularly in countries in which the state was unwilling or unable to uphold its own labor laws, multinationals like these found themselves in the difficult position of having to assess and enforce human rights standards in their suppliers' workplaces. As a result, these companies adopted codes of conduct and supplier standards and they created processes to monitor supplier performance. These early codes drew primarily on standards of the International Labour Organization (ILO) as their fundamental underpinning. In particular, these codes reflected ILO standards encompassing freedom of association, collective bargaining, discrimination, forced labor, and safety and health. As a consequence, human rights began to find its way into business practice—serving as a useful, internationally recognized, defensible set of standards against which companies could assess their business partners.

These early social compliance efforts were largely focused on sending auditors to supplier workplaces to conduct assessments against the company's code. Business used a tool it was familiar with—auditing—to enforce its social compliance rules. These efforts largely fall into what corporate responsibility expert Simon Zadek calls the second stage of corporate responsibility—compliance (Zadek 2004; see Table 1). In this stage, Zadek explains that companies will do "just as much as we have to," adopting a policy-based, compliance-driven approach to human rights as a cost of doing business.

TABLE 1
Zadek's Five Stages of Corporate Responsibility

Stage 1: Defensive. "Its not our job to fix that."
Stage 2: Compliant. "We'll do just as much as we have to."
Stage 3: Managerial. "It's the business, stupid."
Stage 4: Strategic. "It gives us a competitive edge."
Stage 5: Civil. "We need to make sure everyone does it."

Source: Zadek 2004.

Meanwhile, the vast majority of companies remained in Zadek's first "defensive" stage of corporate responsibility on human rights issues in the 1990s. These companies remained convinced that labor conditions in faraway countries were simply not their responsibility—that the obligation to take action remained with the state. However legitimate this claim was in principle, many of these companies soon began to see that society's expectations of them had shifted dramatically. They were now expected to assume some responsibilities of the state, particularly in countries with weak or non-existent governance or rule of law.

By the end of the 1990s, the numerous companies taking action on human rights had produced a proliferation of individual company codes, many of which varied in their standards only along the margins. But large suppliers in the developing world soon found themselves being audited by multiple multinationals on a regular basis, each time to slightly different codes. Acting independently, the multinationals were without a strategy for streamlining audits and addressing this problem. They had limited mechanisms and tools to cross-check supplier lists to make the process more efficient. And questions began to arise about whether these efforts at social compliance were actually improving conditions for workers.

Addressing Root Causes

As companies sought to improve the effectiveness of compliance-driven approaches, a new branch of civil society organizations began to form to help them in this endeavor. Rather than campaigning against companies for their failures in this area, these enterprising new organizations decided to seize the opportunity to devise ways to make more effective and long-term improvements in supply chain conditions.

Organizations such as the Fair Labor Association (FLA), formed in 1999 as an outgrowth of the Clinton administration's Apparel Industry Partnership, took on the issue of the lack of a global auditing standard and decided to issue its own cross-industry code, which it hoped would be recognized by a wide range of companies. It also took on the question of audit validity and transparency by vetting its own auditors and requiring that findings from audits conducted through the FLA be made public on its website. The FLA and similar organizations began focusing on standardizing and streamlining human rights auditing efforts and providing transparent audit results to society (Van Heerden 2006).

Thanks in part to the innovative work of organizations like the FLA, and due to companies' ongoing efforts to improve their monitoring models, a new way forward began to emerge. This new approach required, among other things, that businesses take a look in the mirror and commit to addressing their own roles in human rights issues in supplier workplaces.

Here Nike served as a leading example. As the company sought to improve the results it was getting from its workplace monitoring program, Nike's social compliance team began to analyze the root causes of the problematic workplace conditions they were finding—and not successfully correcting—via audits. They were reaching the third stage in Zadek's model—managerial—in which they realized that they needed to understand the links between their business and the issues themselves (Zadek 2004).

The Nike team embarked on an in-depth inquiry to answer this question, and their findings were remarkable. Rather than concluding that all blame lay elsewhere, they determined that, in part, their own procurement practices were exacerbating, and in some cases causing, the chronic workplace problems they were finding in their audits. It soon became clear that this dynamic was embedded throughout the garment industry. Gap, Inc. also publicly reported their finding that their own sourcing practices contributed to the human rights issues their suppliers were grappling with.

As a result of these findings, many leading companies complemented their monitoring work with internal initiatives focused on understanding and addressing the issues caused by their own procurement practices. Many companies took steps to ensure that procurement staff were accountable for social compliance monitoring results, that they were a part of the discussion with suppliers about improving practices, and that they examined their own buying practices to ensure that they were not causing or exacerbating compliance problems.

The Need for Improved Human Resources Management

Another dynamic identified in the search for root causes was the need for improved human resources management at the supplier level. It became clear to many companies engaged in active monitoring that their suppliers often lacked the capacity to understand the business benefits of making basic improvements in the workplace. As a result, these companies began to focus on building suppliers' human resources capabilities to drive improved conditions over the long term. For example, they pointed out how much money suppliers could save in reduced overtime payments by reorganizing their worker shift systems. With more streamlined shifts, suppliers would see their costs drop, driving a self-interested push toward reducing work hours that would benefit the workers and satisfy the company codes.

The FLA also underscored the importance of improved human resource management in its monitoring approach. Its search for a model that effectively addressed root causes resulted in what the FLA now calls "sustainable compliance"—a model in which audits ask the question "why" more often than "what." Today, the FLA's top priorities are capacity building among suppliers and development of human resource management skills. FLA president Auret van Heerden (2006) has noted that this new effort takes greater time, energy, and resources, but it also pays higher dividends in improved conditions.

The first priority of many companies today remains simply monitoring their supply chain—conducting audits to try to ensure that problematic conditions are not present. But leading companies are also complementing these efforts with work to address the root causes of the most chronic and problematic human rights issues they find in their supply chains. This effort is increasingly seen as the only way to sustainably address the problems and provide real return for a company's investment in compliance. These interventions tend to treat suppliers and business partners more as partners in this work, rather than as subjects of punitive audits.

Although still largely in development, this new social compliance model has the potential to overcome many of the pitfalls that plagued the original monitoring approach. These advances can empower companies to move from Zadek's third stage—managerial—to his fourth stage: strategic. In this way, companies can seek out win–win solutions, be less paternalistic, and engage in more collaborative dialogue with their suppliers about how best to address issues. These strategic efforts protect their brands, create a competitive edge, and begin to address the root causes of human rights problems.

Clarifying the Framework for Business

As leading companies were working to improve their monitoring approaches into the early 2000s, a debate was taking place within the United Nations and among civil society groups on establishing a framework for companies on human rights. This debate festered largely because there was no clear path toward articulating the human rights obligations of companies and how they differed from the obligations of states.

The United Nations' first attempt at providing significant guidance to companies on human rights was a document issued in 2003 called the *Norms on the Responsibilities of Transnational Corporations and Other Business Enterprises with Regard to Human Rights.* Beginning in 1998, the UN had appointed a group of experts to tackle the difficult question of what businesses' obligations were with respect to human rights. After many years of work, the group produced its document, containing 23 human rights standards for companies, which came to be known as the UN Norms.

Although the Norms were welcomed by some civil society groups, they were widely panned by business. The offending portion of the document, from a business perspective, was found in its third paragraph, which implied that businesses had the same responsibilities as states to "secure the fulfillment of, respect, ensure respect of and protect human rights." It went on to say that businesses were "obligated to respect" the responsibilities and Norms outlined in numerous state-to-state treaties and conventions on human rights.

This was highly problematic from a business perspective because there were no distinctions made between the responsibilities of states and those of businesses. It introduced a burden of responsibility that most businesses believed was not appropriate. Most agreed that they had an important role to play in respecting rights but maintained that their roles and obligations were different from those of states. Meanwhile, many civil society groups argued that the Norms were a positive step forward and argued that the UN should adopt the Norms as a formal position on business and human rights.

After years of debate and disconnect on this topic, then–UN Secretary-General Kofi Annan appointed a Special Representative on Business and Human Rights to move the debate forward and to provide the clarity that was still urgently needed. Harvard professor John Ruggie, a leading political scientist and expert on corporate responsibility, was given this task. Ruggie began his mandate in 2005 and spent three years conducting in-depth research and holding extensive consultation with business and civil society.

In June 2008, Ruggie presented his findings to the UN Human Rights Council, which endorsed them. The findings were presented in the form of a policy framework that outlined clearly what Ruggie saw as the differing roles of states and businesses with respect to human rights. Feedback on his report from a wide range of stakeholders has been largely positive. Criticism has come from those hoping that he will expand his work in its next three-year phase to further investigate and clarify his positions on key issues. The business community largely found Ruggie's report to be a helpful contribution to the business and human rights debate, and there are indications that companies will now begin to use his framework as their guide as they formulate their own human rights approaches.

Ruggie's framework (2008) is centered around the core concepts of "protect, respect and remedy." He maintains that states have a duty to protect rights, that companies have a responsibility to respect rights, and that access to remedies for victims of human rights abuses must be greatly strengthened. This simple and straightforward approach has succeeded in providing a framework within which these complex issues can be discussed—and progress can be made.

Nevertheless, a number of key questions in this debate remain unanswered, in particular about what businesses are obligated to do under international law. Ruggie explained that states have an obligation to protect rights under international law, but he noted that his research showed that very few states had policies, programs, or tools in place to help them understand, identify, and address human rights challenges related to the private sector. He concluded that states are the most critical players on this point and that they bear the most urgent responsibility to step up their efforts. Companies are increasingly facing legal issues in the North for alleged rights violations in the South, which Ruggie noted is only likely to escalate given the lack of international regulation or law on business and human rights.

Ruggie also noted in his report that, given the lack of an international legal framework on human rights, companies are taking the initiative to self-regulate. The International Chamber of Commerce, International Organization of Employers, and the Business and Industry Advisory Committee issued a comment on Ruggie's report reiterating their belief that companies must obey the law wherever they operate, even if it is not enforced, and follow international standards where law is absent.

Industry and Stakeholder Collaboration

As a result of these developments, companies and industry associations are now seeing that it is in their own interest to define their values and expectations in this area in order to effectively manage risk and avoid complicity in rights violations. To this end, companies have devised a number of industry and stakeholder collaborations.

These collaborations amount to self-regulation, but they should be considered a step forward. These efforts take companies into the final stage of Zadek's model—civil—in which companies realize the value in all relevant actors' addressing rights simultaneously. They seek the "level playing field," often removing incentives for competitive advantage on human rights and intentionally seeking out good practice that reduces risk for all.

Indeed, collaborative approaches are founded on the desire to seek out "shared value" as explained by Michael Porter and Mark Kramer in their seminal *Harvard Business Review* article titled "Strategy and Society: The Link Between Competitive Advantage and Corporate Social Responsibility" (Porter and Kramer 2006). They identify points of intersection between the interests of business and the interests of society, focusing attention on the most critical issues with the highest mutual payoff. They emphasize that businesses must no longer focus on defense or on philanthropic efforts that are only tangentially related to core business objectives. They advocate the creation of shared value in the most sustainable of ways—when companies focus their efforts squarely at the intersection of business and societal benefit.

Many of the voluntary industry and collaborative initiatives currently under way on the topic of human rights seek to create this shared value. One compelling example is the Kimberley Process, whose tagline is "from conflict diamonds to prosperity diamonds" (http://www. kimberleyprocess.com). The process seeks to address the violent conflict, human rights abuses, and arms trade that is linked to the diamond business in certain African countries. It has done so by introducing a certification scheme through which the diamond industry can monitor, address, and come into compliance with a code that is intended to benefit mine workers, communities, and society as a whole while providing an appealing product for retail companies to market to Western consumers.

The initiative has stemmed the flow of conflict diamonds from 15% of the market to less than 1%, and it has benefited diamond retailers and diamond-producing communities alike.

Still other initiatives have sprung up to grapple with the fundamental questions Ruggie took on in his mandate. The members of the Business Leaders Initiative on Human Rights seek to find "practical ways of applying the aspirations of the Universal Declaration of Human Rights within a business context and to inspire other businesses to do likewise" (http://www.blihr.org). BLIHR's member companies, including The Coca-Cola Company, have engaged a wide range of other businesses, civil society, and governments in an effort to examine and find answers to these questions.

In late 2008, BLIHR, with the goal of complementing Ruggie's work, published a *The Guide to Integrating Human Rights into Business Management* (http://www.blihr.org) to help businesses understand human rights principles and apply them in business systems. BLIHR seeks to inspire businesses around the world to act on human rights out of self-interest, to the benefit of society. The guidance is helping to articulate a specific way forward for business on human rights, in the context of Ruggie's framework. This approach helps companies understand the core commitments they can constructively make on human rights, which can include commitments to the following activities:

- Respect human rights.
- Identify their human rights impacts and take action that is appropriate to address them.
- Engage global and local stakeholders on human rights issues.
- Identify and expeditiously resolve human rights issues.
- Focus auditing systems on corrective action and on the identification of win–win opportunities for business partners being audited.
- Address issues that are systemic in nature, building necessary alliances with civil society, government, and multilateral agencies.
- Train and educate business partners and staff on human rights worldwide.

Companies are also finding great value in direct collaboration with civil society on human rights issues. This type of approach is often the only way to get at issues with complex root causes stretching far beyond the scope of any single business.

An example of such collaboration is The Coca-Cola Company's experience in El Salvador. In response to a challenge from its stakeholders in 2004, Coca-Cola began to engage with a wide range of groups in El Salvador on the endemic issue of child labor in sugarcane harvesting. To foster a multisector, multistakeholder response to this complex issue, Coca-Cola encouraged the formation of a diverse coalition of industry, suppliers, civil society, and government. Encouraging a local response to this issue produced very positive returns.

In just four years, the Salvadoran industry and government significantly stepped up their efforts to combat child labor in sugarcane, with the incidence dropping by 50% in that time frame, according to the Salvadoran Ministry of Education. Increased numbers of children were either in school or engaged in alternative forms of labor, benefiting the Salvadoran industry and government by demonstrating their ability to address this local issue over the long term and benefiting Coca-Cola and its global stakeholders by demonstrating that multinational companies can play constructive roles in fostering local solutions to human rights problems.

Looking Ahead

For companies taking action on human rights issues, this effort is not a theoretical exercise. For business, human rights must translate into a pragmatic set of standards and actions to be taken by a company, as well as broader initiatives involving alignment between government, civil society, and the business itself.

As Simon Zadek points out, a company undergoes a major shift when it makes the transition from seeing corporate responsibility as opportunity creation rather than simply as risk mitigation. Although the vast majority of human rights work by companies is still firmly in the category of risk mitigation, there is increasing recognition of the business opportunities posed by respecting human rights.

The most immediate human rights opportunity that business gives to society is the provision of jobs, which enables people to fulfill one of the most basic human rights—the right to work. Companies can also improve peoples' rights in the workplace, including rights to compensation, freedom of association, nondiscrimination, and other core labor rights. When businesses provide goods and services, they also help people realize rights, especially when those goods or services improve health or education. When capitalizing on these natural and mutual benefits, companies are reaching for highly strategic shared value, as identified by Porter and Kramer.

Conclusion

A great deal of progress has been made in the last 15 years toward a better understanding of the role of business in respecting human rights. In our globalized and interconnected world, the media and civil society draw people's attention to rights violations committed in any corner of the world. Faced with negative media coverage of human rights issues related to their brands, companies initially react defensively, denying that they have a role to play in addressing the issues. As pressure increases, they pursue compliance approaches, but with great difficulty and limited returns. As they move to embed their efforts into their management approaches, they begin to see improved human rights outcomes. And as they embrace truly strategic, collaborative approaches, they reach the realm of shared value, where both businesses and societies benefit.

Twenty years ago, the debate about companies' environmental responsibilities was similar—the rationale for action was driven mainly by risk, the understanding of environmental opportunities was limited, and most boardrooms rarely heard mention of environmental issues. Although today human rights topics are similarly absent from most boardrooms, we believe that human rights will increasingly become an aspect of business management viewed by the business community as vital. Beyond simply mitigating risk, we expect that companies will increasingly recognize the opportunities posed by recognizing and respecting human rights.

This increased activity and business commitment will, in turn, result in clearer guidance, parameters, and frameworks on business and human rights. As companies, civil society, and governments increasingly collaborate and innovate, new paths for mutually beneficial action will emerge. Whether called "shared value" or, as John Ruggie remarks in his landmark report, "shared responsibility," this is the frontier of business and human rights. All sectors and actors bear some responsibility for improving conditions, and all have a constructive and appropriate role to play in spurring the realization of human rights.

Acknowledgement

The views expressed herein are those of the authors and do not necessarily represent those of The Coca-Cola Company.

References

Bairoch, Paul. 1979. "Ecarts internationaux des niveaux de vie avant la Revolution industrielle," *Annuales: economies, societes, civilizations*, Vol. 34, no. 1 (January–February), pp. 145–71.
De Long, J. Bradford. 2004. *Cornucopia: The Pace of Economic Growth in the Twentieth Century*. National Bureau of Economic Research Working Paper 7062. Cambridge, MA: National Bureau of Economic Research.
Landes, David. 1998. *The Wealth and Poverty of Nations: Why Some Are So Rich and Some So Poor*. New York: W.W. Norton.

Norms on the Responsibilities of Transnational Corporations and Other Business Enterprises with Regard to Human Rights. 2003. http://www.unhchr.ch/huridocda/huridoca.nsf/(Symbol)/E.CN.4.Sub.2.2003.12.Rev.2.En?Opendocument

Paul, Karen. 1988. "Business and Apartheid: After the Americans Leave, What Next?" *New York Times,* August 7.

Porter, Michael, and Mark Kramer. 2006. "Strategy and Society: The Link Between Competitive Advantage and Corporate Responsibility." *Harvard Business Review,* December, pp. 78–93.

Ruggie, John. 2008. "Promote, Respect and Remedy: A Framework for Business and Human Rights." *Innovations,* Vol. 3, no. 2 (spring), pp. 189–212.

Universal Declaration of Human Rights. 1948. G.A. Res. 217 (III) of Dec. 10, 1948, UN General Assembly Official Records, 3rd. Sess., Resolutions, U.N. Doc. A/810.

van Heerden, Auret. 2006. Remarks at The Coca-Cola Company, August 1.

Zadek, Simon. 2004. "The Path to Corporate Responsibility," *Harvard Business Review,* December, pp. 1–12.

CHAPTER 8

Employment Discrimination

MARIA L. ONTIVEROS

University of San Francisco School of Law

Most discussions of employment discrimination law and policy treat the issue as one of civil rights or work law. In this chapter, I take a different approach, focusing on employment discrimination law and policy from a human rights perspective. I begin with a discussion of the reasons employment discrimination is correctly understood as a violation of human rights. I then discuss the International Labour Organization (ILO) approach to employment discrimination, addressing the ILO principles on employment discrimination and how the organization has applied these principles. I then turn to the approach to employment discrimination in the United States. After a description of the general framework of how the country regulates discrimination in employment, the focus narrows to specific topics of interest: racial discrimination and affirmative action; discrimination based on sex, gender, and sexuality; religious discrimination; and discrimination based on national origin, citizenship, and migrant status. I conclude with a comparative and critical evaluation of U.S. employment discrimination law under human rights principles.

A human rights focus on antidiscrimination law leads to several conclusions. First, the exclusion of certain industries and occupations from statutory protection leaves many workers unprotected from discrimination. Second, the protected-category analysis used in U.S. employment discrimination law results in many people's being denied their human right to be free from discrimination on an irrational basis. This is particularly apparent in discrimination against gay men, lesbian women, and transgendered individuals, because discrimination against them is not prohibited under the ban on sex discrimination or anything else. In addition, migrants and other noncitizens are not protected under the category of either race or national origin. Individuals who are discriminated against because of more than one characteristic may also be left unprotected.

Finally, the definition of discrimination used in U.S. employment discrimination law has also resulted in incomplete human rights protection.

With regard to racial discrimination, courts' skepticism toward "affirmative action" means that much structural discrimination may not be reached. The skepticism comes from the belief in a formal definition of discrimination that insists on equal treatment for all people, even if the people are differently situated. When this formalistic approach is applied to women, especially mothers and caregivers, the definitions of "discrimination" and "equality" fail to provide an equal playing field with men. In addition, the limited language of the Equal Pay Act fails to effectively tackle the wage disparity between men and women. In the area of religion, the interpretation of "reasonable accommodation" fails to meaningfully address the salient differences that result in discrimination against religious minorities. This analysis leads to the conclusion that different laws or interpretations of existing laws may be needed to comply with the international norms of human rights protection against employment discrimination.

Employment Discrimination as a Violation of Human Rights

Human rights violations deny the basic humanity of a person. In the United States, the most obvious example of systemic human rights violations was the institution of chattel slavery practiced in the South before the Civil War. Simply put, slaves were treated legally and practically as property, not as human beings. They were not allowed to earn income for their labor, participate as citizens in society, make decisions about their family structure or welfare, or move freely from place to place. Slaves were treated this way because they were of African descent. Those who captured and forcibly brought them to the United States believed they owned them. U.S. chattel slavery as practiced in the 1700s and 1800s is now universally condemned as a human rights violation.

In contemporary society, certain groups of people are still treated as a caste below other human beings. One example of this type of systemic human rights abuse affects the Dalits in India (International Labour Organization 2007). Once referred to as "Untouchables," this group has been excluded, by virtue of their caste status at birth, from many occupations, including those involving contact with water or food for non-Dalits and those that require entrance to the homes of non-Dalits. As a result, Dalits are excluded from domestic work; from producing, processing, or selling food; and from much of the work in the service sector. In addition, they have limited access to education, training, and other resources for social advancement. Because of this, they are often confined to jobs such as manual scavenging (described as "the removal, under degrading and hazardous conditions, of human excrement from dry latrines that continue to be used throughout the country") and the removal of dead animals (International Labour Organization 2007:36).

Although the Indian government has formally abolished the caste system and the practice of "untouchability," Dalits continue to be treated as inferior and impure.

What makes these examples such clear violations of human rights? There appear to be at least two evils at work. First, in each case, society has singled out a group of people because of a group characteristic and then used that characteristic to deny the group equal treatment with other human beings. The characteristic used as the basis for denying rights does not affect the group's abilities to participate in human society. Further, it is something that is a core part of the group members' identity, something that cannot be changed (such as race) or that should not change against one's will (such as religion). This fact violates our notions of human rights because part of being human is the opportunity to be judged on one's real abilities. Conversely, it is a human right to not be denied equal treatment because of something that is core to one's identity and does not affect one's ability to perform a job.

Second, in these examples, the group is denied access to certain fundamental rights we believe all humans deserve access to. By denying these rights, society is expressing the idea that the group is less than human. When these two evils come together, we say that discrimination—the irrational denial of a fundamental right to a person or group because of an irrelevant trait or characteristic—constitutes an abuse of human rights.

The Centrality to Human Rights of Discrimination in the Employment Arena

American chattel slavery and the treatment of the Dalits in India are particularly compelling examples of human rights abuses because discrimination against members of these groups took place across the full range of fundamental human rights. This chapter addresses why discrimination in just one area—employment—is still a human rights abuse. It is because paid employment is central to our current understanding of being a free human being and because, in our current social system, it is central to the attainment of all other fundamental rights.

Owning one's own labor has always been viewed as integral to the status of being a free human being. Carole Pateman has argued that, in our current democratic welfare state, paid employment has become the key to citizenship. She argues that the equal worth of citizenship and respect of fellow citizens depend on participation as employees (Pateman 1989). Bill Gould put it this way:

> The starting point for evaluation of these issues is the realization
> that in a modern industrialized economy employment is central

to one's existence and dignity. One's job provides not only income essential to the acquisition of the necessities of life, but also the opportunity to shape the aspirations of one's family, aspirations which are both moral and educational. Along with marital relations and religion, it is hard to think of what might be viewed as more vital in our society than the opportunity to work and retain one's employment status (Gould 1986:892).

On the international level, there is a consensus that discrimination in general and particularly discrimination in employment constitutes a violation of human rights. The Declaration of Philadelphia captured these ideas, and they were reaffirmed by the ILO in its preamble to Convention 111 on discrimination in employment: "The Declaration of Philadelphia affirms that all human beings, irrespective of race, creed or sex, have the right to pursue both their material well-being and their spiritual development in conditions of freedom and dignity, of economic security and equal opportunity" (International Labour Organization 1944). The Universal Declaration of Human Rights also states that discrimination constitutes a violation of human rights.

The ILO links discrimination in employment to human rights because such discrimination "entails a waste of human talents, with detrimental effects on productivity and economic growth, and generates socio-economic inequalities that undermine social cohesion and solidarity and act as a brake on the reduction of poverty" (International Labour Organization 2007:7). ILO research has focused on the link between poverty and racism along with the cycle that the two create to hamper the realization of full human potential. The organization has described it this way:

> Very often those who suffer racial or ethnic discrimination are very poor. Centuries of unequal treatment in all spheres of life, combined with persistent and deep ethnic socio-economic inequalities, explain their low educational and occupational attainments. Lower achievements, in turn, make them vulnerable to ethnic stereotyping, while social and geographic segregation perpetuates ethnic inequalities, reinforcing perceptions of "inferiority" or "distastefulness" by majority groups (International Labour Organization 2007:24).

The ILO Approach to Employment Discrimination

The ILO designated the "the elimination of discrimination in respect of employment and occupation" as one of its fundamental principles and rights at work. Two conventions cover this principle: Convention 100, "Equal Remuneration Convention, 1951," and Convention 111, "Discrimination (Employment and Occupation) Convention,

1958." Convention 100 focuses on ensuring equality of pay between men and women. It requires that countries promote the "principle of equal remuneration for men and women workers for work of equal value" and seeks to end discrimination in compensation based on sex. By focusing on equal pay for "work of equal value," instead of equal pay for workers doing the same exact job, the ILO principle incorporates the ideas behind "comparable worth" analysis. To comply with Convention 100, the "value" of different types of jobs must be assessed and compared before a determination can be made if men and women are being paid equally. This approach recognizes that men and women are often segmented into different industries or different jobs within industries. As a result of job segregation, an analysis of equal pay for men and women doing the same exact job will not be able to fully examine systemic discrimination in pay based on sex. Thus, Convention 100 seeks to reach structural discrimination, not just obvious bias in a single workplace.

Convention 111 requires countries to promote "equality of opportunity and treatment in respect of employment and occupation, with a view to eliminating any discrimination in respect thereof." It defines discrimination as "any distinction, exclusion or preference made on the basis of race, colour, sex, religion, political opinion, national extraction or social origin, which has the effect of nullifying or impairing equality of opportunity or treatment in employment or occupation." The convention defines "employment and occupation" to include access to vocational training, as well as access to employment in general and specific occupations, and the terms and conditions of employment. Finally, Convention 111 makes clear that "any distinction, exclusion or preference in respect of a particular job based on the inherent requirements thereof shall not be deemed to be discrimination." It focuses on ending discrimination based on six categories: race, color, sex, religion, political opinion, national extraction, and social origin. It also recognizes that employers may use actual job requirements to exclude people without "discriminating" in violation of the convention.

The Principles Applied

The ILO outlines at least three different types of discrimination addressed by Convention 111. It describes *direct discrimination* as "rules, practices and policies which exclude or give preference to certain individuals just because they belong to a particular group" (International Labour Organization 2007:9). In contrast, it says, *indirect discrimination* occurs when neutral norms have a disproportionate impact on an identifiable group, without justification. The ILO specifically identifies the differential treatment of particular categories of workers, such as domestic workers, as a form of indirect discrimination that often affects "low-income women belonging to racial or ethnic minorities, and who are often for-eigners" (International Labour Organization 2007:9). Finally, it describes *structural discrimination* as inherent or institutionalized social, institu-tional, and legal constructs that reflect and reproduce discriminatory practices and outcomes.

In looking at how to eliminate discrimination, the ILO recognizes that certain differences in treatment are not discriminatory but are, in fact, necessary to achieve equality. "Special measures that entail non-identical treatment of individuals with particular needs, owing to reasons such as their sex, mental, sensory or physical impairment or social origin, do not constitute discrimination. Giving effect to the principle of equal treat-ment and opportunities means more than treating persons in the same way; it also requires special measures and the accommodation of differ-ences" (International Labour Organization 2007:10). The ILO also recog-nizes the importance of special temporary measures or affirmative action that might be necessary to "accelerate the pace of improvement of the situation of groups that are at a serious disadvantage because of past or present discrimination" (International Labour Organization 2007:10).

The United States' Approach to Employment Discrimination

The United States has passed several laws at the federal level that regulate discrimination in employment. (Although many states have also passed employment discrimination laws, this chapter covers only laws at the federal level.) Title VII of the Civil Rights Act of 1964 prohibits dis-crimination in employment on the basis of race, color, sex, national origin, or religion. In addition, the Equal Pay Act of 1963 regulates discrimina-tion in pay between men and women. The Age Discrimination in Employment Act prohibits discrimination on the basis of age for employees over 40 years of age. Finally, the Americans with Disabilities Act prohibits discrimination against qualified individuals with disabilities. These statutes supplement general federal civil rights statutes and con-stitutional provisions aimed at ending racial discrimination in society, but I will focus on the specific federal statutes passed to address discrimi-nation in employment.

Protected Categories

One key aspect of the structure of U.S. employment discrimination laws is that they only prohibit discrimination based on certain protected characteristics (race, color, sex, national origin, religion, age, and disabil-ity). Thus, groups that are not included, such as migrants or gay men or lesbians, may be discriminated against without violating federal law. In addition, the law does not specifically address discrimination based on membership in more than one identity group. Most courts have been willing to prohibit discrimination based on more than one category, if the categories are both protected under a statute (such as discrimination against Asian men or older women). Courts have also prohibited dual or intersectional discrimination if it affects members of a statutorily protected category and a recognized fundamental right, such as marriage or procreation. Thus, courts have prohibited discrimination against married women or women with children (where the employer did not discriminate against married men or men with children). Courts have not, however, effectively been able to conceptualize and recognize claims based on multiple factors outside these boundaries, such as harassment based on sex, migrant status, and occupation (Ontiveros 2007b).

Excluded Categories

Title VII, the major federal antidiscrimination law, does not cover all workers or all workplaces. It applies only to employers with more than 15 employees, which excludes a sizeable percentage of the workforce. In addition, certain industries, such as domestic work and agricultural work, are specifically excluded. Finally, the laws only apply to employees, not independent contractors. These statutory exclusions tend to have a disproportionate effect on women, especially immigrant women, because they tend to work for smaller employers and in excluded industries, and they are often categorized as independent contractors (Ontiveros 2007a).

Disparate Treatment, Disparate Impact, and Failure to Accommodate

U.S. antidiscrimination laws, as enacted by Congress and interpreted by the courts, have resulted in a few distinct frameworks that individual employees can use to prove that discrimination exits. "Disparate treatment" is the term used to describe a situation where an employer intentionally treats an employee differently because of a protected characteristic. "Disparate impact" discrimination occurs when a neutral employment requirement (such as a height requirement) falls more heavily on a protected group (such as women) and is not justified by business necessity. Finally, some statutes require that employers make "reasonable accommodation" to a member of a protected group (such as a person with a disability) and consider the failure to make a reasonable accommodation a form of prohibited discrimination.

Topics of Interest in Employment Discrimination

Racial discrimination and affirmative action. One of the most important tools for addressing racial discrimination is so-called affirmative action. Such help targeted at certain groups is problematic under U.S. law when the help is targeted at racial groups. Such programs can be challenged under both the Fourteenth Amendment to the U.S. Constitution and Title VII. Under the Fourteenth Amendment, affirmative action programs based on race are subject to "strict scrutiny," regardless of whether the racial group being helped is one that has been traditionally disadvantaged or traditionally privileged. Under this so-called doctrine of color blindness, the U.S. Supreme Court has refused to set different standards for judging the constitutionality of race-based affirmative action programs aimed to help blacks, for instance, than those that benefit whites. In order for a race-based affirmative action program to be upheld, the government must show both that there is a compelling government interest behind the program and that the program is narrowly tailored to accomplish that purpose.

Race-based affirmative action programs have also been challenged under Title VII as a form of discrimination in employment based on race. So far, courts have allowed an employer to adopt a voluntary affirmative action program when the program has been created to remedy a manifest imbalance in a traditionally segregated job category and when it does not unnecessarily trammel the interests of innocent employees. Although this standard seems more lenient than the constitutional standard, it appears that many courts are moving toward a merging of the two.

Discrimination on the basis of sex, gender, and sexuality. Title VII prohibits discrimination based on "sex," but courts and law makers have had a great deal of difficulty determining what both "sex" and "discrimination" mean in this context. In defining "sex," there has been general agreement that a straightforward distinction between men and women would be a distinction based on sex. There is much less agreement on whether and how distinctions based on gender or sexuality would be distinctions based on "sex." In one case, *Price Waterhouse* v. *Hopkins,* the U.S. Supreme Court recognized that discrimination based on gender stereotyping (the requirement that men and women fit a socially constructed vision of what a man or woman should be) can be a form of sex discrimination. In that case, Ann Hopkins had not been promoted to partnership at an accounting firm because she did not act femininely enough. The accounting firm sent her a memorandum saying that, in order to be promoted, she needed to "walk more femininely, talk more femininely, dress more femininely, wear make up, have her hair styled, and wear jewelry" (*Price Waterhouse* v. *Hopkins* 1989:235–6). The court easily found this to be discrimination based on sex because "we are beyond the day when an employer could evaluate employees by assuming or insisting that they matched the stereotype associated with their group for in forbidding employers to discriminate against individuals because of their sex, Congress intended to strike at the entire spectrum of disparate treatment of men and women resulting from sex stereotypes" (*Price Waterhouse* v. *Hopkins* 1989:235–6). Lower courts have followed this ruling but have had difficulty in deciding, for instance, whether a requirement that women (but not men) must wear makeup is discrimination based on sex (*Jespersen* v. *Harrah's Operating Co.* 2006). With regard to sexuality, courts have clearly stated that discrimination based on sexual orientation is not prohibited by Title VII. Thus, an employer is free, under federal law, to refuse to hire a gay man because he is gay or a lesbian woman because she is a lesbian. This holding is difficult to justify and apply, however, in jurisdictions that recognize gender discrimination as a form of sex discrimination and where employers discriminate against gay men or lesbian women because they do not fit the gender roles typically assigned to men and women. If, for instance, Price Waterhouse had simply refused to promote Ann Hopkins because she was a lesbian, the court may have been forced to find no discrimination based on sex, even if the accounting firm's discrimination was based on underlying gender stereotypes.

Courts have also had difficulty in determining whether discrimination against a transsexual or transgendered individual is discrimination based on sex. The traditional view, still held by a slim majority of courts, found that the employer was not discriminating on the basis of the employee's sex, but rather on their decision to change their sex or their status as a transsexual. More recently, some courts have found that when a woman is fired because she has become a man (or vice versa), the employer is firing that person specifically because of (the new) sex and view the discharge as sex discrimination. Other courts have focused on a gender stereotyping analysis to strike down the discharge. These courts use the term transgender, instead of transsexual, to focus not on the narrow biological determination of an individual's sex, but rather on the appearance and identity that is claimed by an employee.

When defining discrimination in the area of sex, courts have struggled with the issue of whether providing accommodations for pregnant women and mothers is necessary to level the playing field with men, thereby creating sexual equality, or whether it is prohibited discrimination. Courts that embrace a sex-blind approach, similar to the race-blind approach of the Supreme Court's interpretation of the Fourteenth Amendment, view these types of accommodations as discriminatory against men and other nonpregnant persons. In *General Electric Co.* v. *Gilbert* (1976), the Supreme Court adopted the sex-blind approach. Congress, however, quickly amended Title VII to reverse *Gilbert* and make clear that discrimination based on pregnancy constituted sex discrimination.

Although direct pregnancy discrimination is clearly prohibited, courts are currently being presented with cases of indirect discrimination, arising from pregnancy-related absenteeism and pregnancy-related leave. Some courts find that a discharge for missing work because of pregnancy-related illnesses is prohibited as equivalent to discrimination based on pregnancy. Other courts take the approach that while employers are required "to ignore an employee's pregnancy, [they are not required to ignore] . . . her absence from work, unless the employer overlooks the comparable absences of nonpregnant employees in which event it would not be ignoring pregnancy after all" (*Troupe* v. *May Department Stores* 1994). In related cases, more and more women are bringing cases alleging discrimination based on maternal and caregiver stereotypes (Sloan Work and Family Research Network 2005; Williams and Segal 2003).

With regard to discrimination in compensation between men and women, in 1963 Congress passed the Equal Pay Act (EPA). The EPA prohibits discrimination in pay between men and women who work at the same establishment and who perform equal work on jobs that require equal skill, effort, and responsibility and that are performed under equal working conditions. To prove a violation of the EPA, a woman must show that men and women work in the same physical location, perform substantially equal work, and labor under similar work conditions. Thus, under the language of the EPA, women may not bring claims based on "comparable worth" or the value of their job to the employer.

Religious discrimination. The prohibition against religious discrimination protects individuals against adverse treatment because of their religious beliefs and the practices or observances associated with their beliefs. The letter of the law also requires employers to make reasonable accommodation for these practices and beliefs. As interpreted, however, the courts have not required employers to bear anything more than *de minimus* costs or to take any action that might be seen as disadvantaging other employees.

For example, suppose an employee whose religious observances occur on Saturday is nonetheless scheduled to work on a Saturday. Without any type of accommodation requirement, the employee must choose between termination for failing to report to work as scheduled and observing his or her religious practices. Potential accommodations include scheduling workers on Saturdays who do not have religious conflicts or requiring the employer to offer premium pay to get someone to volunteer to switch shifts with the Sabbitarian.

Courts in the U.S. have not required the first type of accommodation, however, viewing it as privileging religious conflicts over other types of conflicts. In the court's view, this type of accommodation is a form of favoritism or discrimination based on religion and violates nondiscrimination principles. In *Trans World Airlines, Inc.* v. *Hardison* (1977), the U.S. Supreme Court reasoned, "TWA would have had to deprive another employee of his shift preference at least in part because he did not adhere to a religion that observed the Saturday Sabbath. . . . It would be anomalous to conclude that by 'reasonable accommodation' Congress meant that an employer must deny the shift and job preference of some employees . . . in order to accommodate or prefer the religious needs of others. . . ." Thus, a literal definition of nondiscrimination has trumped the statute's requirement for "reasonable accommodation." Courts have not required the second type of accommodation—paying others premium pay to work on Saturday—because they consider it too large a financial burden to impose on employers. In the TWA case, the U.S. Supreme Court stated that "to require TWA to bear more than a *de minimis* cost in order to give Hardison Saturdays off is an undue hardship."

Discrimination based on national origin, citizenship, and migrant status. Title VII prohibits discrimination based on national origin. The courts have distinguished this protected category from migrant status or citizenship status, which they have found are not protected under the law unless they are used as proxies for national origin. In the seminal case, *Espinoza* v. *Farrah Mfg.* (1973), the employer refused to hire noncitizens, even though the workers possessed legal authorization to work in the United States. The workers argued that this constituted discrimination based on national origin. The U.S. Supreme Court disagreed and said that, since the employer hired many employees of Mexican descent (and who were U.S. citizens), the employer was not discriminating based on national origin when they refused to hire noncitizens. Thus, under U.S. law, discrimination based on migrant or immigration status is viewed as something analytically distinct from discrimination based on national origin and is *not* prohibited by Title VII.

Comparative Approaches and Critique

The general structure of the nondiscrimination laws creates concern because it allows certain types of discrimination to go unregulated. In particular, workers who are not members of a protected class (or who are discriminated against because of a combination of protected and unprotected reasons) and those who work in excluded occupations are not protected. For example, discrimination against migrant women is difficult, if not impossible, to reach under the U.S. laws. Migrant women tend to work in exactly those occupations excluded from statutory coverage (domestic work, agriculture) and in employment relationships (such as subcontracting or as independent contactors) that are not covered. In addition, since migration status is not protected, an employer who discriminates against migrant women, but not other women, may go unpunished under current law.

The ILO has specifically designated the exclusion of certain occupations in which immigrant women concentrate as a form of indirect discrimination. It has targeted domestic work, which is often afforded different and inferior treatment by governmental regulation, as a particularly important area for improvement. It concludes that "direct and indirect discrimination based on sex and age, often combined with migrant status or ethnicity, is at the root of the situation of disadvantage of domestic workers" (International Labour Organization 2007:108) and has noted that female migrants around the world are doubly burdened by their sex and migrant status. They are concentrated in dirty, dangerous, and degrading jobs, for which they receive low pay (International Labour Organization 2007). Under the structure of U.S. antidiscrimination laws, this particularly vulnerable group is left unprotected from human rights abuses.

Several things could be used to improve antidiscrimination law in this regard. First, the law should be amended to cover agricultural and domestic workers. In addition, the definition of employee should be interpreted broadly to include those who are called "independent contractors," but who in reality function as employees. With respect to intersectional claims, courts should prohibit discrimination that includes any of the covered bases and a second or third element whenever the plaintiff can show that there is a pattern or history of this type of intersectional discrimination. These fairly easy fixes could markedly improve the protection offered to many workers.

Topics of Interest

Racial discrimination and affirmative action. The ILO recognizes that merely prohibiting discrimination may not be enough to create a level playing field, given the entrenched nature of inequality and the cyclical relationships among poverty, inequality, and racism. It concludes that, in these situations, "different treatment of disadvantaged groups may be necessary until the causes justifying the adoption of these measures cease to exist" (International Labour Organization 2007:61). After surveying a variety of countries, its research led to the conclusion that "in several countries where thorough analyses have been conducted, affirmative action has been shown to improve the representation of protected groups at the workplace, although its impact has varied depending upon the group" (International Labour Organization 2007:63).

The ILO recommends multiple approaches to implementing affirmative action. It argues that the most successful programs impose costs on employers for noncompliance but do not enforce rigid quotas. These types of programs, which are often implemented through government procurement programs, allow employers to develop sophisticated human resource systems that include formal job evaluations, applicant testing, training, career paths, and performance-based compensation systems. Not surprisingly, these types of programs work best when the employers involved are supportive of the goals. In the United States, this type of affirmative action program is implemented through the procurement program authorized since 1965 under Executive Order 11246.

Executive Order 11246 has been approved under the more lenient approach of Title VII jurisprudence (rather than that of the Fourteenth Amendment), which better fits the ILO vision of nondiscrimination as a human right. In addition, Title VII's seeming rejection of a color-blind model and the embracing of a model that focuses on overcoming past entrenched inequality fit the ILO approach to affirmative action. In the ILO view, an affirmative action approach "seeks to address the failure of labor market institutions to provide equal opportunities to all" (International Labour Organization 2007:61). On the other hand, the current interpretation of the Fourteenth Amendment, which judges programs that benefit traditionally disadvantaged groups the same as those that benefit traditionally privileged groups, misses the human rights history of racial discrimination in the United States and fails to embrace the ILO approach. If the U.S. is to comply fully with the ILO approach, it needs to follow a Title VII approach, rather than its Fourteenth Amendment approach.

Discrimination on the basis of sex, gender, and sexuality. When the U.S. approach to defining "sex" discrimination is put in a human rights perspective, many of the distinctions made among sex, gender, and sexuality become meaningless. A focus on human rights would not parse the distinctions among these ideas. Instead, it would focus on each human being's right to claim his or her own identity and not be discriminated against because of it. In this view, gay men, lesbian women, and transgendered individuals deserve the same protection against discrimination because of their status as human beings. This argument becomes even more compelling when the historical discrimination against gender minorities is considered and compared to the historical discrimination against women. Historically, gender minorities were considered and treated as less than human. Even today, in several parts of the world, homosexuality is illegal, subjecting gay men and lesbian women to imprisonment and corporal punishment (International Labour Organization

2007:42). Regarding women, early case law considered married women to be the property of their husbands, and they were denied self-determination. Both groups faced similar human rights abuses. To prohibit discrimination against one group and not the other allows for continued human rights abuses.

One approach to resolving the matter is to leave the statutory language of "sex" unchanged but to make clear that discrimination based on "gender" is also prohibited by the language. This interpretation should protect gay men, lesbian women, and transgendered individuals who are discriminated against because they do not fit the social roles prescribed for men and women. It should also address discrimination that results from requirements that men or women dress or groom themselves in socially prescribed ways. This approach, however, does not address discrimination based on prejudice directed at gay men, lesbian women, or transgendered individuals that is analytically distinct from prejudice based on gender divergence. It is also unlikely to be accepted by U.S. courts, which have consistently held that a gender approach cannot be used to "bootstrap" protections for gay men and lesbian women when Congress has not extended coverage to these individuals. A better approach is to change the language of the law to include gay men, lesbian women, and transgendered individuals. This is the best way to ensure that their human rights are protected.

In looking at the definition of discrimination, the ILO recommends that non-identical treatment of individuals with particular needs, owing to reasons of sex, may be necessary to give effect to principles of equal treatment. When U.S. courts examine cases involving pregnancy-related illness and caregiver bias, for example, a sex-blind approach will simply not adequately protect the human rights of women and mothers. Absenteeism due to these reasons must be treated differently than absenteeism caused by other things. Differential treatment in this regard is not discrimination. Rather, it is necessary to ensure equality between men and women. Courts need to recognize an accommodation principle to comply with international norms.

When comparing the U.S. approach to the ILO approach on equal pay, the language of the Equal Pay Act only reaches clear cases of direct discrimination between men and women in the same establishment. Thus, U.S. federal law does not meet the standards of ILO Convention 100. As a result, the U.S. has not been able to sign off as being in compliance with the convention. The ILO identifies significant inequalities in pay between men and women as one of the most persistent and resilient types of discrimination around the world. It has concluded that "even though the gender pay gap narrowed in some places and stagnated in others, women continue to work, on average for lower earnings than men. This trend continues despite the striking advances of women in educational attainments relative to men" (International Labour Organization 2007:20). In industrialized countries, it found that discrimination (rather than differences attributable to objective factors, such as education, experience, and hours worked) accounts for 5% to 15% of the gender pay gap between men and women (International Labour Organization 2007:23). This discriminatory disparity is caused by both direct discrimination, such as when employers pay men higher wages for doing the same work as women, and by indirect discrimination, such as when employers undervalue the skills, competencies, and responsibilities of female employees or use other types of gender bias in job evaluation methods. The ILO suggests that a greater understanding of how to value different jobs is the key to eliminating this form of discrimination.

In order for the U.S. to comply with the ILO norms, the U.S. will also need to change its approach to interpreting its law. Because of its cramped language, the Equal Pay Act can address only direct discrimination. The language of Title VII, however, can be read more broadly to address the type of pay discrimination covered by Convention 100. Since Title VII has a broad prohibition against discrimination based on sex, it could be interpreted to address indirect discrimination through a comparable-worth approach. Unfortunately, the U.S. courts have been hostile to this approach (*County of Washington* v. *Gunther* 1981; *American Federation of State, County and Municipal Employees, AFL-CIO [AFSCME]* v. *State of Washington* 1985). As a result, to ensure that principles of comparable worth are incorporated into U.S. law and indirect pay discrimination is adequately addressed, Congress will probably need to amend Title VII.

Religious discrimination. Because of the narrow reading given to "reasonable accommodation" under Title VII, many religious minorities are forced to choose between practicing their religion and being discharged. These employees are denied the human right to practice their religion and be employed equally with others. Since the dominant religions in the U.S. are all forms of Christianity, the basic work calendar follows the Christian calendar. Few people work on Sundays (the typical Christian day for worship), and most major Christian holidays (Easter, Christmas, etc.) are also observed as holidays. The people who most need accommodations are those who practice minority religions. As a result, most Christians never have to ask for an accommodation for their religious observances or choose between their job and their religion. To ask only religious minorities, or even mainly religious minorities, to make this choice arguably violates their human rights.

The U.S. courts could remedy this problem in two different ways. First, the court could employ a different definition of discrimination, one that recognizes that differential treatment is sometimes necessary to give equal treatment. This shift in how discrimination is defined would also be useful in addressing racial discrimination through affirmative action and discrimination against women due to pregnancy and family care issues. Alternately, the court could change its definition of reasonable accommodation to require employers to incur more than *de minimus* cost in order to accommodate the religious needs of religious minorities. Either of these approaches would better protect the human rights of religious minorities in the U.S.

Discrimination based on national origin, citizenship, and migrant status. Because the U.S. Supreme Court has given such a narrow reading to discrimination based on national origin, finding it analytically distinct from discrimination based on citizenship status, there is no prohibition against discrimination against workers because of citizenship or migrant status per se. Only discrimination based on national origin is prohibited. The ILO approach, prohibiting discrimination based on "national extraction or social origin" and giving that a broad reading to focus on discrimination targeted at migrants, provides an analytical model that does not create artificial distinctions.

The ILO approach is informed by the worldwide history of discrimination against migrants as a human rights abuse. It uses the cases of the Roma people in Europe (formerly commonly referred to as Gypsies) and rural migrant workers in China as two examples of migrant people who suffer discrimination. Due to decades of exclusion and discrimination, unemployment and poverty rates for the Roma are distressingly high, while educational attainment rates are very poor (International Labour Organization 2007). In China, a permit system regulates the distribution of jobs in urban regions, retaining the best jobs for local residents. As a result, rural migrant workers often work without the protection of employment contracts, work in low-paying menial jobs, and are generally treated with little or no dignity or respect (International Labour Organization 2007). Experience with these forms of systemic discrimination against migrants has led the ILO to conclude that discrimination based on migrant status can amount to a violation of human rights. Unfortunately, migrant workers in the U.S., left unprotected by antidiscrimination laws, are also susceptible to this type of human rights violation.

U.S. law can be improved in several ways. Most easily, the holding of *Espinoza* v. *Farrah* could be overturned. Discrimination based on citizenship could be prohibited as discrimination based on national origin. Given that the motive and effect for both is likely to be the same, this conclusion might be a better interpretation of Title VII. Alternately, the terms "race" or "color" could be interpreted to encompass discrimination based on migration status or citizenship. Again, the motives between these various types of discrimination may be analytically similar. A final approach would be to amend the statute to comport with the language of the ILO convention.

Conclusion

Examining employment discrimination as a human rights issue provides a different lens through which to examine and critique U.S. law. Using the ILO principles on nondiscrimination as a comparative standard, I have argued that U.S. law falls short of providing full protection for the human rights of American workers. Different laws or different interpretations of existing laws are necessary to fully comply with these international norms.

References

American Federation of State, County and Municipal Employees, AFL-CIO (AFSCME) v. *State of Washington,* 770 F.2d 1401 9th Cir. 1985.
County of Washington v. *Gunther,* 452 U.S. 161 (1981).
Espinoza v. *Farrah Mfg.,* 414 U.S. 86 (1973).
General Electric Co. v. *Gilbert,* 429 U.S. 125 (1976).
Gould, William B. 1986. "The Idea of the Job as Property in Contemporary America: The Legal and Collective Bargaining Framework." *Brigham Young University Law Review,* pp. 885–918.
International Labour Organization. 1944. ILO Constitution, Declaration Concerning the Aims and Purposes of the International Labour Organization, Annex, article V, <http://www.ilo.org/ilolex/english/iloconst.htm>. [April 16, 2009].
International Labour Organization. 2007. *Equality at Work: Tackling the Challenges.* Global Report under the Follow-up to the ILO Declaration on Fundamental Principles and Rights at Work. International Labour Conference, 96th Session 2007 Report I(B). Geneva: International Labour Office.
Jespersen v. *Harrah's Operating Co.,* 444 F.3d 1104, 9th Cir. 2006.
Ontiveros, Maria L. 2007a. "Female Immigrant Workers and the Law: Limits and Opportunities." In Dorothy Sue Cobble, ed., *The Sex of Class: Women Transforming American Labor.* Ithaca, NY: Cornell University Press, pp. 235–52.
Ontiveros, Maria L. 2007b. "Harassment of Female Farmworkers: Can the Legal System Help?" In Sharon Harley, ed., *Women's Labor in the Global Economy.* New Brunswick, NJ: Rutgers University Press, pp. 103–15.
Pateman, Carole. 1989. *The Disorder of Women: Democracy, Feminism and Political Theory.* Stanford, CA: Stanford University Press.

Price Waterhouse v. *Hopkins,* 490 U.S. 228 (1989).

Sloan Work and Family Research Network. 2005. "Caregiver Bias: Work/Life Issues as Diversity Concerns." Interview with Joan Williams. *The Network News,* Vol. 7, no. 4 (April). <http://wfnetwork.bc.edu/The_Network_News/10/interview.shtml>. [April 26, 2009].

Troupe v. *May Department Stores,* 20 F.3d 734, 7th Cir. 1994.

Trans World Airlines, Inc. v. *Hardison,* 432 U.S. 63 (1977).

Williams, Joan, and Nancy Segal. 2003. "Beyond the Maternal Wall: Relief for Family Caregivers Who Are Discriminated Against on the Job." *Harvard Women's Law Review,* Vol. 26, pp. 77–162.

CHAPTER 9

The Human Rights of Workers with Disabilities

SUSANNE M. BRUYÈRE
Cornell University

BARBARA MURRAY
International Labour Office

Focus on Disability a Critical Need

The rights of workers with disabilities have been increasingly recognized in recent years, with a growing emphasis on the social and physical environmental factors constraining their participation in the world of work. This contrasts with the earlier predominant focus on personal impairment and on providing services catering to medical and associated rehabilitation requirements as well as on providing welfare and social security benefits. Underlying this change is a transformation in understanding disability. Rather than being seen as a personal problem or tragedy, there is now a recognition that very many barriers to participation arise from the way society is built and organized and the way people think and make assumptions about disability. At the same time, it has become clear that persons with disabilities have valuable contributions to make in the workplace and to the national economy, in jobs suited to their interests, abilities, and skills with adaptations as required. Their potential often remains untapped, however, to the detriment of society as a whole.

This chapter traces the growth in attention to disabled workers' rights as human rights at national and international levels and examines the underlying reasons why attention must be paid to disability issues. We outline the provisions that have been made in domestic legislation and policy and the key concepts of modern antidiscrimination law and then focus on case studies of U.S. and European Union legislation as examples, before finally turning to the implications of recent developments for policy, programs, services, and research.

Recent Recognition of People with Disabilities
as a Previously Marginalized Group

The rights of workers with disabilities, long overlooked in the United Nations' (UN) Bill of Rights, have recently been brought into the limelight through the negotiation, adoption, and entry into force of the UN Convention on the Rights of Persons with Disabilities (CRPD). Whether a disability dates from birth or an early age or was acquired in the course of working life, the entitlement of persons with disabilities to work and employment on an equal basis with others in work that they freely choose or accept is spelled out in the CRPD, the principles of which include nondiscrimination, equal opportunity, and accessibility.

The invisibility of persons with disabilities in the three instruments comprising the International Bill of Human Rights—the Universal Declaration of Human Rights of 1948, the International Covenant on Civil and Political Rights of 1966 (ICCPR), and the International Covenant on Economic, Social and Cultural Rights of 1966 (ICESCR)—has been the subject of frequent commentary in recent years (see, for example, Byrnes 2008; Degener and Quinn 2002; Kayess and French 2008; Lawson 2007). Where disability was mentioned, it was in relation to social security and preventive health policy. The implications of this oversight did not go unnoted within the UN itself. In 1994, the UN Committee on Economic, Social and Cultural Rights (UN CESCR) pointed out that the effects of disability-based discrimination had been particularly prominent and persistent in the field of employment (UN Committee on Economic, Social and Cultural Rights General Comment No. 5, 1994).

This situation reflected the widespread perception of disability as the problem of individual disabled persons, to be treated medically and with medical rehabilitation, so that the individual might adapt as much as possible to his or her surroundings, whether the person had a disability from birth or later in life. Both the problem and the solution were seen as lying within the individual. An exception to this pattern is the early ILO Recommendation concerning Vocational Rehabilitation of Disabled Persons (No. 99), adopted in 1955, which emphasized the preparation of persons with disabilities for and their effective retention of suitable employment in all fields of work as well as equality of opportunity and equal pay for equal work (see, for example, O'Reilly 2007). Building on the core provisions of earlier instruments regarding vocational training, equality of opportunity, and equal pay for equal work, Recommendation No. 99 served as the basis for national legislation and practice in relation to vocational guidance, vocational training, and placement of disabled persons for almost 30 years, until the adoption of ILO Convention No. 159

concerning Vocational Rehabilitation and Employment of Disabled Persons in 1983. Convention No. 159 requires States Parties to develop a national policy on vocational rehabilitation and employment, based on the principles of equal opportunity and treatment. It states that affirmative measures should not be regarded as discriminating against other workers and that existing services for workers generally shall, wherever possible and appropriate, be used with necessary adaptations (International Labour Organization Convention No. 159, 1983).

It also requires states to consult with representatives of employers, workers, and disabled persons in planning the implementation of national policies concerning the vocational rehabilitation and employment of disabled persons.

Why Needs of People with Disabilities Must Be Addressed

Historically, those with disabilities have globally been among the most economically impoverished, politically marginalized, and least visible members of their respective societies. Yet this group represents approximately 10% to 12% of the world's population, or more than 650 million people (Mont 2007). Of this number, 80% live in low-income countries. Approximately two-thirds of this group—470 million people with disabilities—are of working age, and yet the majority of them do not work (World Health Organization 2005).

Further, people with disabilities represent every ethnic and racial group, religious affiliation, and socioeconomic status. Yet despite these diverse backgrounds, many people with disabilities continue to be the subjects of prejudices and restrictions, as has been true for centuries. The need to address the issues of people with disabilities will only increase in the future, as the number of those who will be counted among them continues to rise dramatically, due in part to an aging population and the rise of people becoming disabled by HIV/AIDS (Pineda 2005).

In the United States, for example, the Census Bureau projects that the populations aged 45 to 54 and 55 to 64 will grow in the next 10 years by nearly 44.2 million (17%) and 35 million (39%), respectively (U.S. Census Bureau 2004). By the year 2010, this group will account for nearly half (44%) of the working-age population (aged 20 to 64), and the number of people with disabilities between the ages of 50 and 65 will almost double (Weathers 2006).

There is a growing global recognition of the need to broaden the labor pool to address the shrinking of available talent resulting from aging and the subsequent changing demographics of the workforce. People with disabilities represent a labor pool that is as yet largely untapped.

According to U.S. statistics from the American Community Survey (ACS), in 2007 the employment rate of people aged 16–64 with sensory, physical, mental, and/or self-care disabilities was 36.3%, compared to 75.2% for people in the same age group without disabilities (Erickson and Lee 2008). In addition, the percentage of working-age men and women with a disability in the United States with incomes below the poverty line was 28.6% in 2007 (Bjelland, Erickson, and Lee 2008). In developing countries, the link between disability and poverty is also strong. Of all people living on less than a dollar a day, 20% are disabled (World Bank 2005), and more than 80% of disabled people in such countries live below the poverty line (Hope 2003).

Similar employment and income disparities for people with disabilities compared to their nondisabled peers can be seen elsewhere. In the European Union of 25 countries in 2002, people with disabilities had an employment rate of 40%, compared to 64% for people without disabilities (Eurostat 2003). Approximately half of people with disabilities were economically inactive (78% for those with severe disabilities), compared to 28% in the nondisabled EU population.

In developing countries, labor markets are often largely informal, with many workers being self-employed. When they work, persons with disabilities are more likely to be self-employed than people in the overall working age population (Mitra and Sambamoorthi 2006). Self-employment and microenterprise opportunities are seen by many as a way to significantly change the lives of individuals with disabilities and often those of entire families who live in poverty and have limited access not only to income-generating activities, but also to education and health services (Handicap International 2006).

Despite increasing recognition of the significant employment and income disparities between people with disabilities and their nondisabled peers, people with disabilities are still largely absent from national and international mainstream agendas to address employment and poverty needs of other marginalized populations. For example, people with disabilities are noticeably absent from the current 2015 Millennium Goals set out by the United Nations to address a number of critical areas of global concern, including hunger and poverty.

U.N. Convention on the Rights of Persons with Disabilities

The UN CRPD, in force since May 2008, heralds a new era not only for persons with disabilities, but also for society more broadly (McKay 2007). It constitutes a paradigm shift in international policy, from a predominant focus on rehabilitating persons with disabilities to a much broader goal of changing or rehabilitating society; a change from expecting people with disabilities to adjust to a socially defined norm to an acceptance of diversity as normal and of differences as part of the human condition; from the exclusion of disabled persons who have long been on the margins of society to their inclusion, full participation, and citizenship. The provisions of the CRPD, which are legally binding on member states that have ratified it (58 as of June 23, 2009), are based on the social model of disability in which barriers to full participation are seen to arise largely from a combination of barriers in the social and physical environment—including inaccessible buildings and information, inaccessible public transport, rules and regulations that exclude, mistaken assumptions about the working capacity of persons with disabilities, and underlying widespread prejudices, stereotypes, and negative attitudes. In defining persons with disabilities, the CRPD includes those with long-term physical, mental, intellectual, or sensory impairments that, in interaction with various barriers, may hinder their full and effective participation in society on an equal basis with others. In the social model evident in the CRPD, the notion of systemic disadvantage is central. Persons with disabilities are discriminated against by social structures and practices that exclude them from full participation in society (Kayess and French 2008).

The word "special" does not appear in the convention, although this word has been traditionally attached to many policies, programs, and services associated with disabled persons—special education, special needs assessment, special training, sheltered employment. At the insistence of the disability caucus representatives during the negotiation of the CRPD, there is no provision in the convention for special services in the traditional mold. Instead, there is an acknowledgment of specific requirements that need to be accommodated. This is a real and dramatic shift at the level of international policy, as it implies that implementing the provisions of the CRPD will require changes in ways of thinking and behaving as well as in the practical ways that policies, programs, and services are designed and delivered in order to make this revolution on paper also a revolution in practice.

The CRPD provides for an approach to work and employment for persons with disabilities that is very new for many countries. Article 27 requires States that have ratified it to recognize the rights of persons with disabilities to work on an equal basis with others, including their right to gain a living by work freely chosen or accepted, in a labor market that is open, inclusive, and accessible. This is a right that is guaranteed in Article 23 of the Universal Declaration of Human Rights (UDHR) on the right of people to work:

> Everyone has the right to work, to free choice of employment, to just and favourable conditions of work and to protection against unemployment. Everyone, without discrimination, has

the right to equal pay for equal work. Everyone who works has the right to just and favourable remuneration ensuring for himself and his family an existence worthy of human dignity, and supplemented, if necessary, by other means of social protection. Everyone has the right to form and to join trade unions for the protection of his interests.

The provisions of Article 27 of the CRPD cover people with disabilities seeking employment, those advancing in employment, those who acquire a disability while employed, and those wishing to return to work after a period of absence. The CRPD also recognizes that for many disabled persons in developing countries, self-employment or micro-business may be the first, and in some cases the only, option. States are called on to promote such opportunities. The right to exercise labor and trade union rights is promoted. States are also called on to ensure that people with disabilities are not held in slavery or servitude and are protected equally with others from forced or compulsory labor.

A central requirement for labor market inclusion is nondiscrimination against people with disabilities in their search for work and employment as well as equality of treatment between men and women with disabilities. The CRPD emphasizes that the right to work applies to "all forms of employment." Thus, the provisions of Article 27 also apply to sheltered workshops, which are common in developing countries and are also operational in countries with advanced economies. This is a major change, as sheltered workshops to date have generally not been covered by employment legislation.

The CRPD does not create new rights, but it does contain a number of innovations (Byrnes 2008; Kayess and French 2008). One of these is the right to an accessible environment. The concept of "reasonable accommodation" is a key provision in this, referred to throughout the CRPD—in Articles 2, 5, 14, and 24 concerning education and 27 concerning work and employment. It is now a requirement that employers take steps to ensure that work environments are accessible and that information is available in accessible formats in the workplace. Denial of reasonable accommodation is considered discrimination in the CRPD and is thus illegal.

Two other requirements for labor market inclusion provided for in the CRPD could pose challenges to the international community. One is the accessibility of the built environment, transport, and information. This is both a general principle of the convention and the subject of a specific article (No. 9). Accessibility has been discussed for many years, yet disabled persons still have difficulty getting into and out of buildings and using public transport, and people who are blind or visually impaired often have difficulty accessing information, whether in print or electronic form. States are thus required to take appropriate measures to identify and eliminate obstacles and barriers to accessibility and to promote "universal design," meaning the design of products, environments, programs, and services to be usable by all people, to the greatest extent possible, without the need for adaptation or specialized design. The second requirement for labor market inclusion is awareness of the capacity and rights of persons with disabilities. States are required to take immediate steps to promote a fundamental change in societal attitudes by fostering respect for the rights of people with disabilities and by combating stereotypes and prejudice (Article 8).

National Legislation

The trend toward a rights-based approach to disability matters is reflected in the adoption of antidiscrimination legislation concerning persons with disabilities in more than 40 of the 189 UN member states (Degener and Quinn 2000). This number may have increased in recent years, as countries have reviewed and revised their legislation, anticipating the entry into force of the UN CRPD (see Degener 2008).

Disability Rights in the U.S.—A Case Study

In the U.S., disability rights have been a part of the regulatory framework since the passage of the Rehabilitation Act in 1973. A decade or more after civil rights legislation protecting the rights of women and ethnic and racial minorities was passed in the 1960s, people with disabilities began to see their civil rights protected—initially in the provisions of the Rehabilitation Act of 1973 and later by the Americans with Disabilities Act (ADA) of 1990.

The Rehabilitation Act of 1973 as amended. The congressional intent for the Rehabilitation Act of 1973 (P.L. 93-112) was to develop and implement—through research, training, services, and the guarantee of equal opportunity—comprehensive and coordinated programs of vocational rehabilitation and independent living for individuals with disabilities to maximize their employability, independence, and integration into the workplace and the community (Burgdorf 1995).

The Rehabilitation Act, as amended, prohibits discrimination on the basis of disability in programs conducted by federal agencies, in programs receiving federal financial assistance, in federal employment, and in the employment practices of federal contractors. Entities that receive federal funding and the federal government must continually review their programs and activities to ensure that they are effectively serving people with disabilities. For purposes of this chapter, the employment nondiscrimination provisions, which were the precursor for the Americans with Disabilities Act, are the focus. Section 503 requires affirmative action and prohibits employment discrimination by federal government contractors and subcontractors with contracts of more than $10,000 (Rehabilitation Act of 1973, 29 U.S.C. §793).

The definition of disability under the Rehabilitation Act was the basis for the definition of disability under the ADA. It includes any person who (a) has a physical or mental impairment that substantially limits one or more major life activities, (b) has a record of such an impairment, or (c) is regarded as having such an impairment. Major life activities include walking, seeing, hearing, speaking, breathing, learning, working, caring for oneself, and performing manual tasks.

Americans with Disabilities Act of 1990. Title I of the Americans with Disabilities Act of 1990 extended the prohibitions against discrimination in employment on the basis of race, sex, religion, and national origin to persons with disabilities, beyond just employers who are federal contractors (as covered under the Rehabilitation Act; Equal Employment Opportunity Commission 1992). The goal of the ADA employment provisions is to provide equal rights to people with disabilities, thus increasing their labor market opportunities. Title I regulations apply to private employers with at least 15 employees, but where state laws are more inclusive, they may cover employers with fewer employees. The ADA employment provisions prohibit job-related discrimination against people with disabilities and require that employers provide reasonable accommodations. Those involved in vocational counseling and job development and placement for persons with disabilities thus must understand who is covered by the law and the principles of reasonable accommodation.

The ADA protects qualified individuals with disabilities from employment discrimination. In determining whether ADA employment provisions cover an individual, it must first be determined whether the ADA's very specific definitions of "disability" and "qualified individual with a disability" are met. This is always a case-by-case assessment. As just described, under the ADA an individual with a disability has a physical or mental impairment that substantially limits one or more major life activities, has a record of such an impairment, or is regarded as having such an impairment. A qualified individual with a disability satisfies the requisite skill, experience, education, and other job-related requirements of the employment position that such an individual holds or desires and can perform the essential functions of such position with or without reasonable accommodation.

Providing a necessary reasonable accommodation for an individual with a disability is considered a form of nondiscrimination under the

ADA. Reasonable accommodation is a modification or adjustment to a job, the work environment, or the way things usually are done that enables a qualified individual with a disability to enjoy an equal employment opportunity. The ADA requires reasonable accommodation in three aspects of employment: the application process, the performance of the essential functions of the job, and the benefits and privileges of employment. Examples of reasonable accommodations include making facilities accessible; restructuring a job by reallocating or redistributing marginal job functions; altering when or how an essential job function is performed; creating part-time or modified work schedules; obtaining or modifying equipment; modifying exams, training materials, or policies; providing qualified readers or interpreters; or reassigning someone to a vacant position.

ADA Amendments Act (ADAAA). It is also important to be aware of changes in interpretation of these definitions that occur over time based on court rulings. For example, in 1999 the U.S. Supreme Court ruled that factors that mitigate the disabling nature of an impairment may be considered when determining whether a person is covered under the ADA (Sutton v. United Airlines, 1999). More recently, based on the assessment that the Supreme Court decision has resulted in some individuals with substantial impairments incorrectly being found not to be people with disabilities, amendments to the ADA (ADAAA/S. 3406; Public Law No. 110-325) have been passed that attempt to reinstate a broader interpretation of protections available.

The ADAAA leaves intact the first prong of the disability definition language of the ADA, so that a person will still need to show that he or she has a physical or mental impairment that "substantially limits" one or more major life activities in order to be protected under the ADA. But the new interpretation acknowledges that the term "substantially limits" established a greater degree of limitation than Congress had intended and should be interpreted less severely. ADAAA also now prohibits consideration of mitigating measures in determining whether an individual has a disability, with the exception of ordinary eyeglasses and contact lenses. In other words, employees will be evaluated without regard to the hearing aids, medication, prosthetic devices, and other measures they use to manage their impairments. The ADAAA also provides that an individual is "regarded as" having a disability if the employee establishes that he or she has been discriminated against because of an actual or perceived physical or mental impairment. This new provision ensures that people who are fired or suffer other adverse employment actions because they are regarded as disabled can prevail if they prove that they were discriminated against. However, the "regarded as" prong would not apply to transitory and minor impairments where the impairment is expected to last less than six months. The legislation also makes clear that employers will not be required to provide a reasonable accommodation to individuals who are "regarded as" disabled (Equal Employment Opportunity Commission 2008).

In summary, the implications of the ADAAA amendments for employers going forward are that they will restore protections against disability discrimination to a broader range of individuals, including those with mental illness, epilepsy, muscular dystrophy, cancer, diabetes, cerebral palsy, and *perceived* disabilities. The definition "substantially limits" now needs to be interpreted more broadly, with regard to effect on a major life activity. Also, mitigating measures can no longer be considered when determining whether a person has a disability covered under the ADA.

Europe as a Case Study

Up to the late 1990s, a variety of laws was in place in European countries under which disabled people were entitled to access to education, training, employment, and rehabilitation services without expressly prohibiting discrimination on the basis of disability. There were some exceptions to this—the Scandinavian countries, for example, have consistently opted for an employment equity approach, regulating employer responsibilities regarding disabled persons through general labor or work environment legislation (Organisation for Economic Co-operation and Development 2003), and in the United Kingdom, the Disability Discrimination Act of 1995 replaced the quota scheme in existence under Disabled Persons (Employment) Act of 1944. Many countries have relied on quota legislation or regulations as the main tool for enhancing labor market prospects for job seekers with disabilities (International Labour Organization 2006). European countries with this type of provision include Austria, France, Germany, Greece, Italy, Luxembourg, Poland, Portugal, and Spain. Under the quota schemes, employers with a certain size of workforce are obliged to employ people with recognized disabilities in a specified proportion of jobs. In many countries, a contribution is payable into a central fund by employers who do not meet this obligation, to be used to promote the accessibility of workplaces or for vocational rehabilitation purposes. In some cases, employers are offered other options to partially meet their quota obligations, including the option of providing on-the-job training opportunities, offering apprenticeships for persons with disabilities, or subcontracting work to enterprises employing persons with disabilities.

The European Union, now comprising 27 member states, actively promotes equality of opportunity for people with disabilities in employment and in society more generally through a disability strategy, a directive, and a plan of action. A key feature of the approach to promoting the labor market inclusion of people with disabilities is the involvement of social partners and disabled persons as representatives in promotional activities. Following the revision of the EU treaties to include an article (No. 13) concerning the combating of discrimination on the grounds of disability among other grounds (European Union Treaty of Amsterdam 1997), an EU Directive on Equal Treatment in Employment and Occupation (2000/78/EC; European Commission 2000) was adopted in 2000, outlawing discrimination on the basis of disability, among other grounds. EU member states were given a time frame of three to six years to implement this directive in their national legislation. The directive requires employers to develop and implement an action plan to give effect to its provisions, involving them actively in the process of promoting employment opportunities for disabled persons, in some cases for the first time.

With the negotiation and adoption of the EU directive in 2000, the legal landscape began to change noticeably regarding the employment of persons with disabilities in European countries. In Germany, for example, a series of legal reforms was completed in November 2001, aiming to tackle discrimination against people with disabilities in all aspects of life (Eurofound 2001b). Social law regulations for disabled persons and persons in danger of becoming disabled were consolidated and further developed in Book 9 of the Social Code of July 2001 (Bundesministerium für Arbeit und Soziales 2006). The Act on Equal Opportunities for Disabled Persons of May 2002 provides for measures to implement the ban on discrimination in areas not covered by the social code, including provisions for barrier-free environments, nondiscriminatory wording of profession-related regulations, and equal opportunities for university studies. Book 9 of the Social Code defines disabled persons as "persons whose physical functions, mental capacities or psychological health are highly likely to deviate for more than six months from the condition which is typical for the respective age and whose participation in the life of society is therefore restricted" (Bundesministerium für Artbeit und Soziales 2006:9). A revised quota provision is included in Book 9 of the Social Code, aiming, as before, to promote employment prospects for people with severe disabilities, with a reduced quota requirement (5% rather than 6%) on employers of 20 or more workers, a reduced compensatory payment requirement on employers who partially fulfill the quota obligation, and a significantly higher payment by companies that completely fail to comply (Eurofound 2001b).

The UK Disability Discrimination Act of 1995 deals with the rights of disabled people in employment as well as in other areas, including education and access to goods, facilities, and services. A disabled person is defined as someone with a physical or mental impairment that has a substantial and long-term adverse effect on the ability to carry out normal day-to-day activities. The provisions relating to employment and most other areas also apply in relation to a person who has had a disability in the past. Amended several times up to the adoption of the Disability Discrimination Act of 2005, the act makes it unlawful for employers to discriminate against a disabled person in the terms of employment offered, as well as promotion, transfer training, or any other benefit, or through dismissal or subjecting the person to any other detriment unless the differential treatment can be justified. Employers are obliged to make reasonable adjustments to the workplace and the way work is done to overcome the effects of disability on a person's capacity to perform a job. Originally applicable to employers of 20 or more employees, the act now applies to all employers.

In addition to legislation to promote opportunities for job seekers with disabilities, legal provisions to protect people with disabilities against dismissal are in place in Austria, France, Germany, Spain, Sweden, and the UK (Eurofound 2001a). In the case of Germany, for example, the protection commences six months after the start of employment.

The pay of persons with disabilities is the subject of legislation or regulations in a minority of EU member states. In Austria and Ireland, there is a legal provision that workers' pay should not be reduced on the basis of disability. In Germany, the Social Law Code (Third Book) provides for wage subsidies to compensate for lower productivity so that all disabled workers can receive the same pay as nondisabled workers. The amount granted depends on the severity of disability and other factors that hamper integration into the open employment sector (such as age). Wage subsidies are granted for a duration of three or eight years depending on other contributory factors, such as whether the disabled person belongs to a group that is difficult to integrate (Degener 2004).

In new EU member states that are emerging from a system of central planning under which people with disabilities either did not work at all or worked in special centers, the move to a nondiscrimination approach is at an early stage of implementation, although legislative reform has already occurred.

Changes Needed Going Forward

Change the Overarching Philosophy

The increasing recognition that people with disabilities deserve the opportunity for equal rights and self-determination can be seen in the rise of a person-centered approach in the delivery of rehabilitation and disability services. Stemming from this change is the furthering of disability employment rights. Employment may be necessary for income, but it is also a direct reflection of individual fulfillment, achievement, and the constitution of one's identity and social inclusion (Arendt 1958; Beck 2000; Muirhead 2004; Mundlak 2007; Murphy 1993; Phelps 1997; Schultz 2000; Solow 1998). As a result, employment and the opportunity for its advancement has become a key aspect of disability rights policy and empowerment.

The United States, like many other countries, is still struggling with how best to coordinate policies and programs to support people with disabilities in achieving employment and community living and participation outcomes commensurate with their nondisabled peers (Golden, Zeitzer, and Bruyère, forthcoming). The policy issues currently faced by the United States are not unique and are based on the reality that the experience of disability is considered separate from mainstream issues. The service delivery construct created in the past 30 years of well-intentioned disability policy has continued on some level to perpetuate static continuum-based services and supports that appear to have limited utility to serve as a conduit between disability and nondisability systems (Golden, Blessing, and Bruyère, 2009).

Changes in the regulatory environment set to take place as states implement the UN CRPD will be dramatic in some jurisdictions. The shift from a predominantly medical- or welfare-focused approach to a social and rights-based model of disability will require that a disability audit be undertaken of all relevant laws and that revisions be made as required to reflect the CRPD provisions. To expedite these changes, and to make a difference to persons with disabilities seeking work and employment, a campaign of sensitization and induction training is required for those enforcing the laws (such as judges and lawyers) and those monitoring the implementation of the laws on the ground (such as labor inspectors).

Address Inconsistencies in the Philosophical
Approaches of Different Laws

In the United States, the problems of continuing employment and income disparities that exist for Americans with disabilities are not new—rather, they are the result of often disparate past policies that treated disability and employment as two separate issues only marginally related. Disability standards and definitions often operate in contradiction to employment, its severity often negating the possibility of work. This has been a long-standing issue, one that has been in discussion for close to 25 years.

The (U.S.) National Council on Disability (at that time "National Council on the Handicapped") provided a report in 1984 on *National*

Policy for Persons with Disabilities to then-president Ronald Reagan. The report called for a consistent review of disability-related laws, regulations, and enforcement that would refine and improve their harmony with the public good and the developing situation of disabled people and society (National Council on the Handicapped 1984). More recently, this same organization released a report that reiterates the call for needed efforts to create seamless services among the numerous specialized employment systems now available for people with disabilities (e.g., Vocational Rehabilitation, Ticket to Work, Social Security waivers, supported employment, and others; National Council on Disability 2006).

In other countries within the Organisation for Economic Co-operation and Development (OECD), concern also exists about how to reconcile the potentially contradictory goals of disability policy. One of these goals is to ensure that disabled people are encouraged and empowered to take part as fully as possible in economic and social life, and in particular in gainful employment. The other goal is to ensure that people with disabilities are not denied the means to live decently because of restricted earning potential linked to their impairment. A recent OECD study calls for a fundamental rethinking and restructuring of the legal and institutional framework of disability policy in many countries, and for "unbundling" of disability and benefit receipt, with a shift away from a passive disability policy to a stronger emphasis on activation measures (Organisation for Economic Co-operation and Development 2003).

Enforce Equitable Employment Opportunities Legislation

Even with success in getting legislation that provides employment protections for people with disabilities, problems in enforcement and implementation can limit the intended effectiveness of any laws that are enacted.

An example has been in implementation of the employment provisions (Title I) of the Americans with Disabilities Act. Moss et al. (1999) discussed the benefits of using data on disability employment discrimination charges collected by the Equal Employment Opportunity Commission (EEOC) in its enforcement of Title I of the ADA, as a way to identify who files charges, over what issues, and with what outcomes. These authors described the limitations of being able to use this data confidently for such analyses, due to inconsistencies in data reporting. They cited findings from a 1995 EEOC Task Force to assess the state and local Fair Employment Protection Agencies (FEPAs) that the EEOC contracts with and shares responsibility for receiving and investigating employment discrimination charges (State and Local Task Force 1995). These findings document reports on the perceived weaknesses of the FEPA reporting processes at that time due to inadequate access to needed computer equipment for reporting purposes.

In a separate but related study, Moss et al. (2001–2002) also reviewed the implementation of the ADA Title I by the EEOC. These authors' findings raise questions about the effectiveness of the EEOC's efforts, concluding that Congress had not given the EEOC the resources needed to ensure an investigation of cases when needed. "As a consequence, the Agency has always struggled with more complaints than it could properly handle, while for most of its existence it has also tried to develop and maintain an effective program of enforcement litigation" (p. 3).

Implications for Employment and Training

The recent trend toward mainstreaming employment and training opportunities for persons with disabilities, which has been given new momentum at the international level through the entry into force of the UN CRPD, will require mainstream vocational training centers to review their premises as well as their policies and practices and to provide induction training and supports to instructors and other staff in order to ensure that inclusion is effective and that all students benefit. The implications for the current special training centers are less clear, though these services will undoubtedly go through a process of change, and some may decide to provide specialist advice to the mainstream training centers. A similar process of change is required in relation to work and employment—sensitizing employers, trade unionists, and the workforce in general will be an important first step to accommodating workers with different disabilities in the open workforce. The positive experience of many employers to date in recruiting and retaining workers with disabilities will contribute to this process. It remains unclear what will happen to the sheltered workshops that exist in countries at every level of economic development, as the requirement "to facilitate the movement of more and more workers to more "open" options becomes more widespread and these workshops become subject to employment legislation.

Implications for Labor and Employment Relations Professionals and Related Research

The disparities in employment for people with disabilities presented here illustrate the tremendous loss to business of willing and able talent as well as the loss to people with disabilities globally of income and social and economic participation. In the last two decades, the issue of disability in the workplace has garnered a great deal of attention. In the United

States, the passage of the ADA broadened the concern over disability and work to the fields of law, sociology, economics, and rehabilitation psychology (Colella and Bruyère, forthcoming). The UN CRPD and similar disability nondiscrimination and disability rights–based legislation in other countries are now also fueling applied concern and scholarly activity about these issues more broadly around the world.

Related research on disability and employment has been less developed in the field of labor and employment relations, despite the fact that many issues pertaining to the functioning of this field are relevant; among these are labor and employment law interpretation, conflicts about accommodations, performance issues and disability and health-related considerations, equity in leave and benefits policies, and other issues relevant to the domain of labor and employment relations professionals. Although research on employment of people with disabilities has been conducted for many years, much of this research has been conducted in the field of rehabilitation counseling and rehabilitation psychology and not in the labor and employment relations field per se. There are many fertile new areas for application of research in this area, and labor and employment professionals can play a significant role in assisting with the full realization of the local, state, national, and now international laws that now provide protections for people with disabilities.

At the local level, employers need legal guidance as well as practical assistance with required implementation of these nondiscrimination requirements, such as reviewing existing policies and practices to identify places where discrimination might occur, implementing related human resources and supervisory staff training on disability awareness and regulatory requirements, and addressing conflicts when they arise regarding accommodation requests. Continued research is needed to assess which kinds of workplace policies minimize disability employment discrimination and maximize inclusion for employees with disabilities. Analyzing changes in levels of grievances around issues of accommodation over time within organizations, monitoring equity in pay levels and career advancement opportunities for people with disabilities relative to their nondisabled peers, and identifying the specific characteristics of environments where people with disabilities can function maximally will be of significant assistance in guiding employers in the future to successfully navigate disability employment nondiscrimination and accommodation requirements.

At the national level, continued review of the kinds of charges being filed and their outcomes is needed. As disabilities of emerging interest become evident—autism, learning disability, chronic fatigue syndrome, and the needs of returning veterans with, for example, post-traumatic stress disorders and traumatic brain injury—new guidance will be needed to promote appropriate workplace responses to these issues. Input to public policy formulation by those knowledgeable about these workplace issues and their implications for minimizing employment nondiscrimination going forward will be imperative.

The recent passage of the ADAAA will necessitate new attention to these issues in the United States. Labor and employment relations professionals are uniquely experienced to bring an added perspective about effective workplace policies and practices to these efforts in formulating public policy and supporting regulations. Some of the areas for consideration will be dealing with the increased need for accommodation and flexibility in policies that will be presented by an aging workforce, as well as possible new considerations raised by the proposed Employee Free Choice Act and unionized environments. (The Employee Free Choice Act, legislation pending in the United States, would amend the National Labor Relations Act to establish an easier system to enable employees to form, join, or assist labor organizations. The latest version was introduced into both chambers of the U.S. Congress on March 10, 2009. Further information is available at http://thomas.loc.gov/cgi-bin/query/.)

With the entry into force of the CRPD, there is also an opportunity for countries to share experiences, whether or not they have ratified. For the U.S., for example, experiences in attempting to increase efforts to minimize employment disability discrimination and maximize inclusion for people with disabilities can be shared with other countries that are now working to implement the provisions of the UN CRPD. In addition, Americans will now be able to learn from the efforts of other countries how to improve related U.S. public policies and workplace practices. Similar opportunities will be open to countries around the world. There will also be significant need for help in interpreting the requirements of the CRPD in each country setting where it is being adopted. Internationally oriented labor and employment relations professionals with significant knowledge of disability employment nondiscrimination have a newfound forum for applying their perspectives to the implementation of employment rights for a population whose rights and employment needs were in most cases not previously addressed.

Labor and employment relations personnel may also perhaps be able to contribute to helping the U.S. reach a decision regarding ratification of the UN CRPD, which to date has not occurred. The U.S. has often historically been slow to ratify international treaties and has not, for example, ratified the Convention on the Rights of the Child or the Convention on the Elimination of All Forms of Discrimination against Women. This should not dissuade us from continuing to promote ratification by the

U.S. to the Obama administration leadership, as there is some precedent for this. The U.S. ratified 14 ILO conventions, between 1936 and 1999, including the Worst Form of Child Labor Convention (No. 182) of 1999. The U.S. also was a strong advocate for development of the International Bill of Human Rights and has a strong record in promoting human rights at the domestic level. Many countries look to the U.S. and its disability community for guidance on disability rights issues, often modeling their domestic legislation after the ADA. The U.S. has a unique responsibility to engage in this important international process and may now more likely be persuaded to sign and ratify the UN CRPD, based on awareness of the U.S. international reputation regarding disability rights. There is an indication that this may happen, based on a commitment made by Barack Obama during the 2008 presidential election campaign.

Acknowledgments

We acknowledge the efforts of Erika Eckstrom and Sara VanLooy, research/administrative assistants in the Employment and Disability Institute at Cornell University, and Liesbeth Van Parys, ILO intern, in the preparation of this manuscript.

The views expressed in this chapter are those of the co-author Barbara Murray and do not necessarily reflect the views of the International Labour Office.

References

Arendt, Hannah. 1958. *The Human Condition*. Chicago: University of Chicago Press.

Beck, Ulrich. 2000. *The Brave New World of Work*. Cambridge: Polity Press.

Bjelland, M.J., W.A. Erickson, and C.G Lee. 2008. *Disability Statistics from the Current Population Survey (CPS)*. Ithaca, NY: Cornell University Rehabilitation Research and Training Center on Disability Demographics and Statistics (Stats RRTC). November 8. {http://www.disabilitystatistics.org}. [April 19, 2009].

Bundesministerium für Arbeit und Soziales. 2006. *Rehabilitation and Participation of Disabled Persons*.

Burgdorf, Robert. 1995. *Disability Discrimination in Employment Law*. Washington, DC: Bureau of National Affairs.

Byrnes, Andrew. 2008. *The Disability Discrimination Ordinance, the UN Convention on the Rights of Persons with Disabilities and Beyond: Achievements and Challenges after Ten Years of Hong Kong Anti-Discrimination Legislation*. University of New South Wales Faculty of Law Research Series, Paper 13, Sydney, Australia.

Colella, Adrienne J., and Susanne M. Bruyère. Forthcoming. "Disability and Employment: New Directions for Industrial/Organizational Psychology." In *American Psychological Association Handbook in Industrial/Organizational Psychology*. Washington, DC: American Psychological Association.

Degener, Theresia. 2004. *Germany Baseline: Study*. <ec.europa.eu/employment_social/fundamental_rights/pdf/aneval/disabfull_de.pdf>. [November 10, 2008].

Degener, Theresia. 2008. *Employment Discrimination as a Human Rights Violation: Comparative Overview of Current Disability Discrimination Legislation.* Paper presented at subregional meeting on disability legislation, "Decent Work for Persons with Disabilities in Africa," University of the Western Cape, Cape Town, South Africa, May 12–14.

Degener, Theresia, and Gerard Quinn. 2000. *A Survey of International, Comparative and Regional Disability Law Reform.* In M.L. Breslin and S. Yee, eds., *Disability Rights Law and Policy: International and National Perspectives* (Papers conceived and commissioned by the Disability Rights Education and Defense Fund [DREDF]). <http://www.dredf.org/international/book.shtml>. [April 19, 2009].

Degener, Theresia, and Gerard Quinn. 2002. *Human Rights and Disability: The Current Use and Future Potential of United Nations Human Rights Instruments in the Context of Disability.* Geneva: Office of the UN High Commissioner for Human Rights.

Equal Employment Opportunity Commission. 1992. *A Technical Assistance Manual on the Employment Provisions (Title I) of the Americans with Disabilities Act.* Washington, DC: Equal Employment Opportunity Commission.

Equal Employment Opportunity Commission. 2008. *Notice Concerning the Americans with Disabilities Act (ADA) Amendments Act of 2008,* October 6. <http://www.eeoc.gov/ada/amendments_notice.html>. [October 20, 2008].

Erickson, W.A., and C.G. Lee. 2008. *Disability Statistics from the American Community Survey (ACS).* Ithaca, NY: Cornell University Rehabilitation Research and Training Center on Disability Demographics and Statistics (StatsRRTC), November 8. from <http://www.disabilitystatistics.org>. [April 19, 2009].

Eurofound. 2001a. *Workers with Disabilities: Law, Bargaining and the Social Partners.* <http://www.eurofound.europa.eu/eiro/2001/02/study/tn0102201s.htm> [November 10, 2008]

Eurofound. 2001b. *New Laws Seek to Improve Employment Prospects of Workers with Disabilities.* <http:/www.eurofound.europa.eu/eiro/2001/12/feature/de0112238f.htm>. [November 10, 2008].

European Commission. 2000. Council Directive 2000/78/EC, November 27. <http://ec.europa.eu/employment_social/news/2001/jul/dir200078_en.html>. [November 10, 2008].

European Union Treaty of Amsterdam. 1997. <http://www.eurotreaties.com/amsterdamtext.html>. [November 10, 2008].

Eurostat. 2003. "Employment of Disabled People in Europe." *Statistics in Focus, Population and Social Conditions, 26/2003.* <http://epp.eurostat.ec.europa.eu/cache/ITY_OFFPUB/KS-NK-03-026/EN/KS-NK-03-026-EN.PDF>. [April 19, 2009].

Golden, Thomas P., Carol J. Blessing, and Susanne M. Bruyère. 2009. "Evolution of Employment and Disability Policies and Practices in the United States: Implications for Global Implementation of Person-Centered Planning." In C. Marshal, E. Kendall, M. Banks, and R. Grover, eds., *Disability Insights from across Fields and around the World. Vol. 3: Responses—Practice, Legal, and Political Frameworks.* Westport, CT: Praeger, pp. 1–16.

Golden, Thomas P., Ilene Zietzer, and Susanne M. Bruyère. Forthcoming. "New Approaches to Disability in Social Policy: The Case of the United States." In Tuncay Guloglu, ed., *Social Policy in a Changing World.* Munster: MV Wissenschaft.

Handicap International. 2006. *Good Practices for the Economic Inclusion of People with Disabilities in Developing Countries: Funding Mechanisms for Self-Employment.* Sussex, England: Handicap International.

Hope, Teri. 2003. "Disabilities: Aid Groups Call for a UN Convention to Protect Rights." *UNWire*, February 14, 2003. <http://www.unwire.org/unwire/20030214/32057_story.asp>. [April 30, 2008].

International Labour Organization Recommendation concerning the Vocational Rehabilitation of Disabled Persons (No. 99). 1955. <http://www.ilo.org/ilolex/english/recdisp1.htm>. [November 10, 2008].

International Labour Organization Convention concerning the Vocational Rehabilitation and Employment of Disabled Persons (No. 159). 1983. <http://www.ilo.org/ilolex/english/convdisp1.htm>. [November 10, 2008].

International Labour Organization. 2006. *Achieving Equal Employment Opportunities for People with Disabilities through Effective Legislation*. Geneva: International Labour Organization.

Kayess, Rosemary, and Phillip French. 2008. "Out of Darkness into Light? Introducing the Convention on the Rights of Persons with Disabilities." *Human Rights Law Review*, Vol. 8, no.1, pp. 1–34.

Lawson, Anna. 2007. "The United Nations Convention on the Rights of Persons with Disabilities: New Era or False Dawn?" *Syracuse Journal of International Law and Commerce*, Vol. 34, no. 2, pp. 563–619.

McKay, Don, 2007. "The United Nations Convention on the Rights of Persons with Disabilities." *Syracuse Journal of International Law and Commerce*, Vol. 34, no. 2, p. 323.

Mitra, Sophie, and Usha Sambamoorthi. 2006. "Employment of Persons with Disabilities: Evidence from the National Sample Survey." *Economic and Political Weekly*, Vol. 41, no. 3, pp. 199–203.

Mont, Daniel. 2007. *Measuring Disability Prevalence*. SP Discussion Paper No. 0706. Washington, DC: The World Bank. <http://siteresources.worldbank.org/DIS-ABILITY/Resources/Data/MontPrevalence.pdf>. [November 3, 2008].

Moss, Kathryn, Scott Burress, Michael Ullman, Matthew Johnsen, and Jeffrey Swanson. 2001–2002. "Unfunded Mandate: An Empirical Study of the Implementation of the Americans with Disabilities Act by the Equal Employment Opportunity Commission." *University of Kansas Law Review*, Vol. 50, no. 1, pp. 1–110.

Moss, Kathryn, Michael Ullman, Matthew Johnsen, Barbara Starrett, and Scott Burris. 1999. "Different Paths to Justice: The ADA, Employment, and Administrative Enforcement by the EEOC and FEPAs." *Behavioral Science and the Law*, Vol. 17, no. 1, pp. 29–46.

Muirhead, Russell. 2004. *Just Work*. Cambridge, MA: Harvard University Press.

Mundlak, Guy. 2007. The Right to Work: Linking Human Rights and Employment Policy. *International Labour Review*, Vol. 146, no. 3-4, pp. 189–215.

Murphy, James B. 1993. *The Moral Economy of Labour: Aristotelian Themes in Economic Theory*. New Haven, CT: Yale University Press.

National Council on Disability. 2006. *National Disability Policy: A Progress Report, December 2004–December 2005*. Washington, DC: National Council on Disability.

National Council on the Handicapped. 1984. *National Policy for Persons with Disabilities*. Washington, DC: National Council on the Handicapped.

Organisation for Economic Co-operation and Development. 2003. *Transforming Disability into Ability: Policies to Promote Work and Income Security for Disabled People*. Paris: Organisation for Economic Co-operation and Development.

O'Reilly, Arthur. 2007. *The Right to Decent Work of Persons with Disabilities*. Geneva: International Labour Organization.

Pineda, Victor. 2005. "A World Enabled: Fighting for the Human Rights of Persons with Disabilities." *UN Chronicle,* Vol. 4, no. 4, pp. 12–13.

Phelps, Edmund. 1997. *Rewarding Work: How to Restore Participation and Self-Support to Free Enterprise.* Cambridge, MA: Harvard University Press.

Rehabilitation Act of 1973, 29 U.S.C. §793. <http://www4.law.cornell.edu/uscode/29/793.html>. [June 29, 2009].

Schultz, Vicki. 2000. "Life's Work." *Columbia Law Review,* Vol. 100, no. 7, pp. 1881–964.

Solow, Robert M. 1998. *Work and Welfare.* Princeton, NJ: Princeton University Press.

State and Local Task Force. 1995. *State and Local Task Force Report.* Unpublished report prepared for Equal Employment Opportunity Commission Chairman Gilbert. F. Casallas. Washington, DC: Equal Employment Opportunity Commission.

Sutton v. United Airlines, 527 U.S. 471 (1999).

UK Disability Discrimination Act. 1995. <http://www.opsi.gov.uk/acts/acts1995/ukpga_19950050_en_1>. [April 19, 2009].

UK Disability Discrimination Act. 2005. <http://www.opsi.gov.uk/Acts/acts2005/ukpga_20050013_en_1>. [November 10, 2008].

UN Committee on Economic, Social and Cultural Rights General Comment No. 5, 1994.

U.S. Census Bureau. 2004. *U.S. Census Bureau Population Projects.* <http://www.census.gov/ipc/www/usinterimproj>. [November 2, 2008].

Weathers, Robert R. II. 2006. *Disability Prevalence Rates for an Aging Workforce.* Ithaca, NY: Cornell University, Rehabilitation Research and Training Center on Employment Policy.

World Bank. 2005. *Development Outreach: Disability and Inclusive Development.* July. Washington, DC: World Bank.

World Health Organization. 2005. *Disability, Including Prevention, Management, and Rehabilitation.* 58th World Health Assembly. <http:www.who.int/ nmh/a5817/en/>. [November 3, 2008].

ABOUT THE CONTRIBUTORS

Susanne M. Bruyère is associate dean of outreach and director of the Employment and Disability Institute, Cornell University School of Industrial and Labor Relations (ILR). She is project director and co-principal investigator of numerous research, dissemination, and employer technical assistance efforts focused on workplace disability nondiscrimination. Susanne has a Ph.D. in rehabilitation counseling psychology from the University of Wisconsin-Madison, is a Fellow in the American Psychological Association, an executive board member of the American Psychological Association Division of Rehabilitation Psychology (22), chair of GLADNET (the Global Applied Disability Research and Information Network on Employment and Training), and past-chair of the CARF (Rehabilitation Accreditation) board of directors.

Lance Compa is a senior lecturer at the Cornell University ILR School, where he teaches U.S. labor law and international labor rights. He is author of the Human Rights Watch reports *Unfair Advantage: Workers Freedom of Association in the United States under International Human Rights Standards* (2000) and *Blood, Sweat, and Fear: Workers Rights in U.S. Meat and Poultry Plants* (2005) and of reports on workers' rights in Cambodia, Chile, China, Haiti, Guatemala, Mexico, Sri Lanka, and other developing countries.

James A. Gross is a professor at the Cornell University ILR School, where he teaches courses in labor law, labor arbitration, workers' rights as human rights, workers' health and safety as a human right, and values, rights, and justice in economics, law, and industrial relations. He received an M.A. from Temple University and a Ph.D. from the University of Wisconsin-Madison. He has authored and edited numerous articles in academic journals and law reviews and volumes, including *Workers' Rights as Human Rights* (2003, Cornell University Press), a three-volume study of the National Labor Relations Board and U.S. labor policy, and a forthcoming volume from Cornell University Press, *Transforming the American Workplace: The Case for Human Rights at the Job.*

Jeff Hilgert is a Ph.D. candidate in industrial and labor relations at Cornell University and a visiting Fulbright student at McGill University in Montreal. His dissertation examines the right to refuse unsafe work and its origins and treatment in North American labor relations policy and under international human rights standards. He has an M.Sc. in labor studies and is a graduate of the Labor Center at the University of Massachusetts, Amherst and the University of Minnesota, Duluth.

Barbara Murray has worked in the area of disability for over 20 years in Europe, the Asian and Pacific region, and Africa; she is familiar with international disability-related legislation, policy, and services. Currently she is senior disability specialist in the International Labour Office (ILO) Skills and Employability Department. Prior to coming to the ILO headquarters in Geneva in 2000, she worked as ILO senior vocational rehabilitation specialist for the Asian and Pacific Region in Bangkok, and before that in the research department of the National Rehabilitation Board in Dublin. Barbara has a doctoral degree in sociology from the University of Zurich and a master's degree in economics from University College, Dublin.

Tonia Novitz is a professor of labour law at the University of Bristol. Her research interests lie in international labor standards, EU social policy, and mechanisms for the protection of human rights. She is author of *International and European Protection of the Right to Strike*, co-author of *Fairness at Work: A Critical Analysis of the Employment Relations Act 1999 and Its Treatment of Collective Rights*, and co-editor of *The Future of Remedies in Europe*. She is also a member of the editorial board of the *UK Industrial Law Journal*.

Maria L. Ontiveros is a professor at the University of San Francisco School of Law, where she teaches employment discrimination, labor law, and international/comparative labor and employment law. She co-authors the casebook *Employment Discrimination Law: Cases and Materials on Equality in the Workplace*. Her research interests focus on workplace issues affecting women of color, the organization of immigrant workers, and the Thirteenth Amendment to the U.S. Constitution. She received an A.B. in economics with university and departmental honors from the University of California, Berkeley; a J.D. cum laude from Harvard Law School; an MILR from Cornell University; and a JSD from Stanford Law School.

Edward E. Potter joined The Coca-Cola Company in 2005 as director of global workplace rights. Prior to that, he was an attorney and partner with the law firm McGuiness, Norris & Williams, LLP in Washington, D.C. for 26 years. Potter has served as the U.S. employer delegate to the annual International Labour Organization Conference since 1997. He has frequently testified before the U.S. Congress and has published several books and articles. He has a master's degree in labor economics and collective bargaining from Cornell University and a law degree from the Washington College of Law at American University.

Marika McCauley Sine is manager of global stakeholder engagement at The Coca-Cola Company, on whose behalf she engages with the United Nations Global Compact, the Business Leaders Initiative on Human Rights, and other international organizations and initiatives. Before joining Coca-Cola, Marika worked for nongovernmental organizations including Oxfam America and The Asia Foundation on economic development, human rights, and agricultural sustainability issues. She also served as an AmeriCorps Congressional Hunger Center Fellow, focusing on addressing hunger and poverty in the United States. She has a master's degree in public policy from Harvard University's John F. Kennedy School of Government.

Rebecca Smith is coordinator of the Justice for Low-Wage and Immigrant Workers Project of the National Employment Law Project. She has been actively involved in promoting migrant workers' rights as human rights before the Inter-American Commission on Human Rights, the Inter-American Court on Human Rights, and the UN Committee on Migrant Workers; in proceedings under the North American Agreement on Labor Cooperation; in shadow reports on U.S. compliance with the International Covenant on Civil and Political Rights and the Committee on the Elimination of Racial Discrimination; and in the annual Global Forum on Migration and Development Civil Society Days.

Burns H. Weston is the Bessie Dutton Murray Distinguished Professor of Law Emeritus and senior scholar at The University of Iowa Center for Human Rights. His primary research interests lie in issues of human rights law and policy, particularly in respect of jurisdictions that resist human rights on cultural or ideological grounds. Weston has authored, co-authored, and edited many books on human rights, including *Child Labor and Human Rights* (Lynne Rienner Publishers, 2005). He is an honorary member of the board of editors of the *American Journal of International Law* and a member of the editorial review board of *Human Rights and Human Welfare*.

The publisher would like to especially acknowledge the following people who worked behind the scenes to produce this volume: Rhonda Clouse of Cornell University for coordinating manuscripts and editor-author communications; Molly Bentsen as copyeditor; Peggy Currid as proofing editor; Karen Higgins for the cover layout; our friends at the ILO for granting use of the cover photo; Kelly Applegate of Publication Services, Inc. who managed the project in the composition phase; Jeff Gallagher, Bruce Boyd, and the able crew at the University of Illinois Printing Department; and Fran Benson, Susan Barnett, and Mahinder Kingra from Cornell University Press for the helpful and timely advice they periodically offer to promote and distribute LERA Research Volumes.